920
FEW

Cre C2 ✓

A few small candles.

5/99

$28.00

DATE		

A FEW SMALL CANDLES

A

FEW

SMALL

CANDLES

War Resisters

of World War II

Tell Their Stories

EDITED BY

LARRY GARA &

LENNA MAE GARA

THE KENT STATE UNIVERSITY PRESS

Kent, Ohio, and London

©1999 by The Kent State University Press, Kent, Ohio 44242
All rights reserved
Library of Congress Catalog Card Number 98-31253
ISBN 0-87338-621-3
Manufactured in the United States of America

05   04   03   02   01   00   99   5   4   3   2   1

Library of Congress Cataloging-in-Publication Data
A few small candles : war resisters of World War II tell their stories
   / edited by Larry Gara and Lenna Mae Gara.
        p.   cm.
     Includes bibliographical references (p.   ) and index.
     ISBN 0-87338-621-3 (alk. paper) ∞
     1. World War, 1939–1945—Conscientious objectors—United States.
2. Service, Compulsory nonmilitary—United States.   3. World War,
1939–1945—Personal narratives, American.   4. Conscientious
objectors—United States—Biography.   5. Political prisoners—United
States—Biography.   I. Gara, Larry.   II. Gara, Lenna Mae, 1926–   .
D810.C82F48   1999
940.53'162—dc21   98-31253

British Library Cataloging-in-Publication data are available.

For all those men and women who,
through the ages,
resisted the wars of their time.

All the darkness in the world
cannot put out the light of one small candle.

Contents

Preface

THE TERM "GOOD WAR" was not used during the years of World War II. To the generation that came of age during that terrible time, it was just another war, a war that would take lives and destroy the futures of millions throughout the world. The war followed years of disillusionment with World War I and two decades of antiwar writing and activity in the United States. Even after fighting began in Europe, there was an intense debate in the United States over America's role. A combination of antiwar sentiment and isolationism formed a public opinion determined to keep the United States out of the conflict. It was only after the Japanese attack on Pearl Harbor that the argument ended.

In 1940, a year before the United States entered the war, Congress passed the nation's first peacetime conscription law. The Selective Training and Service Act provided legal options for any objector who "by reason of religious training and belief [was] conscientiously opposed to participation in war in any form." Classification 1-AO was for those objectors willing to serve as medical corpsmen in the military, an option preferred by members of the Seventh Day Adventist Church. The 4-E classification was for those who would not accept military service but who were willing to do civilian work of "national importance." Objectors choosing such service, if they were granted that privilege by their draft boards, were sent to Civilian Public Service (CPS) camps. Nominally under the control of one or another of the historic peace churches, with each objector or his sponsor paying thirty-five dollars a month for his keep, the camps were in fact controlled by Selective Service and headed by the army's General Lewis B. Hershey. The camps were located in parks and other areas removed from large populations, leading some objectors to complain that the program was meant to place them out of public view and awareness. Eventually, selected draftees were permitted to serve outside the camps, primarily in hospitals or medical research centers. Approximately twelve thousand men served in alternative service projects during World War II.

Little of the writing about World War II has focused on conscientious objectors and alternative service. Even less known is the record of the nearly six thousand war resisters who served terms in federal prison for violating the draft law. Some objectors were denied 4-E classification by their draft boards and subsequently refused induction. Others went to CPS camps but later concluded they could no longer accept conscription and walked out of camp. And some men openly refused to register. About a third of those imprisoned as objectors were Jehovah's Witnesses, who claimed and were denied ministerial exemption.

This book relates the experiences of ten men who served prison terms for war resistance. They were not draft dodgers. Their opposition took the form of open resistance, not evasion. It is an aspect of the war that has been virtually ignored, yet the record is part of the larger picture of American reform and the history of nonviolence. These are individual stories related some fifty years after the fact. While a few had access to contemporary documents for verification, specific inaccuracies due to the passage of time and the vagaries of memory are inevitable.

Each contributor was asked to relate his reasons for opposing the war, what happened to him as a result of that opposition, and how he feels about the experience today. While this is by no means a comprehensive history of that chapter in our history, these memoirs open a window on World War II resistance and provide source material for future historians. The stories are personal and poignant and are worth reading for themselves.

Each of the individuals included in this volume remained active in various causes relating to peace and social justice. All of them served prison terms, but their backgrounds and early experiences were strikingly different in terms of religion, class, ethnicity, and political perspective. A few World War II resisters who went on to significant post-war careers are no longer living. They include Bayard Rustin, who became a major figure in the civil rights movement;

Jim Peck, who was an energetic nonviolent fighter for peace and civil rights; Robert Lowell, who twice won the Pulitzer Prize for poetry; and Igal Roodenko, who became a roving prophet of nonviolence, spreading the message at home and abroad. While many resisters later made important contributions to their chosen professions, during wartime they served as symbolic candles in a world of darkness, keeping alive a belief in nonviolence when most of the world had descended into a maelstrom of hatred and death.

We are grateful to John Hubbell, director of The Kent State University Press, for his steady encouragement of this project and for his patience as we untangled the knots and snags. To the men who contributed their stories to this volume, our special thanks. Bringing up memories that are often painful and always difficult to document is a daunting task that they all performed cheerfully and with generosity.

Larry and Lenna Mae Gara

A FEW SMALL CANDLES

Prison Memoir

*Our principle must be to build, not destroy, to create,
not to crush.*

THE CLOUDS OF World War II were already gathering in 1936 when
I entered Antioch College in Yellow Springs, Ohio, as a freshman.
The vision and integrity of President Arthur E. Morgan and several
faculty members were strong influences as I moved into a lifelong
commitment to working for peace and justice. In 1940 I was part of a
group that founded Ahimsa Farm, a cooperative study center near
Cleveland. Following Gandhian methods, we helped integrate a
public swimming pool and promoted two Food for Europe Pilgrim-
ages to protest the Allied embargo of food shipments to European
countries then under German control.

In 1941, Eleanor Meanor and I were married, and while I was
working as New England Youth Secretary with the Fellowship of Reconciliation under the direction of John Swomley, we lived at 8 Rock-
well Street in Cambridge, Massachusetts. There were a host of visitors coming and going, including Bayard Rustin, who was destined
to serve time with me in the Federal Prison at Ashland, Kentucky.
Eleanor worked in a nearby nursery school. A number of us working in the area became interested in the approaching date of January 26, India's Independence Day. Even though they had not yet
received their independence, they had proclaimed it thirteen years
previously.

A group of us, including longtime friend and Antiochian Bill Hefner, went to Washington and promptly began our picketing in front
of the British Embassy. We gave advance notice to the press and had
handbills on the issue of Indian independence. A sign referred to one

BRONSON P. CLARK (b. 1918)
Since prison and parole to a civilian hospital, then to the Friends
Ambulance Unit in China, Bronson Clark has been active in
business and peace-related work. After the war he began a long
association with the American Friends Service Committee,
becoming executive secretary in 1969. He has traveled widely as
consultant, lecturer, and writer. With his wife, Harriet Warner, he
now lives in North Carolina and Maine. *Photo courtesy of the
Antiochiana Collection, Antioch College.*

of President Roosevelt's war goals of "Freedom of Expression." Another said, "Free India Today for a Free World Tomorrow." It was against the law in Washington to bring a foreign embassy into "public odium." We said, "Where there is empire there is odium." We were quickly arrested and taken by paddy wagon across the Potomac River to the D.C. jail. We had arranged ahead of time for bail, but when we were brought back to the courthouse we were fined twenty-five dollars each, which, being low, we decided to pay. As I left the courthouse and stepped out on the sidewalk, I was arrested by two FBI agents and taken before a federal judge at another courthouse, where it was noted that I had refused to report to Civilian Public Service at Big Flats, New York. This was a violation of the Selective Training and Service Act of 1941, and bond was set at two thousand dollars. So I sat in a D.C. jail while my friends got on the phone with George Lyman Paine, in whose Boston Park Street office I had my FOR desk. He paid my bail, and I shortly returned to Boston.

Even though I knew I would not accept CPS, having been denied conscientious objector status by my draft board, which I learned later never granted CO status to anybody, I wanted to establish that I was a CO first for future treatment within the prison and parole system. As I prepared my CO Form 47, I added a copy of "Antioch Notes," written during Arthur E. Morgan's tenure as president of Antioch College; it contained the following statement:

> Public Officials, when they deal with a sincere conscientious objector, do well to respect his position, for in his own way he is undertaking to make a contribution to human society which must be made if mankind is not to destroy itself by violence. In 1918 the Allies achieved overwhelming victory in the "war to end war." The tragic aftermath of that victory suggests tolerance and respect for those who sincerely and thoughtfully seek a different solution. Most great social advances were begun by a few persons. A wise society will not destroy a minority that, without violence to society is committed to finding a better way.

On March 7, 1942, I attended a hearing on my claim as a CO in the company of my brother, Sheldon, who was an attorney. We also brought along a court reporter to take notes. This reporter was promptly ejected from the meeting. There was a lot of mixed-up FBI junk in the file; my CO claim was denied, and I was classified 1-A, a classification that I promptly appealed to the president. The appeal was actually handled by Brig. Gen. Lewis B. Hershey. Sometime earlier I had written my Cleveland Heights, Ohio, draft board for permission to join Gandhi's nonviolent army to defend India. I shortly received the following reply: "Dear Sir: At a recent meeting of this Board your request for permission to leave this country to join the non-violent army in India has been refused. Yours very truly, F. A. Needham, Chief Clerk."

At least we were dealing with the right language!

Working through the appeal system, I was finally classified as a CO. I refused, however, to report to CPS at Big Flats in New York, feeling it was a government conscript labor camp. On April 6, 1943, with a well-known attorney, William Thomas, by my side, I was given a sentence of three years. All the other cases that day, mostly Jehovah's Witnesses, received five. So the judge gave a nod to Thomas. (Later on, William Thomas became a federal judge. Over the years I used to pass him walking in Cleveland, and he would say, "Bronson, you are the only case I ever lost.")

I spent three weeks in the bedbug-infested Cuyahoga County Jail, often in the company of raving drunks, horrible food, and impossible lighting conditions for reading. There was no recreation. And while Eleanor could visit me—alas only once a week—it was difficult to see or hear her because of thick screening and the din of other visitors. She never missed her visit, in spite of a new job as director of the Huron Road Nursery School. I was glad when they called me to gather my things for departure.

It turned out that I was transferred to the Federal Prison in Chillicothe, Ohio. As we approached the entrance, the guard lifted the phone: "A marshall and three prisoners." "Prisoner"—he was speaking of me! As I approached the steel doors, I thought, "Three years, am I to spend three years here?" The marshall spoke up, "Well, boys, this will be your home for some time to come." The auto thief handcuffed on my left arm looked dour and said nothing. An eighteen-year-old youth and war objector handcuffed on my right arm looked rather solemn, but we exchanged wry smiles.

After handing over all personal items, including my wedding ring, we were stripped, showered, and put in brown jumpsuits until we were issued prison-blue trousers and shirts. We were then led to the quarantine block where a prisoner stays for thirty days while he is being classified. This block had some outside cells, one of which I entered. I heard at the far end of the tier the guard pull a lever and the bolt lock. Four stone walls, one with a door and one with a window. A stone ceiling and a cement floor. The room had a bed, a small metal table, a metal chair, a wash basin, a toilet with no seat, and a whisk broom.

Occasionally I could see the face of another prisoner opposite me appear at his small cell window. He waved, but of course no communication was allowed. I learned later how prisoners scooped the water out of their toilets and conversed from cell to cell and floor to floor that way. As time began to pass, I felt lonely, cut off, and depressed. I had a vast number of friends and helpers, and also enemies. My fellow convicts. They knew when I arrived, how long my sentence was, what I was in for.

But the inevitable grapevine now helped me. I heard a scraping noise at the front of my cell door. A book was being shoved under the door, opened up to fit, and a grinning face appeared at my window and was gone. Pearl Buck's *The Exile!* It was a wonderful read, and Buck took me out of that prison to China.

After three weeks in quarantine, I wrote a letter to the warden asking about mail and why I was not being processed. It turned out that in some of the material I was carrying I had mentioned a hunger strike at the Federal Prison in Danbury, Connecticut, and they concluded I would be starting one in Chillicothe. After a month they let me out into the prison population.

Before every meal in quarantine, the inmates would line up in two long rows of about fifty men each and then the "count" would be taken; during this the guards used military-type commands and enforced strict silence. One day the mass conformity of such a regime was glaringly broken when a new prisoner stood in the line without shoes or stockings. This created a sensation among guards and inmates. The chap in question was a freckled, red-haired, youthful lad with a boyish face. A glance at him was enough to suggest that here was an extremely sensitive soul who looked less like a convict than any of us present. His smiling blue eyes gazed with earnest sincerity at the guard when the officer ordered, "Go back to your cell and put on your shoes!"

Stanley (later to be known as "the Barefoot Boy"), did not move, and we held our breath. Part of Stanley's pacifist philosophy objected to killing animals, so he was a vegetarian and would not wear leather shoes. In this he was like St. Francis. But ah! A St. Francis within a modern prison! The guard paused, realizing this was entirely new in his experience and that consultation with "higher-ups" was in order. The guard stepped back and blew his whistle. "Right face, forward march." A double line of men in blue walked at a quick pace out of the cell block leading into the dining room. Blue shirts, blue trousers, and brown army shoes—all alike. Except one, and he was barefoot.

For three days the head guard would approach Stanley holding a pair of shoes and socks. Stanley refused to utilize socks because it would wear them out, and this was wasteful. The guard saw the humor of it and kidded him, as did his fellow inmates. Naturally, anyone taking on the prison authority was supported by the inmates, even though in talking with Stanley they came away shaking their heads at his answers to questions about his beliefs. This situation prevailed for thirty days of quarantine, and then came the thunderbolt: Stanley was sent to the "Captain's Hole," which consisted of three separate cells below ground level under the administration building. There he was cut off from all prison life, movies, the library, and, worst of all, his growing number of friends. The other two cells were occupied by lewd types, and eighteen-year-old Stanley was forced to witness various forms of sex play through the bars. And their talk was hardly elevating.

After about three months at Chillicothe we were summoned for transfer to who knew where. Five of us, including Stanley, who was finally released from the Hole, sat on a bench awaiting our departure. The guard who had taken care of Stanley approached with a pair of socks and leather shoes. It was evident that Stanley had won the respect of this guard, because in full view of many other guards, this officer knelt down and put socks and shoes on Stanley.

This act so moved Stanley that he did not resist and he left Chillicothe wearing leather shoes.

A leg iron was attached to my right leg, which in turn was attached to the left leg of my good friend Charles Butcher. We already knew each other because we were both from Boston. Charles was a graduate of Harvard; he had a brilliant mind and had edited the *Harvard Crimson*. He and his wife, Agnes, were knowledgeable about the law, and Charles filed a test case in which he attempted to prove that CPS camps were not under civilian control as provided by law but were being operated by Gen. Lewis B. Hershey and other military officers. This gambit failed.

I recall that when we were all in the long limo with "Department of Justice Federal Bureau of Prisons" emblazoned on the doors, we stopped at a town in the middle of our trip. The guards rode forward with guns while we were in a heavy wire cage with doors and windows without handles. Thus chained and locked in, we gazed out at some of the townspeople who paused to look at us. Charlie pushed the visor of his blue prison cap up, raised his handcuffs, and snarled at them. They jumped back in horror. It's a fact that when one is a prisoner in this kind of situation, you begin to think, "How do I break out of this mess?" Being treated like bank robbers, it was hard not to act like them. It gave us all a laugh and a minor scowl from a guard.

As we were being processed at the Federal Correctional Institution at Ashland, Kentucky, I met Antiochians who advised me not to request an open dorm, which was noisy and lacked privacy, but to choose a cell block. Stanley, on arrival at Ashland, took off his shoes and socks and became the "Barefoot Boy" again. I should say that Ashland had a much-improved atmosphere over Chillicothe, which had a large population of youthful offenders. Ashland had a large number of COs, Jehovah's Witnesses, older bootleggers, a few men charged with cheating on federal taxes, and a progressive warden.

The prison administration did a little passive resistance of its own and chose to ignore Stanley. Thus he was assigned to the yard maintenance crew where he pushed a lawn mower. His feet became sore and blistered in the sun. As a result, he began to "ride the sick line," where he came in contact with the prison doctor who was also the institution's psychiatrist. One day Stanley was ordered to take a wheelbarrow over some ground that was covered with many stones and cinders. He refused and was taken before the disciplinary board of which the doctor was a member. Stanley was placed in a "strip cell" (i.e., with nothing in it) for "mental observation."

This attempt to smear Stanley as a "psycho" caused quite a reaction among the COs who, while not agreeing with his position, felt that it was sincerely held. Charles Butcher then proposed to the COs that if Stanley were crazy, then Butcher was also crazy and would take off his shoes. This was indeed a serious step, inasmuch as parole and credit off your sentence for "good time," usually as much as a third, might be lost. Most COs had received five years, a few of us less, so this was a real dilemma. Most were hesitant about joining Butcher. However, on the appointed day, five of us removed our shoes and proclaimed, "We're crazy, take us to the Blue Room."

Our shoes had been removed just before the noon meal, and as we marched into the dining room our fellow inmates exclaimed, "Why, there's another barefoot boy!" "Yeah, and look over there: see, another one!" There was a great buzz in the dining hall. Most guards looked serious, but some smiled a bit. For myself, as I padded along the cement floor, the little rule buried among a maze of regulations ran through my head: "Clothes shall be worn in the conventional manner." We had written the administration protesting Stanley's treatment and asking that he be released into the general population. While the administration did not discipline us, they did not ignore what we had done either, as a united action by any group is carefully followed by officials. No doubt our Gandhian tactics of nonviolent direct action concerned the administration.

The next day Stanley's Blue Room door was opened and he received mail, writing paper, and books. His feet were under treatment for burns and his condition was much improved. I was one of four who felt the administration had made a good step and could not release Stanley without "losing face." So we put our shoes back on. However, Butcher felt we should have held to our original demand that Stanley be released into the population, and he kept his shoes off. Butcher's job was on the construction crew, and he suffered considerable discomfort. However, after another day Butcher was of a divided mind, and as a symbol of this position and a tribute to his sense of humor, he put one shoe on. This caused considerable mirth.

Meanwhile, we had proposed that Stanley be permitted to purchase tennis shoes. On the fourth day Stanley was released from the Blue Room and admitted to the hospital for foot treatment. Upon release from the hospital, he was handed a pair of tennis shoes and the case of "the Barefoot Boy" was closed. There were some aftereffects. Three of us who had pretty good jobs in the medical department were dismissed by the doctor, whose methods of psychiatry we had challenged. Two of the fellows were placed on labor gangs, while I went to the education department to teach. Much later the Bureau of Prisons replaced this doctor, which was to its credit.

My first class consisted of fifteen inmates. Most of them were in for making moonshine, and there was one dope peddler and one auto thief. Most of the men were between twenty and thirty years of age, with two-thirds serving second or third sentences for the same offense. One long, lanky briar hopper had done six years in a Tennessee prison for murder. Once, in response to a guard's statement that in prison he was warm and well fed, he said, "Aw, I wanta go home where the hound dogs lick the skillets." These men had IQs that ranged from sixty to ninety, a few up to one hundred. They were unable to read anything as advanced as a daily newspaper, and for the most part they were unable to write letters home or read those they received. In math, all but a few could add; half could subtract, but only a few could multiply and divide.

I started off by informing the class that I had a license plate across my car just as they did. This was an effort to assure them that I would not play the role of a "screw" or a "rat" and that, even though I was their teacher, I was still one of them. It was clear that class discipline had to be voluntary, since I would never report any problems. The majority were anxious to learn and were willing students in arithmetic, reading, and writing. There was a minority of gold brickers who merely attended to avoid work on the labor gangs. I pointed out to these men that, in fairness to the others, they should keep quiet, and then I went about attempting to interest them.

An incident of cheating was defeated by my saying out loud to the whole class, while addressing the inmate whose work was being copied, "Dokes, would you help James? He seems to be having trouble." My policy was one of urging cooperation and encouraging the men to help each other. They soon saw I was not interested in grades, and, in fact, I gave them none. With rare exception, the cheaters soon took pride in doing their own work without help. In spelling, one man would open his speller on his lap to copy out the words. I said, "For heaven sakes, Rhodes, put the book on the table in front of you, it's much easier to read." I insisted he do this, and for the next three classes Rhodes copied from his book in full view. He soon saw I had no objection, but he was unable to fit into the open competition with his fellow classmates, since they quickly ruled him out. Soon Rhodes closed his speller and struggled along as best he could.

While our study consisted of reading, writing, spelling, math, and some English, I soon saw how being cut off from reading even the daily newspapers contributed to the students' profound ignorance. One day I asked, "Is the world flat or round?" It will perhaps astound some to learn that half of the class did not know. Truly, the experience of what early astronomers and explorers felt when they attempted to convince their fellow citizens that the world was round became mine.

"Smith, what holds the world up?"

"Well, Clark, I guess it floats on water."

"All right, what holds the water up?"

"Hmmmm, well the water rests on a base."

"What holds that base up?"

At that point the class began laughing, for it was clear to all how illogical it was. I then gave a brief and simple talk on astronomy that they were extremely interested in. When I stated that we were traveling through space around the sun at eighteen miles per second, they shook their heads in doubt. "If we are moving that fast why isn't the wind blowing?" inquired one man. Newton's laws of gravity were briefly pointed out and I used the simple illustration of a fly walking along the inside of a window of a fast-moving car. "Do you think the fly knows he is traveling at fifty mph? So we are unaware of our speed on this earth." Once I held a class on "How to stay out of jail."

In one math class, trying to get through to them, I said, "If you had a still, and you had a forty-gallon drum, and you put in twenty-five gallons of mash, then added twelve gallons of water, how many gallons would you have in the still?" They replied, "Ah, Clark, if you made liquor that way, you'd blow up the still!" One has to be rather ingenious to keep twenty or so adults interested for three and a half hours. But my efforts had their reward when, at one point, two of the men said they had written home for the first time and were able to read the family reply.

In late August 1943, I had a brief visit with Dr. Arthur E. Morgan, former president of Antioch College, who was now operating a nationwide program to strengthen our communities. He was arranging with the warden, Dr. Hagerman, to teach a twenty-unit correspondence course on this subject. This was approved, and he sent in a sizable number of books for our course, complete with a syllabus that directed us to write a five-page response each week. I recall receiving back Dr. Morgan's comments on my paper, one of which exceeded five pages. My fellow classmates consisted of about twenty COs. Dr. Morgan was really dedicating himself to this effort. Later, I received credit from Antioch College and a grade of B+, all at no charge.

One of the most remarkable things that can happen in prison happened to me. Front and center, wife Eleanor. She was director of the Huron Road Nursery School, an important and challenging job for her. She was experiencing waves of nausea in the morning that she attributed to stress. After a time the nausea let up, but one day my mother, Hazel, with whom Eleanor was living in Cleveland Heights, said, "I think you are pregnant." Eleanor was positive she was not, but knew something was wrong and went to her doctor. She mentioned that she thought she had gastric disturbances. Dr. Irwin replied, "Since when does gastric disturbance have a heartbeat?" Eleanor was told to quit work in about a month (women were handled very differently in those days!). Eleanor said she felt very stupid for not knowing, but she had been quite irregular in menstruating. She was by no means stupid.

Here is my reply to this news:

My Dearest Wife, Your beautiful and moving letter has brought me a happiness that space, steel, and stone, cannot reduce. The life within you is a physical demonstration that though we are apart, yet a part of me—physically—will be with you—and so now spiritually and actually we have been joined together in spite of manmade laws. In my situation I feel as if the gates have swung open and part of me has gone home to you. In the days ahead I shall be with you every minute. . . . What satisfaction to know that in spite of the troubled times our business of building a family is not going to be interrupted. I feel I've gotten the "drop" on somebody! . . . You asked me to help you on date of arrival. I don't think so but April 6 my trial date to January 6 equals 9 months. Therefore the baby would arrive before January 6, probably in December. All I can say is we have just gotten under the "wire." . . . You are such a lovely wife and I know will make one of the best mothers. The fellows here will soon find me hard to live with, but I don't care. All my love.

As one of the older cons said in speaking of my arrest, "Clark said, 'Pardon me, Marshall, but may I go back for my hat?'"

On December 29 I was informed by a telegram from my mother that daughter Mallory had been born without complications, weighing six pounds, three ounces. When Warden Hagerman handed me this wire, he congratulated me and I staggered out of the office. I was really nervous, my hands shook and I could hardly open a pack of cigarettes. (Alas, in those days I smoked!) It took me about an hour to settle down.

Some of the negatives of prison life were offset in a major way by a sterling and courageous group of COs who shared the prison experience. A fellow Antiochian greeted me at Ashland when I came to work in the front area. Later on Bayard Rustin came in, a towering addition and one involved in a major integration effort. Another friend was Wilbur Burton, former copy editor for the *New York Times*. He was extremely knowledgeable about the Far East, especially the Chinese situation, where for a period of time he had served as an adviser to Chiang Kai Shek. He was a totally political objector who believed that U.S. foreign affairs were grossly flawed, especially as they functioned in the Far East. He used to say he did not want to be colonized by the French in Indochina, as they were vicious in their methods. He also took his copy of the *Times* and underlined great sections of the international news, scrawling commentary in the margins.

Larry Gara was a CO who was preparing to teach. He was active in prison protest life and refused parole with strings, serving his full sentence. He later became one of Wilmington College's superior and long-term faculty members. Wilmington, a Quaker college, found Larry a firm peace advocate despite some unease among those around him. However, in 1996 Larry received the annual Distinguished Faculty Award from the Alumni Council.

Fran Hall, a CO from New York, was a deeply spiritual individual and a strong support to everybody. He was noted for setting his very thick-rimmed glasses aside, refusing to use them for longer and longer periods each day, taking a series of eye exercises to strengthen his muscles to change the shape of his eyeballs. Tough man. He later devoted most of his life as secretary to the New York Yearly Meeting of Friends (Quakers).

Ashton Jones, a Southerner, had total dedication to challenging the war system at home and abroad. He joined most protests and later in life outfitted a stationwagon with an amplifier, camping equipment, and large signs with peace messages, traveling thousands of miles and showing up at major demonstrations. He spent a fair amount of time in local lock-ups. He recounted to me time spent in jail in Cairo, Egypt. In response to my concern about how rough that must have been, he replied, "Why no, Bronson, do you know there were fellows in that jail from all over the world? It was a deep spiritual experience for me, a kind of worldwide brotherhood."

Meredith Dallas, a tall, handsome actor and fellow Antiochian, was deeply spiritual—not in the conventional sense, but in a humanitarian view at the deep center of his mind. After prison, Dallas returned to the Antioch theater program and for years was a towering figure as an actor and teacher of theater arts. Bill Hefner was also in Ashland, a fellow Antiochian and partner in starting Ahimsa Farm, where we studied nonviolent methods for social change until most of us ended up in prison.

Bayard Rustin, an African American CO from New York, was a staff member of the Fellowship of Reconciliation and an exponent of nonviolent direct action. Bayard spread the message of peace and reconciliation via the spoken word and through the magic of his tenor voice. Before he came to Ashland, he was riding across Texas in a train on which seven German prisoners of war were guarded by a military policeman. The military police (MP) had the Germans eat early to avoid contact with other passengers in the diner, though one woman got angry because they were to eat before her. As the MP and his prisoners filed by, she stood and slapped a German across the face. The Germans became tense, drawing into themselves as they passed. At this point Bayard swung into action. He asked the MP for permission to speak to the Germans. The MP replied that it was against regulations for civilians to speak to prisoners of war. Bayard then said, "But there is no regulation saying I cannot sing to them." The MP said he knew of no such order. So Bayard sang, in German, Schubert's "Serenade" followed by "A Stranger in a Distant Land." Later, as the Germans filed by, the one whose face had been slapped put his hand on Bayard's shoulder and said in broken English, "I thank you."

Bayard later came into Ashland with a three-year sentence. We were all cheered by his arrival, but a major problem loomed ahead. I was elected by fellow inmates to the Inmate Representative Committee that Warden Hagerman had set up. We met at regular times and discussed various changes in prison life. Since individual radios would result in bedlam, we had a prison amplification system. Our committee arranged to schedule symphony programs on Sundays, and we changed the manner of leaving the dining room. Before, we all waited until everyone had finished eating, then marched out at the sound of a whistle. Now, as each man finished, he returned to his dorm or cell.

At that time all federal prisons were racially segregated, though at Ashland, Protestant and Quaker Sunday morning worship groups were integrated. We pressed the Catholic priest, a Kentuckian, to integrate his service, but he refused. We next attempted, with Warden Hagerman's agreement, to open the door between upper and lower floors of our cell blocks so that Bayard could join his friends for games in the recreation area. This was opposed by inmate Judge Huddleston, the considerably overweight former treasurer of Kentucky who was serving time for IRS delinquencies. When Bayard entered the recreation room, fellow COs surrounded him. Huddleston suddenly stood up, grabbed a thick-handled mop, and brought it down on Bayard's head. From the other end of the cell block, I witnessed Huddleston strike three blows. Not wishing to show panic, I did not run. The mop handle broke in three places, but nobody said anything. Huddleston finally threw down what was left of the mop and simply shook all over until I thought he would have a heart attack. The guards heard the ruckus but, unfortunately, instead of removing Huddleston, they removed Bayard to his floor below and locked the gate.

A. J. Muste, executive secretary of the Fellowship of Reconciliation, received word of this event and wrote to Bayard:

> The other day I completed the reading of Lillian Smith's *Strange Fruit* with a very troubled spirit. I was overwhelmed by the intricacy of the pattern of race relationships as she depicted it, its deep roots in the social-historical soil and in the human soul, and the fatal precision with which, almost without any individual actually willing evil, a climactic horror such as lynching came about. What, one asked, what force can possibly avail to overcome this evil and to change the individuals involved in it? Now I have just finished reading the account of the demonstration of nonviolence by our friends in Ashland a couple of Sundays ago. It is difficult to put into words the joy I feel over the fact that their spirits under severe testing remained pure and true. If they were the sons of my flesh, I could not feel more closely bound to these young men than I do. . . . May they be spared suffering and may [they] have humility, wisdom and strength sufficient under the day. . . . They . . . use the method which can break the barriers of race and caste.

Later, Charles Butcher wrote a clever musical based on Gilbert and Sullivan's music about a prison utopia with Bayard the lead singer and me as the worst singer. The band of prison inmates used washtubs and other improvised instruments, and it was a smash hit, poking ironic fun at prison life. When the musical was performed for the prison staff, it went so long the guards finally shut it down.

In late October 1943, Meredith Dallas undertook a fast until death in protest of the methods of censoring his mail. It is one thing to read about Gandhi's fasts, and it is another to see a colleague fasting every day, drinking only water, and carrying on his work, day by day growing thinner and weaker. I knew Warden Hagerman was concerned, but Meredith was taking on a very large order.

After twenty-seven days, our progressive warden began holding meetings with the Inmate Committee and announced new censorship policies. There would be no censorship of religious, political, economic, or social matters, and, further, we could discuss institutional matters, even writing critical as well as uncritical statements about the institution. I wrote to Eleanor describing the new policy: "So Meredith came off his fast starting slowly with fruit juices much to the relief of all. I should say that five COs in Lewisburg were also on a fast protesting not only censorship but the right of free access to books, papers, et al. for all prison inmates. Here at Ashland one of the former members of the Newark Ashram has joined the Lewisburg fast and [has] not been eating for two weeks and Dr. Hagerman, who all along has said he would never force feed anybody, is trying to work solutions to this CO. So all gave credit to Meredith for our new censorship policies."

On May 10 I sent a long letter to Eleanor for infant Mallory. "I want to tell you, Mallory," I wrote in part, "of my faith in 'good.' I have been in actual situations where violence was met with nonviolence and a profound thing was evident. . . . But the supreme tragedy of my fellows is [that] they follow the footsteps of their fathers, representing an unending human chain, which is twisted and caught in a morass of revenge, hate, slaughter and bitterness. . . . Our principle must be to build, not destroy, to create, not to crush. If in any way I have helped these immortal truths, then my being in prison is a thing I hope you shall be proud of."

After many letters to Eleanor planning how I might apply for parole using a hospital as an employment place for me, and after Eleanor made a trip, babe in arms, to visit the parole board in Washington, I was granted parole as of May 20, a date ten days away.

In the Quaker meeting on Sunday, I was asked to say a few parting words. It is very hard for someone so close to leaving prison to talk to those who face endless days. Of course, I'd done more time than many, but that did not help. In a way, having a wife and child gave me responsibilities that many did not have, and they were glad that I made parole. Still, a part of me would remain there with those splendid fellows. I told them that my companionship with them would remain forever.

Originally my parole was granted for employment in a Manhattan hospital, but Eleanor so charmed Howard Gill, the deputy director of the Federal Bureau of Prisons, that he changed my assignment to the Sandy Springs, Maryland, Hospital, just down the road from his home. He also arranged for Eleanor, Mallory, and me to live in his home at no expense. Coming out of prison I did not question this arrangement, although I wondered about being that close to a person with so much power over me.

Howard Gill's wife was a psychiatrist at Washington's St. Elizabeth Hospital. They were a brilliant pair with two sons in the military. In the evening, the conversation around the dinner table reflected the day's news of the war, and I was not one to be self-effacing in my views of these matters. One evening Gill exploded, and we promptly moved out, renting a tiny apartment over a drugstore within walking distance of the hospital. To get away from Gill's oversight, I applied for a parole change to a farm run by an Antiochian friend's husband, but Gill blocked that assignment.

With my parole requiring an acceptable job, the heat was on! I had become aware that the American Friends Service Committee was part of the British Friends Ambulance Unit, China Convoy, and that a number of American COs were already at work there. After Eleanor and I thought it over, I applied and was accepted. We were given lodging at Pendle Hill, a Quaker study center near Philadelphia, while I was in training for China. In the meantime, the United States dropped two atomic bombs on Japanese cities and the war came to its bloody end. I briefly considered not going, but I had signed a two-year contract, and China's civil war between the Communists and the Nationalists raged on.

At this point I felt, due to my personal contacts with many Friends, my new association with the American Friends Service Committee, and my shared feeling of affinity with Quakers, that I would apply for membership at Germantown Friends Meeting before I left for China. Eleanor and I had attended the Germantown Friends Meeting on many occasions. I was promptly accepted into membership, with special congratulations by Esther Rhodes.

What a wonderful breath of air my service in China was. All those who had various war objections in the United States were at sixes and nines about Selective Service, CPS, and prisons. In China, we had a well-organized international team of British, Canadian, New Zealanders, Welsh, Australian, Chinese, and American men and women. A council, with Colin Bell as chair, administered job assignments that everyone accepted willingly. The motto was Go Anywhere, Do Anything (GADA).

I found myself quickly assigned to administration, and when the main headquarters moved to Chengchow, Honan, I was left behind on the west bank of the Yangtze River in Chungking. I was the West China Agent, responsible for the truck convoys carrying medical supplies that had been flown over the hump to Kunming and for delivering them all over western China, then under the control of the Nationalist government. Later I was sent to Yenan to investigate the feasibility of establishing a team of doctors, nurses, and "medmecs," a term for bright team members who could fix almost any broken-down hospital equipment, including the building itself. I met Chairman Mao and Chu Teh, the top military figure, when I sat in on a long interview with a *New York Times* military writer. My purpose in being in Yenan was to determine what medical supplies were needed and to ensure that Yenan officials would accept our team.

The result of this was a meeting in Nanking with an aide to Gen. George C. Marshall in which we secured three U.S. Air Force planes to move our Honan office to Shanghai. A frustrated UN agency gave us medical equipment from its bulging warehouses, such prime items as microscopes and new sulfa drugs, which we loaded on the planes. Our team was flown into Yenan, where they were assigned to the civilian hospital. They were cut off for two years, emerging in 1949 with the Communist forces after the fall of Peking.

The administration assigned me and a British colleague to visit various projects to see which should continue into the postwar period. At a large conference, all our team leaders made decisions about the future work. By this time, many British team members who arrived in China after I did were demobilized in London and went home. I began to press the administration to release me about nine months early, since I had been in prison and absent from my family for long years.

And so I rejoined my family, and shortly found that President Harry Truman had granted me a full pardon, with no application from me, restoring all my civil rights. Years later a joke went around AFSC that you could not be executive secretary unless you had been to China—first Colin Bell, then Lewis Hoskins, and then Bronson Clark.

After the war, Eleanor and I had three more daughters and traveled widely as I worked in business and for the American Friends Service Committee, becoming executive secretary in 1969. Eleanor died in 1987, and in 1989 I married Harriet Warner.

Davıd Dellinger

Why I Refused to Register in the October 1940 Draft and a Little of What It Led To

While in Spain during the Civil War, I knew I had to find a better way of fighting, a nonviolent way.

I BELIEVE THAT THERE are mysterious spiritual factors that influence who we are and what we do. For me, beginning in early childhood, these were the solitary experiences of the ecstasies of Nature and having to deal with the racism and classism of many of the well-to-do adults in the suburb of Boston where I grew up (even as I saw indications that they were not as happy as they would have been had they lived a more egalitarian and sharing life-style). I can think of four other influences that led me to become an objector to World War II long before the United States officially entered.

First, I was influenced by my exposure to the lies and failures of World War I and the examples of persons who fought in that war or went to prison for resisting it. A second influence included my visits to Nazi Germany in 1936 and 1937 when I was anti-Nazi and the U.S. government, banks, and major corporations were supporting Hitler. A third was my experience, after returning from Europe, going "on the road," penniless, riding the rails, and staying at missions and hobo jungles. The fourth influence was the inspiring example of grass-roots practitioners of nonviolent resistance to oppression and injustice. The practitioners included radical Christians, Jews, Buddhists, atheists, anarchists, Native Americans, African Americans, the labor organizers with whom I worked in the thirties, and Gandhians in India. I mention Buddhists, anarchists, and Native Americans, even though I knew none of them personally. But I read widely, and all the major influences I have listed were broadened and deepened by this.

DAVID DELLINGER (b. 1915)
David Dellinger began his lifelong work for peace and justice while a student
at Yale, from which he graduated in 1936. Since World War II he has been a printer,
editor, author, and lecturer. An antiwar leader during the Vietnam era, he
was one of the defendants in the Chicago Eight trial, which later became the
Chicago Seven after the trial of Bobby Seale was separated from the other
seven. The trials followed the police riot at the Democratic Convention
of 1968. With his wife, Elizabeth, he now lives in Peacham, Vermont.

One of my most vivid memories is of the widespread rejoicing I observed—and felt—when World War I came to an end in November 1918, about three months after my third birthday. "Now no one will have to kill other people," is the way my father put it at the time. When I was thirteen, a German officer from that war was invited to speak in our Wakefield, Massachusetts, town hall in a celebration of the tenth anniversary of the ending of the war. Many people spoke out against allowing an "enemy" to speak, but my father and I went to hear him. I was profoundly moved by the German's appeal for the people of the world to work across national boundaries to solve their differences rather than going to war and doing the terrible things that he had done. And it was an early lesson on the gains to be made by following one's own common sense and conscience, rather than being intimidated by self-styled patriots.

Sometime during college I read a book that contained a moving account of something that happened during the Christmas season among soldiers in rival trenches. One night the Germans, as I remember it, started singing Christmas carols. After a while the British also began singing carols. Soon a few soldiers started climbing out of their trenches and singing on the strip of land that separated them. Others joined in and together they shared the Christmas spirit. When dawn came they climbed back into their trenches. I don't remember if the story relates whether or when they resumed shooting at one another. But soldiers in many wars often shoot over the heads of their enemies when they receive orders to fire. My guess is that that's what most of those soldiers did.

Harry Rudin, a history teacher at Yale, participated in that war. He was the first person who told me that quite a few disillusioned soldiers made a point of firing over the heads of opponents rather than trying to kill them. He didn't do this at first, but he soon became horrified enough by the senseless slaughter to start doing so. Though I had no courses with Rudin, we became good friends and he strengthened my determination never to support war. He also had a historical perspective that supported my early antinazism.

An even more inspiring example to me than Gandhi (who offered military support to the British during World War I) was Eugene Victor Debs, the charismatic labor leader who was sentenced to ten years in federal prison for his antiwar speeches. In the end he served

only three years because the country had begun to realize that entering the war had been a terrible mistake. Even Woodrow Wilson, the
president who had demanded U.S. participation in "A War to Make
the World Safe for Democracy," reached a point of utter disillusionment when he said, "Is there any man, woman or child in America—
let me repeat, is there any child—who does not know that this was
an industrial and commercial war?"

I knew those words by heart long before the United States came
close to entering what is known as the Second World War. And I also
knew the words of Debs which told me that going to prison could
have desirable spiritual consequences. At the time of his sentencing
he said, "While there is a lower class I am in it; while there is a criminal element I am of it; while there is a soul in prison I am not free."
Debs also said something that encouraged me long before World
War II to develop my own conscience and to follow it rather than becoming a follower of role models: "I would not be a Moses to lead
you into the Promised Land, because if I could lead you into it someone else could lead you out of it." This became especially relevant
when most of the peace leaders from whom I had learned valuable
lessons tried to persuade me to register for the 1940 draft.

Even Roger Baldwin, the head of the American Civil Liberties
Union who had been jailed in the earlier war, appealed to me to register. Otherwise, he said, I would embarrass the peace organizations
that had secured passage of a special nonmilitary assignment for
draftees whose religious training forbade them to kill. Primarily the
exemption was for Quakers, Mennonites, and Brethren, the so-called
"peace churches." And indeed, the head of the American Friends
Service Committee, whom I had long admired, tried to persuade
me to register so that I could become the director of one of the camps
for such draftees. Under my leadership, he argued, it could become
a worldwide example of the importance of nonviolence. But I was
working with youth gangs in a racially conflicted inner city, and to
leave that to supervise nonviolent religionists raking leaves in an isolated geographical area wasn't the kind of nonviolence I believed in.
To make it even worse, the rules were set by Gen. Lewis B. Hershey,
and he forbade the residents to use their weekends or other spare
time to go where other people lived and speak against the war. For
a final example, Reinhold Niebuhr, who had inspired me at Yale with

his brilliant, deeply religious, anti-imperialist pacifist sermons, went through a subsequent spiritual crisis. He became obsessed with the sinfulness of human beings, including himself, and condemned sinful "addiction" to nonviolent soul force as "arrogant utopianism." The day that I and seven other students at Union were carted off to prison, he preached a sermon in the chapel saying that his greatest failure as a Christian had been his inability to educate us as to the true nature of Christianity.

Shortly after Hitler came to power, I became an anti-Nazi. One of my favorite poets at the time was Archibald MacLeish, who expressed his condemnation of fascism in 1933, both verbally and in his "frescoes for Mr. Rockefeller's City." But there were other influences as well: Jewish friends; E. Fay Campbell, an adult adviser at the University Christian Association; and other radicals I have mentioned. And opposition to nazism flowed naturally from my early opposition to lynching and other racial oppressions. This had developed as a result of the "mistake" I made in junior high school of falling in love with a poor Irish girl and having a poor Italian boy for my best friend. That was in the twenties, when there were no Negroes in town; but in my neighborhood the Irish and Italians were treated as if they were inherently inferior members of worthless races.

When I graduated from Yale in 1936, I had won a graduate fellowship to study at Oxford University for two or three years. Before I entered Oxford, I made two trips to Nazi Germany, with a visit to Spain and Italy in between. In Spain I was so impressed with the grass-roots soldiers who had been attending the People's University in Madrid, where I stayed for a time, that I seriously considered joining them in fighting Franco. This is how I put it in my book *From Yale to Jail:* "If my friends were going to die I was ready to die with them, and who knows, maybe we'll win. But by then I knew that the Communists were shooting the Trotskyists, both were shooting the anarchists, and the anarchists had shot at the car in which I had been riding in Barcelona when it made a wrong turn into their sector. Whoever won that way it wouldn't be the people. I knew that I had to find a better way of fighting, a nonviolent way."

Earlier that summer I had read the book *The Conquest of Violence,* which gave historic examples of how even idealists who pick up the gun for a just cause tend to become corrupted, much as some of the

Communists, Trotskyists, and anarchists had. The book was written by a Dutch anarchist named Bart de Ligt, who advocated the kind of nonviolent anarchism I soon became attracted to.

Between Spain and Germany I spent a week or more tracing one of the routes of Francis of Assisi through southern Italy, stopping to spend solitary time in each of the little chapels identified with him. Like me, Francis was the son of a rich man but became committed to nonviolence, justice, and sharing. Of course, he went much further than I have in sharing worldly goods with the poor. But after Spain, and from what I had already learned about the challenges of being an anti-Nazi in Germany, I wanted to absorb as much as I could of Francis's spirit before going back for a second visit.

Before my first trip to Germany, I knew that the U.S. government and banks were supporting and arming Adolf Hitler, much as in later years they armed and supported Saddam Hussein before waging war against Iraq. As Thomas Mann wrote in his diary in 1934, "Russian socialism has a powerful opponent in the West, Hitler, and this is more important to Britain's ruling class than the moral . . . climate of the continent . . . the governor of the Bank of England was sent to the United States to obtain credits for war materials for Germany, armament credits."

I also knew that a number of major U.S. corporations had set up plants in Nazi Germany for reasons similar to those that more recently have led corporations to set up plants in dictatorships supported by the United States in Central and South America. General Motors, ITT, and Ford come most readily to mind as having plants protected by Hitler, but there were others. In all my visits the pro-Nazis used these activities by the United States as an example of why I should support the Nazis, while the anti-Nazis cited them as an example of what they were up against in their efforts to get rid of Hitler. Some middle-of-the-roaders agreed with some of my complaints about the Nazis, but said that if Hitler was as dangerous as I claimed, the United States would not support him as strongly as it did. Others argued that Hitler's main purpose was to get rid of the Versailles Treaty, which extorted German reparations long after the end of World War I, imposed repressive restrictions on the German economy and armed forces, and robbed Germany of some of its traditional territories.

When I first entered Germany, I went to bookstores and asked for the works of Heinrich Heine, one of my favorite poets, whose works were banned because he was Jewish. This led to some fascinating discussions. One was with a Jewish manager who, after getting the book from the store's cellar, suggested that I stay in a bed-and-breakfast near his home in the ghetto. After that I often stayed in similar places in other cities. Especially in the ghettoes, but elsewhere as well, I was asked why the United States had a limited quota on German immigrants and was turning away Jewish refugees and other anti-Nazis, except for well-known individuals like Thomas Mann and Albert Einstein. Many times I was urged to go back to the United States to work against this and other evil practices that supported the Nazis. Later I canceled the last two years at Oxford in order to do some of these things while also working against lynching. Lynching was on the increase during that period, and the pro-Nazis frequently cited it as the American equivalent of their country's occasional mistreatment of Jews.

When I finally got to Oxford, I learned that Jobst von der Gröben, a German Rhodes scholar, was a member of my residential college, New College. Since the Nazis had not vetoed his selection, I assumed that he was pro-Nazi. But when we met, I found that Jobst was strongly anti-Nazi. Apparently he came from a leading family and had a brilliant record. So, for public relations reasons, the Nazis decided not to oppose his selection. We became good friends, discussing, among other things, what we could do to strengthen the anti-Nazi movement inside Germany, which was far stronger than most Americans realized, then or to this day. Also, what we could do to get the United States to work with the anti-Nazi movement rather than the Nazis. When I went back to Germany in the spring and summer of 1937, Jobst felt that because of his publicized anti-Nazi activities in England it was not safe for him to return to Germany. He did give me the names and addresses of a number of anti-Nazis, and I was able to carry a few messages from those in one city to those in another. He also told me that a number of anti-Nazis worked in the German Foreign Ministry, and he gave me the names of two or three who were apt to be sent to the United States from time to time, in case I could help them in any way. The only one I ever saw in the United States said that the U.S. officials he talked with liked the similarities between German fascism and the U.S. system, so they didn't want to hear any of his criticisms of the Nazis.

It was clear to me during this period that England, France, and the United States were working with Hitler not only for the profits to be gained by U.S. banks and corporations, but also with the major aim of influencing the Nazis to expand militarily to the east, destroying, or at least crippling, the Communist enemy. On the other hand, the Soviet Union was wooing the Nazis in the hope that they would expand westward and engage in a war with its capitalist enemies. When the Nazi-Soviet Pact was signed in August 1939, the United States knew that it had lost this diplomatic war and for the first time Roosevelt and other top capitalists began to prepare for war against their German ally.

During the Great Depression of the thirties, people who lost their jobs or their homes were often called "lazy" by people in the middle and upper classes. Based on my unorthodox Wakefield friendships, studies in economics, and a number of limited contacts with such people, I tended not to believe this. But when I returned to the United States in the fall of 1937 and worked at the Yale University Christian Association, I wanted to test my beliefs more thoroughly than I could at the Yale Hope Mission. And I wanted to share the lives and problems of down-and-outers in a more comprehensive way than I could when I responded to a person who had asked me for money for food by inviting him to share a meal with me at a nearby restaurant.

So I left Yale during a three-week vacation, dressed in my oldest clothes, carried no money, and stayed at missions, municipal lodging houses, and hobo jungles. I had fascinating experiences in all these places, as well as while "riding the rails." This latter experience happened when a fellow hobo invited me to join him for a couple days' trip and showed me how to get into a boxcar while evading the railroad police. Some police would arrest attempted riders while others preferred to use their clubs against them. The trick was to hide a little beyond the railroad yard (and the police) but near enough to jump on while the train was still going relatively slowly. The only catch was that someone had to prepare a boxcar ahead of time, at the risk of being seen by the police. Usually we took turns doing this.

My most serious personal crisis occurred in New York City on the third day, when I needed to walk several miles from the Bronx, where a truck driver had let me off, to the municipal lodging house in lower Manhattan. In return for the ride I had helped him unload his heavy cargo and was exhausted. Reaching Central Park and falling asleep on a park bench, I woke to the sounds of two children calling me a "funny man," and the mother shouting for them to get away from me. "It's a bum. I told you to stay away from them." These portrayals of how I looked—and felt—made it almost impossible for me to do what I desperately needed to do, to ask passersby for money for food. I needed to eat in a way that I never had before, or would ever need again, even in my hunger strikes later in prison. My head ached, and when I stood up and tried to walk I was dizzy; I also itched all over from the lice and bedbugs that had feasted on me at the missions. In addition to my physical needs, I had a spiritual need to ask straightforwardly for what I genuinely needed. Before I finally managed to do that, I learned how much more difficult it is to ask for badly needed help (particularly to beg for it) than to be asked for it; how much easier it is to give from one's surplus than to receive something that one cannot survive without.

After a couple of occasions when people looked at me (or away from me) with total disgust, or said "Get way from me, you bum," a woman gave more than I had requested—namely, a miraculous spiritual release of inner tension, together with feelings of expanding freedom and joy. Perhaps the woman gave because she sensed this in my face or in the manner in which I approached her.

Any doubts I may have had about the laziness of the majority of men on the road were dissipated by that first night in "the Muni." It seemed as if I had just gotten to sleep when I was wakened by a low roar. Everyone was getting out of bed, grabbing their things and rushing to the exit. My first thought was of fire. Jumping up, I was relieved not to smell smoke or see other danger signs. Puzzled, but fully awake and still apprehensive, I followed the others. In the dim light I could barely see a clock on the wall. It said four-thirty. "Where's everyone going?" I asked a man who was rushing by me. "To look for work, you dope." Four-thirty was the time the staff opened the doors, which had been locked the night before to keep out late arrivals. On my way out I talked to someone else. He explained that everyone was hurrying to get a good place in the lines on certain street corners where middlemen came in pick-ups or stake-body trucks to gather a few workers. Some were taken to out-lying districts for a day's work on farms or country estates; others would be taken to closer areas to distribute phone books or circulars or to work at other jobs for a few hours, such as unloading trucks.

Previously I had lived in a world that seemed to exalt material things but robbed them of some of their magic by treating them as private possessions to be sought and consumed without sufficient regard for our kinship with all living beings. Now, living in a society of the homeless, I was amazed to find how many of them shared in a comradely way with those who had been less successful, whether in begging or in convincing employees in food stores and restaurants to leave bags of food in garbage cans or other designated places. Per-haps that is the reason that the coffee and food tasted better than it had at the most luxurious private homes or expensive restaurants. For whatever reason, I definitely experienced material delights that were more deeply and fully satisfying than most of the ones I had previously savored. And I knew that I would always cherish the people with whom I spent those days and nights. Whatever their oc-casional shortcomings, they strengthened my faith in human nature in a way that most of the rich people did not.

When I returned to Yale, I suffered for a week or two from the sores from the lice and bedbugs. But my spirit had been cleansed. I knew that I had to work harder to fashion a way of life that would not accept either the spiritual poverty of most of the rich (including many who attend church and mouth religious words) or the mate-rial poverty of the poor. Instead, I would have to do my best to draw on the true insights and riches of both.

Based on that first trip, I made a series of others. And after my first semester at Union Seminary in New York City, I moved with four other students to live in Harlem. It was another way of liv-ing closer to those who were looked down on by so many of the privileged people with whom I had been associating at Yale, Oxford, and Union. It turned out to be a complicated experience in which we were initially treated with more suspicion than I had met on the road. But it was a healthy suspicion, one that helped me under-stand the problems of people of color in a deeper way. And it added

firsthand experiences that reinforced my natural skepticism of a government that shortly afterward claimed to be drafting its youth in
case it became necessary to go to war against a racially prejudiced
Hitler. Also, it brought me closer to people who are victimized by the
country's undemocratic economy and sometimes engage in acts of
desperation that cause a prejudiced criminal justice system to fill our
jails and prisons with them, including the two federal prisons where
I was soon to be sent.

The thirties was a time when the nonviolent Gandhian movement against the British occupation and rule in India was heavily
publicized in the U.S. media. In part this was because the revolt was
against the British rather than against U.S. imperialism in Cuba,
Puerto Rico, Central America, and the Philippines. Also, the rulers
of the United States were already aiming to replace British colonialism in much of the world by "more enlightened, more democratic"
American imperialism, which was the underlying reason they entered both world wars. In any event, I got more extensive details of
the spirit, methods, defeats, and triumphs of the Gandhian campaigns than today's media ever prints about nonviolent campaigns
for justice within the United States or its territories. In addition,
there were radical visitors from the United States to India who sup-
plied additional information that I savored. Primary among them
were Richard Gregg and a number of nonviolent activists who, as
teaching missionaries, became a part of the Gandhian movement.
These included Ralph Templin and Jay Holmes Smith, who were
expelled from India when they refused to sign the oath of allegiance
that the British rulers required of all foreigners in 1939. When they
returned to this country, I learned from them of a number of books
by Indian nonviolent activists that had a profound influence on me.
I particularly remember *War Without Violence* by Krishnalal Shridharani. So, whereas U.S. Communist party members were thrilled
to "know" (despite evidence to the contrary) that the Soviet Union
was a shining example of Leninist successes, I was thrilled to know
that a creative and powerful nonviolent movement for justice and
equality existed in India, even if it had not yet achieved most of
its objectives. And soon the radical intentional pacifist community
that I was a part of in the inner city of Newark was sharing experi-

ences with the Nonviolent Ashram that Smith had helped start in Harlem and with the communitarians in Yellow Springs, Ohio, with whom Templin was working.

Equally important to me were efforts to organize a union at Yale for the nonacademic employees, beginning in the fall of my freshman year, and my arrest in 1937 for a nonviolent action against racial segregation in a northern movie house. Naturally, these led to other examples of working with and learning from labor unions and anti-segregation forces, whether they called themselves Gandhian or not. Most obvious were the massive sit-ins by auto workers (including the one in Flint, Michigan, in 1936) and the nonviolent activities in defense of the Scottsboro Boys (nine black youths who had been condemned to death for allegedly raping two white women). When I lived in New Haven in 1937 and 1938–39, a variety of incipient or newly formed unions were trying to organize and I worked intermittently with them. Particularly at the beginning, I managed to penetrate and leaflet in a variety of stores and other establishments where known union organizers were banned. And in 1938 I spent a vacation from Yale working with the Steel Workers Organizing Committee in a number of risky nonviolent activities in a tightly controlled company town in New Jersey. In 1939 I attended antiwar rallies organized by John L. Lewis, the leader of the frequently striking United Mine Workers, who had broken with Franklin Roosevelt because of the president's decision to maneuver the United States into the war.

Finally, during every April since 1934, there was a day whose growing list of sponsors called for a National Student Strike Against War. Originally it was in response to the Oxford Pledge, in which a large number of students at Oxford pledged that they would never take part in an international war. Soon the pledge and the day of observance grew in this country and became very powerful. I can't remember whether I began to observe this strike in my sophomore year at Yale or slightly later. But for many years before the draft law was passed, many of my friends and I stayed away from classes on that day, holding a variety of public vigils, rallies, and demonstrations. And of course we did this in prison in April 1940, with the ultimately exciting results noted by George Houser.

We eight Union Seminary students spent the first week of our imprisonment in New York City's West Street Jail. There we mingled with Leo Lepke, the head of the Mafia, and several of his adjutants. To our surprise, they were friendly to us while saying to me such things as "I am in jail for killing people but you are here for refusing to kill anyone. It doesn't make sense." Or, "I just gave my lawyer a few thousand dollars to give to the judge to lessen my sentence, but all you guys had to do was to sign a paper that wouldn't have required you to do anything, and yet you refused. WOW!" Later, after one of my arrests, I stepped between another Mafioso and a guard who was roughing him up. He thanked me and said something like this: "Like us, you know that the system is based on stealing as much as you can from anyone you can, but unlike us you are trying to work out a better way of living." That was before I temporarily shared a cell with a bank robber, who told me that with the right pieces of paper (stocks, bonds, property deeds) he wouldn't have had to use guns, knives, and jimmies. Instead of becoming a bank robber, he could have been a banker who robbed people legally.

After West Street, we were transferred to the Federal Correctional Institution at Danbury, Connecticut. None of the top officials there showed any interest in making it a genuine correctional institution. I walked into the first Saturday night movie with a black man with whom I had been talking. The guard pointed to the white section for me and the black section for him, but I sat next to my friend in the black section. It was not a planned protest, just the instinctive, natural thing to do. Soon I was carried out and placed in a solitary cell in the maximum security "troublemakers" cell block. Later, war objectors organized a number of protests against racial segregation, both at Danbury and in other prisons, including Lewisburg Penitentiary, where I did two years. When we took such actions, or did other things that I thought were in accord with the best teachings of Jesus and the Jewish prophets, we never received any support or understanding from the Christian chaplains at either Danbury or Lewisburg. But I developed a fruitful relationship with the rabbi at Danbury, who stimulated me spiritually and encouraged me to be true to what I saw as the prophetic heritage.

One aspect of my working with John L. Lewis was that Eleanor Roosevelt proposed that I be included in the list of organizers of the biggest antiwar demonstration where Lewis would speak. After the event she invited me into the White House and we had a friendly talk in which she expressed her support for my nonviolent efforts for justice and equality and for changing from a greedy, selfishly competitive society to a more communal one. After I had been in Danbury a short while, I got a letter from my brother, who was a student at Swarthmore College. He had been part of a committee that had lunch with Mrs. Roosevelt when she came to the college to speak. When she heard his name she asked if I were his brother and pumped him for prison news about me. She also said, "When you write Dave, tell him that I admire him. Tell him that I think he is right in the stand he has taken." Knowing the attacks she was under for attitudes and practices that differed from those of her opportunistic husband, I decided to view this as a personal message that I would not publicize because of the difficulties it might cause her. I did this because of my belief that true nonviolence requires special sensitivities not only toward one's opponents but also toward persons with whom one shares many convictions but who have to decide for themselves when they will go public about some of them. I don't know if my decision was a correct one, but looking back now I wonder if she might have sent the message both personally and with the hope that I would release it and put her antiwar sentiments in the context that she associated with me, instead of the selfish isolationism of those who wanted to let the Europeans fight while the United States profited. Perhaps I lacked the faith in Mrs. Roosevelt that I should have had.

The other reason I mention the message is that the censors had decreed that I should not see the letter in which my younger brother wrote the words that Mrs. Roosevelt had asked him to send me. When his letter arrived, I was in solitary confinement, but a lieutenant with whom I had become friends showed it to me, saying that I should read it but never tell anyone that he had shown it to me. If I did, he would be in dire trouble, perhaps discharged or worse. His willingness to show me the letter came out of a friendship that we had gradually developed as he and I each tried to live up to our best selves. For the lieutenant that meant not blindly accepting the prison system's condemnation of criminals as evil subhumans who could never be trusted. For me it meant trying to treat each prison guard as an individual with a potential humanity that lay beneath the surface but was usually frustrated by the routine cruelties he was supposed to inflict on prisoners. I understood why so many prisoners called the guards "hacks" and why they would not consider being friends with any of them, except as a way to obtain dope or other forbidden items. But, in addition to my understanding of the need to treat every person, in or out of prison, as a potential friend, I also realized that most of the guards were working-class people who had taken the job as the only way they could earn a living and support their families, especially during the depression. So sometimes I tried to get into a discussion about that aspect of their employment, hoping that later I would be able to suggest that even as they were sometimes forced to do terrible things that the prison system required, similarly many of the prisoners were there because they had done terrible things that society required in order for them to feed their families or provide them with other forms of security. This led to several good friendships with guards who did their best to be as decent as possible with their "fellow prisoners."

My belief in the submerged humanity of prisoners who had committed the most heinous crimes was strengthened in a Hudson County, New Jersey, jail shortly before I landed at Lewisburg's maximum security prison. I was in the jail because I had refused to pay bail during the period between my arraignment and trial. I do this as often as I can because I don't believe that the inability to raise money for bail should force people to spend weeks, months, sometimes a year or more in jail before they have even been tried. This time my wife, Elizabeth, called the judge after a week or two and explained why I had refused bail. He responded by releasing me on my own recognizance. And when he sentenced me to two years, which was less time than the court sentenced most war objectors at that time, he suggested that I spend the evening at home with my wife and voluntarily return to the federal building the next morning to meet a sheriff who would drive me to Lewisburg.

But at my arrival at the New Jersey jail, the officials had concluded that I must be "yellow," since I was refusing to defend my country militarily. Saying this to my face and to the prisoners in my assigned cell, they asked the prisoners to "take care of this unpatriotic guy." The men they said this to were in a small, overcrowded cell where the most violent prisoners were kept. Later, when I was leaving on my own recognizance, a slightly nicer guard said that he hadn't approved of where I had been put but hoped that I had learned how evil prisoners and Nazis can be and had given up my ideas that nonviolence is a practical way of combating them. Despite all this, I was clearly saved from what might have happened to me— not by my own efforts, but because this was the prison where, on my arrival, I had intervened when a Mafioso was being roughed up by a guard. Word of what had happened came rather quickly to the "worthless, evil" prisoners in the cell where I had been assigned and, step by step, several of them became my friends.

Not long after I arrived at Lewisburg, five of us conducted a long hunger strike for abolishing "the Hole" and eliminating the censorship of mail, books, and magazines. Winning the issue on censorship and feeling that the issue of the Hole had reached a fairly wide audience on the outside through prison visitors and progressive publicity, we stopped the strike on the sixty-fifth day (after a month of force feeding). The next day I was put in the "fuck-up dorm," which had a high percentage of southern military prisoners who had committed violent crimes. One of the two guards who took me there addressed the prisoners as follows: "This guy is one of those phonies who says he's too good to be in regular prison with you." This was a total lie. Unlike a few war objectors, I had always opposed special classification and treatment as a political prisoner. "He's a nigger-lover who says that you guys should eat and sleep with the niggers and use the same toilets and showers as niggers do." True. "And he's a Nazi who spits on the flag and refuses to fight for our country." And, after a pause, as if to let his words sink in, "We're leaving now so that you guys can take care of him." Just before they closed the door, the other guard spoke for the first time: "When we come back, we hope you give him to us with his head in his hands."

Here I will have to paraphrase what I said because I don't remember it word for word the way I remember what the guards had said; but this was the general line of attack, using street language and drawing on things I had learned from my earlier prison experiences: "You guys know enough not to believe those hacks. That's a lot of bullshit they're trying to shove down your throats and you know it. It's the hacks who act like Nazis, not me. You know how they treat you. I've been up there in solitary fightin' for you guys. Five of us have been up there fightin' to get rid of the goddam Hole. We're fightin' for the cons and the hacks don't like it. I know a lot of you guys have been in the Hole, so I don't have to tell you what it's like. I don't have to tell you why we've been on hunger strike demanding that they stop acting like Nazis and do away with the Hole once and for all. You want to know why they're tellin' all those lies about me? To get you and me fightin' amongst ourselves instead of stickin' together against them. Anyone who has been doin' time like you guys have won't fall for that shit. You know the score. And so do I."

I survived, though there were times, especially that night after the lights went out, when I didn't expect to. But it was more than a month before I made a request to be transferred to a cellblock, where I desperately needed the relative quiet of a cell after that noisy "fuck-up dorm." I waited that long because the one thing you can't do as a serious nonviolent activist, especially in prison, is to run away from threats or danger. If you do, the wrong reputation will follow you wherever you go or are moved.

This was only one of several times in Lewisburg when prisoners were asked to "take care of Dellinger," sometimes with the offer of parole if they did. But this was the most difficult occasion for me to handle because of my exhaustion from the long hunger strike. A few years later I wasn't surprised at something Dorothy Day, the cofounder of the Catholic Worker movement, said when she visited me and Elizabeth at our intentional pacifist community. It was the day after William Remington, a former commerce department official who was a victim of the McCarthy era, had been killed at Lewisburg. "You don't believe the official version, do you?" she asked. "That he was killed by a prisoner who was stealing his cigarettes when Remington came back to his cell and caught him?" Based on our similar prison experiences, we agreed that the officials had asked some prisoners to kill him, probably saying something like, "He's a dirty Communist, so why don't you get rid of him. If you do, we'll reward you with parole, or time off your long sentence."

Is it any wonder that in my resume I included under "Education" the following: "Three years' imprisonment at Danbury, Connecticut, Federal Correctional Institution (1940–41) and Lewisburg, Pennsylvania, Federal Penitentiary (1942–45) [for refusal to register for the draft, though I was militarily exempt as a divinity student]. Occasional refresher courses in other jails. Yale University B.A., magna cum laude, 1936; Henry Fellow to New College, Oxford, 1936–37; year and a half of courses at Yale Divinity School and Union Theological Seminary (1937–39)."

RALPH DiGia
_____

My Resistance to World War II

*World War II reenforced my belief that in war one
becomes what the enemy is accused of being.*

A DAY IN EARLY MARCH 1943. A loud whistle. A shout, "On the
count." It was time for the hacks (guards) to take the count of the
prison population to make sure that no one was missing. I shouldn't
have been surprised (and I wasn't) that I found myself in a prison
cell. After all, my father had given me a good start in that direction.

My father, a barber, was an immigrant, and in this country he
belonged to a group of Italian socialist immigrants—barbers, shoe-
makers, tailors, and laborers. As a youngster I was taken to many
meetings where I heard talk about the exploitation of the poor by the
rich and how in war the rich got richer and the poor died. There was
much talk about opposing Mussolini's fascist government. Every
Columbus Day there would be an outdoor meeting attended by representatives from the American and Italian governments praising
Italy and the Italians here. But my father would take me to the meeting held by people opposing Mussolini. I remember going with my
father to protest the trial and execution of two Italian anarchists,
Sacco and Vanzetti, whom many believed were framed on murder
charges.

At home we had a book that had photos of the horrors of war
resulting from the use of mustard gas. Later, reading *All Quiet on the
Western Front* and *Johnny Got His Gun,* two powerful antiwar novels,
certainly made an impression on me. The thirties was a period of
antiwar sentiment. In college I participated in demonstrations against
ROTC, then called "Mili-Sci" (Military Science). I joined the thousands of students who signed the Oxford Pledge not to participate

38

RALPH DiGia (b. 1914)

Ralph DiGia (*at left*) has been a lifelong pacifist. While a student at City College of New York in the thirties, he signed the Oxford Peace Pledge and took part in antiwar demonstrations. Yet in 1940, because his pacifism was not religiously based, he was denied classification as a conscientious objector. After serving two and a half years in prison for refusing induction, Ralph began his long association with the War Resisters League, first as a volunteer and then as a staff member. Since World War II he has participated in numerous antiwar and civil rights actions, sometimes committing civil disobedience. Since his official "retirement," he has continued to serve WRL as a volunteer. He lives in New York City with his wife, Karin.

in war. There were many demonstrations throughout the country against war up to the time of Pearl Harbor. Feelings ran so high that in late 1940 the draft law only narrowly passed the House of Representatives.

But the draft was now a fact. It was time to make a decision. I had read about the conscientious objectors in World War I and how they had remained true to their beliefs. Their actions were an inspiration to me in my decision to register as a conscientious objector. There was no question for me; war was not the way.

On registration day in October of 1940, I registered and informed the draft board that I was a conscientious objector. They didn't have much of a reaction (this was before Pearl Harbor) and told me I would have to fill out a form. As of that day I had never met a pacifist nor known of a pacifist organization. Yes, I had antiwar friends, but they were not pacifists. So when the draft came, my friends entered the military and I remained behind to do what I believed in. Soon after I registered, I read a headline which mentioned that seven seminarians had refused to register and would be sent to jail. I suppose that if they had not been religious, I would have followed up on them. (Later I met two of them in jail and we became friends.)

I presented my case in writing to the appeals board, writing about my background in opposition to war, that war was contrary to all the ideals in which I believed, that we must look to the example of Gandhi and nonviolence as a substitute for war. Without a religious background, I didn't expect to be classified as a conscientious objector, and I was right. In the spring of 1942, I was ordered to report for induction, and then came the discussion with my parents. My mother's feelings were that I go neither to jail nor the army. My father, who had supported me up to this point, now advised me to report for induction. He was afraid that going to jail would ruin my future and believed that, as a college graduate, I could get a good job in the army. One must remember that going to jail in those days didn't have the same acceptance that it had during the civil rights and Vietnam eras. So, in retrospect, I can understand my father's reaction. Anyway, I argued that I had gotten many of my ideals from him, and now that the moment had arrived for me to live up to them, he was asking me to give them up. And what would ideals mean if one gave them up when they were put to a test? It was a very upsetting discussion, and we both went to bed unhappy. The next morning my father had already gone to work when I got up, and my mother told me he had said I should do what I had to do.

This having been decided, the next question for me was how to handle the induction day. Having proceeded this far without help from anyone or any organization (I don't know why I never sought help), I decided that I would go to the office of the U.S. attorney on the day I was supposed to be inducted. I wasn't sure how the government would proceed, whether the FBI would come knocking at my door to arrest me. Since I didn't want to involve my parents in such a scene, I decided to turn myself in.

The U.S. attorney's office asked what he could do for me. I told him that I was supposed to report for induction and that I was refusing to do so. He wasn't upset or angry, as I thought he would be; as a matter of fact, he was very helpful. He told me that he didn't have any papers about me and he could do nothing. At that point I wasn't sure what to do. After all, I had said all my goodbyes. Then the attorney told me something that marked a turning point in my life—that I should go to see Julian Cornell, a Quaker lawyer who handled conscientious objector cases, and that he could be reached at the office of the War Resisters League.

I went immediately to the War Resisters League, operating out of a small office in lower Manhattan. There I told Abe Kaufman, the executive secretary, why I had come to the office. Although I had no idea that there was such an organization, I sure was happy that it existed. He told me there were other objectors in the area and that he would arrange for me to meet them. What a relief to find out that I was not alone and that I would have some support. I made an appointment to see Julian Cornell. We met and discussed my case. Since I was not religious, he said he had three other such cases of nonreligious objectors that he was appealing, and he would combine theirs with mine. He would prepare all the paperwork and let me know when I would have to be in court. The four of us appeared before a judge for a hearing and were released without bail in the custody of our lawyer pending appeal.

In the meantime, I met with other objectors, who had not yet been called for induction, to discuss our beliefs. I had previously read about Gandhi's use of nonviolence to achieve India's independence but had not really studied it thoroughly enough to understand it completely. I learned a lot in my conversations with my new friends. My belief in opposing war was strengthened. I remembered those brave men who had stood up against the government in World War I and their importance in the fight against war. I knew that if those who opposed war were to accept induction anyway, there would be no chance of achieving the goal to end war.

In early 1943 we lost our appeal on the grounds that our beliefs did not come under the religious definition of the Selective Service Act. The judge sentenced each of us to three years in prison.

In March I entered the West Street Jail in New York to be held there to await transfer to another federal prison. It was overcrowded, gloomy, and, during the day, constantly noisy. Visiting conditions were terrible, which upset my parents. A glass partition separated the visitor from the prisoner and conversation was carried on by phone. Since I was awaiting transfer, I was not assigned to a job. Although I was there only about thirty days, the time went very slowly.

An ironic situation developed at West Street. Louie Lepke of Murder, Inc., was being held in a solitary cell and was awaiting sentencing (later he was executed) for murder. So here was someone in prison for killing while others were there for refusing to kill.

In April some other COs and I were transferred to Danbury Prison (classified as a Federal Correctional Institution) in Connecticut. The conditions there were an improvement over West Street. It was relatively new, clean, bright, and not overcrowded. There was the usual thirty-day quarantine period during which prisoners were instructed about rules and procedures, answered questionnaires, got physical exams, and learned how to make a bed—to make sure the covers were so tight that they'd bounce a quarter. Finally, I was sent out to join the prison population. I was assigned to a dormitory and to work on a labor gang. There were two types of housing, cells and dormitories. Most lived in dormitories. Cells were mostly for "trouble-makers" or for men who requested them for a good reason. As a matter of fact, after a lengthy stretch in a noisy dormitory with little privacy, one preferred a cell for a change.

I hate to say this, but I was relieved to be in Danbury, where there were many COs and a sense of solidarity. I was with a community. And the prison was not like the ones I had seen in Hollywood movies. On my parents' first visit they were quite relieved, especially after their visit to the West Street Jail. Visits at Danbury were held in a large room, sitting in chairs face to face without interference. And the warden walked his dog around the room and smiled, thereby assuring visitors that everything was cozy. My parents were relieved, and this made me feel better.

I didn't mind working on a labor gang. It was good exercise. I used up a lot of excess energy, and it made the time pass. That's the way it was at the beginning. As for the make-up of the prison population, conscientious objectors made up the largest segment. Others, all in for nonviolent violations, were butchers and gas station owners (convicted of violating wartime rationing laws), numbers runners, bootleggers, and bad check artists. All the latter had sentences of thirty days to a year. Sentences for war objectors ranged from two to five years.

After a few months we began to discuss the existing racial segregation in the dining hall and whether we could do something about it. We discussed it among ourselves during yard period. Danbury had an education department, with evening classes in arts, crafts, and English. We asked permission to form our own sociology class. There was no objection, for it would look good on the prison's record and for the warden to have such instruction at the prison. This gave us an opportunity to discuss specific plans.

We chose a committee to discuss with the warden our suggestion to integrate the dining hall. He refused to meet with a committee but would meet with two individuals to discuss the problem. The warden argued that prison was a mirror of the outside society and that we should change the outside first. No other federal prison was integrated, he pointed out, and that was the policy of the Federal Bureau of Prisons in Washington. He said that he personally favored integration, but his hands were tied. He could do nothing.

We now had to decide what course we should take. A sit-in in the dining hall? Continue to organize until we had a larger group to participate? Go ahead with a work strike? After a couple of weeks we decided on a work strike. We informed the warden that we had no choice but to refuse to work until the dining hall was integrated. There was no response from the warden. We then chose a day to ask all those interested to meet in the yard after breakfast and refuse to go to work. In the middle of August eighteen of us appeared to strike, and thus the action began.

We were moved to a cell block that contained exactly eighteen cells. There we were isolated from the rest of the population, locked in our cells except for a forty-minute yard period. Food was brought to our cells. In order to communicate we had to lie on the floor and shout through the crack at the bottom of the door. But how to pass notes and reading materials? We found metal collars at the bottom of the radiator pipes. By attaching a string (taken from Bull Durham cigarette tobacco bags distributed by the prison) to the metal disc and tying the other end to a magazine or other paper we were able to pass things to one another. We would send the disc sliding under the door to a cell across the hall where that person would pull the string until he secured the reading material. One of the guards commented that this means of sending things was an "ingenious device." And so it was.

After many weeks our spirits began to sag. Nothing was happening—no publicity, no move by the warden. There was talk of ending the strike, of going back into the population to organize and get more support. Perhaps we should go back and have a sit-in in the dining hall? These were difficult and depressing days. But in the end we decided to hang in a little longer.

Meanwhile, friends at the War Resisters League increased their efforts to publicize the strike through press releases to the African American and liberal press, a visit to Congressman Adam Clayton Powell, and letters to James V. Bennett, director of the Federal Bureau of Prisons. Finally the story appeared in a few newspapers, and the ACLU criticized Bennett. Our spirits were buoyed and there was no more talk about ending the strike.

Just before Christmas the warden dropped in on us. We were released from our cells so he could talk to all of us at the same time. He said he wanted us to know that he had plans to desegregate the dining hall on Feburary first, but we were hindering his plan. He said his hands were tied as long as we remained on strike. We could hardly believe this. We told him we would like to discuss this among ourselves and would let him know our decision. Wondering whether this was a trick, we agreed to take him at his word while committing ourselves to return if the promise was not kept. We sent word to the warden that we were ready to end the strike. We did not mention our committment to return.

On February 1 there was an announcement that prisoners could sit anywhere they wished in the dining hall. The dining hall was desegregated. What a wonderful feeling after more than four months on strike. At first a few whites and African Americans complained of the change, but nothing serious happened. After a month or so, no one paid any attention to the seating.

While on strike I learned something that had nothing to do with the issue of integration. I remember my father denouncing the church and priests, making it clear to my mother, who was a Catholic, that his children were not to go to church. As I was growing up, I noticed that my boyhood friends who went to church were not interested in any of the social issues that interested me. And it seemed to me that the church's attitude was that we should wait for "pie in the sky when you die." I had no reason to believe that religious people were interested in supporting the causes I believed in. Interestingly enough, the strike had the effect of changing my mind. A few religious friends had also been on strike. One of them said that he was amazed that a nonbeliever would participate in the action in which we were all involved. His impression was that one had to believe in God in order to join in social action. So the strike not only eliminated a social injustice, but it also erased misconceptions that some of us had.

In battling the monotony of prison life, I did something very unusual for me: attended the services of the Jewish, Catholic, and Protestant faiths. It was a new experience for me, and a way to break up the monotony.

When you have two to five years to do, you see people come and go, since most of the prisoners had shorter sentences. Then you notice that many people, especially those in for white-collar crimes, are making parole while very few war objectors are being granted parole. So we decided to make an issue of it. In order to bring this to the attention of the authorities, we decided to refuse to work. In discussing how to proceed, we decided that one person at a time should refuse to work instead of all striking at once, as we had in the strike against segregation. In this way the authorities would not know how many might be involved. Someone carved out a wooden numeral "1." We would display the numeral in the prison yard and announce that whoever found it in his bed would have to go on strike the next day. (Of course, we actually had volunteers.) I was the fifth to go, joining the others who were being held in segregation quarters.

Every Wednesday for fifteen weeks an objector joined the strike. But by then I was not there, because five of us had been transferred to Lewisburg Federal Penitentiary. It was a treat to be driven about two hundred miles, to enjoy the scenery, to be in the wide, open spaces.

Lewisburg was not a federal correctional institution like Danbury, but a penitentiary where three- and five-year sentences were considered short time. Many prisoners were there for violent crimes like bank robbery and kidnapping, and fifteen-, twenty-, or twenty-five-year sentences were common.

Since we were still on strike we were placed in the tough cell block in individual cells. Things were uneventful, as we were just getting used to our new surroundings. A few days later one of the other prisoners in the cell block came to the front of my cell and said that we had better get back to work because our presence there was making it hard on them. He said the hacks were hanging around more than usual because of us. I explained that the authorities had deliberately put us there, figuring that the other prisoners would pressure us to go off the strike. They were playing prisoner against prisoner to gain their own ends. He didn't accept that and repeated that we'd better get out or else. This left me uneasy, but fortunately cell bars separated us. The next morning another prisoner approached my cell and asked if I was a friend of Dave Dellinger's. Though I had never met Dave, I had heard of him, so I answered "yes." He replied, "any friend of Dellinger's is a friend of mine." He assured me that if anyone bothered me I should let him know and he would take care of it. This gave me an inkling of how things were handled in Lewisburg. I learned later that Dave had the respect of the general population because he had supported some of them when they were in trouble with the authorities. The next week we were transferred to another cell block and were segregated from others. When other Danbury strikers were transferred to Lewisburg, we were all moved to a dormitory where we were able to move about among ourselves.

Weeks went by and we were getting nowhere with the parole issue. Furthermore, Lewisburg didn't seem to be a place where paroles were easily granted to any prisoners. After about two months we decided to go back into the population.

We were put in different housing units. I was put in a dormitory without any other objectors. Word gets around who you are when you are moved into new housing. I moved in after the evening meal and was greeted by no one. I arranged my belongings, read a little before lights out, and then went to bed. As I was falling asleep, suddenly my bed was moving and I was being doused with water and I heard a flow of words about being a "fuckin' yellow coward." I was frightened, but whoever did it had disappeared. I moved my bed back and got in and then someone said, "Here comes the hack." He stopped at my bed. I pretended to be asleep, and he asked me what happened. I said that nothing had happened, that I was all right. After he left someone said that it was a dirty trick and offered me dry clothes. Someone else suggested we switch my wet mattress with one belonging to a prisoner who was working on the night shift. I objected, but they went ahead with the switch. I was very uneasy, wondering what would happen when that man came back to his bed. When the prisoner got back he began swearing that he would take care of the person who had done this. In the morning I went to the shower room where I had hung my wet clothes. And next thing I knew, someone grabbed my shoulder and swore at me for having taken his mattress. Before I could answer, someone else grabbed his shoulder and told him that he was the one who did it and if there were anything to say, to say it to him. Again I learned that this was the way things were settled in Lewisburg.

That evening I was called down to the office and told that I was being transferred to another dormitory for my own safety. I objected vehemently, saying that would be the worst thing that could happen, giving the impression to other prisoners that I couldn't "take it." I was told that if I didn't move I would be responsible for anything that happened to me. That was okay with me. Later I wondered if the guards might arrange for "something" to happen to me. When I went back to my dorm I told other inmates the story. The incident proved to be very fortunate for me. The fact that I had not ratted on anyone and had refused to move made me an okay guy. I was accepted into the community.

After that things settled into the usual monotonous routine of obeying silly rules—"Roll down your sleeves, straighten out the line, get that shovel moving, quiet!"—the noisy dorm, loud talking, no privacy. Some of this was offset when I was able to do something useful, helping someone write a letter, listening to a hard-luck story, giving some advice.

Always taking orders wears you down and frustrates you because you can't do much about it. But two weeks before I was to be released, I reacted. Once a week we would go to the clothing room for a change of clothes. This hot summer day when I received my clean clothes, I put on everything except my undershirt. Rather than wait until I went back outside to work, I decided to remove it at once. The hack asked me to put my shirt on. I started to explain why I hadn't put it on. Again he ordered me to put it on. Again I tried to explain. He cut me short and asked, "Are you refusing to obey an order?" I hesitated for a moment, then shrugged my shoulders and said, "yes." He took me to the captain and said, "This man refused to obey an order." Before I could say anything the captain said, "Take him to the Hole." My belt was removed so I couldn't hang myself. I spent most of the time walking up and down in my cell, shaking my head—not out of anger, but at the absurdity of it all. The next day I was let out.

After almost three years in prison, I guess I had reached a breaking point. I had endangered the date of my release, which was a few weeks away. But I didn't care. I had to say "no!"

Late in June 1945, I was released. I had a strange feeling on the train ride from prison to my home. Passengers reading, talking quietly, seemingly unconcerned with world events. I didn't feel connected to them. I wondered what they would feel if they knew that I had just been released from prison for refusing induction into the military. I thought I should be celebrating and overjoyed. Instead I sat silently and was slightly anxious about what I would do after

I got home. A former college friend met me at the railroad station, much to my surprise and joy, thus connecting me to the outside world once more, and I felt much better. Then to my family, and I was happy.

Soon after my release I received an invitation from Dave Dellinger, who had been released a few months earlier, to join him in upstate New York where he was staying in a cottage of a friend who was not living there at the time. I joined him and his family and Bill Kuenning (also from Lewisburg) to give myself time to readjust to the outside world and to be with my prison friends again. Dave and Bill worked on a farm, and I got a job in a summer resort hotel.

Before long we became active again. Dave had secured possession of an old printing press and we decided to publish a magazine that we called *Direct Action*. Just about this time the A-bombs were dropped on Hiroshima and Nagasaki. This prompted a *Direct Action* editorial headlined "Declaration of War," which stated that the United States could have no claim "to being a democratic or a peace loving nation. Without any semblance of a democratic decision the American people awoke one morning to discover that the United States government had committed one of the worst atrocities in history." The editorial called for "total war against the infamous economic, political and social system which is dominant in this country." We published two issues of the magazine. With the arrival of winter we had to leave, moving back to our homes in the city.

Needless to say, after prison I continued my involvement with the War Resisters League. Beginning in 1946 I became a volunteer; I then joined the staff in 1955 and remained on staff until my retirement. Today I am again a volunteer. My years included countless demonstrations and many arrests for protesting bomb testing, civil defense drills, nuclear weapons, nuclear power plants, the Vietnam War, Central America intervention, and the Gulf War. During the Vietnam War I also counseled war resisters.

There are some interesting stories attached to many of those demonstrations, but there's one in particular. In the summer of 1951, it was headlined "4 Americans Bicycling From Paris to Moscow." I joined Dave Dellinger, Bill Sutherland (also from Lewisburg prison), and Art Emory, and we sailed to Europe on a ship laden with students, arriving in France in about ten days. Our first job was to find a printer to publish our leaflet, which explained that we had served prison sentences in the United States as conscientious objectors to war. We appealed to people in both East and West blocs to join together in nonviolent resistance to war and injustice. The leaflet was always printed in English on one side with the other in French, German, or Russian, depending on where we were distributing it.

In Paris we visited the Soviet and German consulates to request visas for our trip. In each case we explained who we were and the purpose of our trip. The German consul was visibly upset. This request obviously had to be discussed with American authorities, no matter what the German government might desire. We were told to fill out an application and we would be informed of the decision at a later date. We visited the Soviet consulate and were well received. The consul agreed with some of the things we said, explaining that the Soviet army was a peace army and that we probably would be welcome. Of course, we were told, we would have to wait until he had consulted with his government.

In a short time we were refused a visa by the Germans—I should say by the Americans, because this was 1951 and the Germans were still not free of U.S. control. The Soviet consul told us that we had to wait a little longer. We were not told "no," but we felt we couldn't wait any longer. We began to doubt that we would ever be granted a visa. We decided we would bicycle to Strasbourg at the German border to protest the denial of a German visa. We knew we would be unable to get into Germany, but we did want to call attention to the fact that the United States was setting up a barrier to making known our message. And from there we would continue our attempt to get a Soviet visa.

We bicycled from Paris to Strasbourg, passing out our leaflets on the way. We tented near the bridge over the Rhine. We distributed leaflets and fasted for a week, which drew the attention of the press.

Our next plan was to head for Vienna, where the four Allied powers were situated, and there we would check on our visa application at the Soviet consulate. We bicycled to Switzerland where we boarded a train for Vienna. There we consulted with some Quakers for information and advice. They were very fearful of having any contact with the Soviets. We got in touch with the Soviet consul in

Vienna, who was also happy to meet us and encouraged us to be patient. But after a couple of visits we felt we were getting nowhere. We had applied in July, and it was now October. We decided on a plan to go to the Soviet-controlled section of Austria and distribute our leaflets. We would buy train tickets to go to the British zone, which was legal, but we would get off at the stop before that, the Soviet zone in Baden, which was illegal. The Quakers warned us that we would disappear and that no one in Baden would dare take a leaflet from us. Well, we discounted their fears, thinking we might be detained and maybe imprisoned, but not disappear. We did write letters home about our plans, suggesting that they could be in touch with our New York friends if they didn't hear from us.

So we went ahead with our plan. The four of us got off in the Soviet zone, and no one questioned us. We had decided to go two together so as to appear less conspicuous. We began to pass out our leaflets as we met soldiers in the streets. We would smile and say a few words in Russian—"friend," "peace." There was no problem with passing out the leaflets; no one questioned us. We walked through the town twice without incident, passing out leaflets to soldiers. And then we decided to do something that wasn't in our plan: to catch the next train back to Vienna. We had accomplished more than we had expected.

Much to the Quakers' surprise (and ours), we returned safely to Vienna. Why hadn't we been arrested? I believe that the people in Baden figured that no one in his right mind would be doing what we were doing without the approval of the authorities, and therefore they accepted the leaflets. But whatever the reason, they had taken our leaflets. And what was the effect? Who knows? We hope it planted a seed in some that affected a future decision.

Having lived through the years of World War II, I am more convinced than ever that war is not the method to solve conflicts. When I refused induction I had no illusions that I was going to have any effect on the current situation, but I hoped that I might contribute something to future situations. I did want to help keep alive the ideal of nonviolence and resistance to war. If every pacifist went to war when called, the ideal of nonviolence would lose its power.

World War II reenforced my belief that in war one becomes what the enemy is accused of being. Compare the atrocity of Hiroshima to what I was taught in school, that one of the worst atrocities of World War I was the German submarine attack on the Lusitania, an unarmed ship with civilians aboard. Americans, as well as other nationals, think of themselves as decent people, but they will sink to any level to destroy others in war. No matter how people justified war in the past, we are now in the nuclear age, and even from a pragmatic view we must look to other ways to solve our conflicts.

There is a long, long history of developing efficient weapons of extermination. And where has it left us? Compared to this history, nonviolence is in its early stages. We need to put more resources and effort into developing nonviolent alternatives. Let us consider what our professed ideals are. Is war the method to achieve these ideals? Or is nonviolence the way? Some say nonviolence is idealistic and unrealistic, but studying the history of war and violence, we must conclude that nonviolence is pragmatic. Whatever we choose to call it, let it be. Nonviolence is the way.

ARTHUR A. DOLE

My War and My Peace

*I am therefore hopeful that war and conscription,
like slavery and the duel before them, eventually
will become obsolete.*

WHAT DID YOU do during World War II?

I was a civilian.

That's the short answer. A much longer, but still abbreviated, reply is that while I was a student at Antioch College in Yellow Springs, Ohio, in 1941, before Pearl Harbor, I registered as a conscientious objector and my draft board classified me 1-AO (noncombatant). I refused this classification; pled *nolo contendere*; was sentenced in 1942 to five years' incarceration in the Federal Correctional Institution in Ashland, Kentucky; and in 1943 was paroled to Civilian Public Service (CPS). I was first assigned to Powellsville, Maryland, a camp whose mission was primarily to cut trees and drain swampland. Then I transferred to the Vital Economics Department of the University of Rochester Medical School to study the effects of temperature, high altitude, and yeast diet on volunteer subjects. Finally, I transferred to the unit at Eastern State Hospital in Williamsburg, Virginia, whose mission was to care for patients diagnosed as psychotic. I walked out of CPS in August 1945 and worked in the clothing room of the American Friends Service Committee in Philadelphia until ordered by the Justice Department to report to Lewisburg, Pennsylvania, Federal Penitentiary. In 1946, after the war ended, I was paroled back to my former job at the American Friends Service Committee and then returned to complete my bachelor's degree at Antioch College.

ARTHUR A. DOLE (b. 1917)
Arthur Dole is Emeritus Professor of Psychology in Education
at the University of Pennsylvania. He is president of People for
Educational Advancement and Community Enhancement, which
raises funds for a college and a nongovernmental organization in
San Salvador. He and his wife, Marjorie, live in Maine.
Photo courtesy of the Antiochiana Collection, Antioch College.

One of my very earliest memories is of the end of World War I, "the war to end wars." I was still very young, but I can clearly recall a dark night in San Francisco, toddling to the window when bells and sirens sounded the good news. War next comes to mind when I was about six and we lived in Weston, a pleasant suburb of Boston. Using a snowshoe for my shield and a stick for my sword, I played at being a knight. I thrilled to the lust of battle with or without play-mates, dying sometimes only to rise up for another duel. I also recall wondering what had happened to the German soldier whose hel-met, a hole in the center of it, hung in our shed. I recall meeting Fred Josefson, a friend of the family who had been a spy for the United States, a big, impressive, jovial chap who recounted his adventures in Europe with zest. In contrast there was Uncle Harold Dole, then a chicken farmer, who was said to have missed a great career as a writer because he had been gassed and shell shocked in France.

In 1929 I watched the movie *All Quiet on the Western Front*, with Lew Ayres. Clearly, World War I had been a terrible and tragic mis-take; innocents killed and were killed. The film touched me at a basic, emotional level. "War is not for me," I said to myself.

During the twenties and early thirties my extended Dole family and many of our friends were Unitarians. At that time the Ameri-can culture included strong currents of isolationism and pacifism. I heard my Great-uncle Charles (my grandfather's brother) preach strongly against war. I found out much later that this distinguished Unitarian minister, who had served briefly in the Union forces dur-ing the Civil War, had opposed America's intervention in the Euro-pean conflict. He spoke out forcefully while visiting his son, James, in Hawaii. The consequences for Jim Dole, a leading citizen and industrialist in a military community, were considered a bit embar-rassing.

Charles Dole's daughter, Winifred, and her husband, Horace Mann, along with their two daughters, Barbara and Kay, became my "alternative" family. While my parents were enmeshed in a bit-ter divorce, the Manns helped me with finances for camp, Phillips Exeter Academy, and Antioch College and offered me hospitality dur-ing vacations. Horace Mann, a retired teacher of foreign languages and a grandson of the famous legislator and educator, was an in-dependent thinker who was at least a hundred years ahead of his time. Discussions with him on current topics during my adolescence sharpened my appreciation for intellectual give-and-take. Quietly, Horace spoke up for democracy, human rights, tolerance, civil liberties, humane socialism, and pacifism. Although he never forced his opinions on me or tried to convert me, he was and remains a powerful mentor and role model.

After my father left my mother in 1930, he became a distant figure. My mother, angry and hurt, sued the other woman for breaking up her marriage. She was very bitter toward most of the Dole family. Because I did not share her feelings about my father and grandparents, I learned quite early in life that strong emotions may lead to illogical and self-destructive acts and thoughts and that there may be more than one side to a quarrel.

Mother was a moderate Republican, liberal in the social sphere. She drank, smoked, was a staunch feminist, and occasionally attended the local Unitarian church. Politically, she was close to a monarchist, anti-Communist, anti-Socialist, anti-union, anti–civil rights and was all for the American way. She was proud of her roots and stressed ancestry, social class, and prestige. Before World War II she was a bit of a libertarian: "The less government the better. Be an independent thinker." Charles Dole and Horace Mann, in her eyes, were "saints," impractical idealists.

I have been told that from infancy I was a skeptic about traditional religion. As a toddler I asked, "Who is God's wife?" I can't recall that I ever agonized over the nature and existence of God, as many do. I rejected most traditional theological concepts: original sin, eternal damnation, heaven or hell in the next life, saints, and devils. I was neither quite clearly an agnostic nor an atheist. I accepted, enjoyed, and found awesome the natural world. The golden rule, the brotherhood of man, tolerance, and turning the other cheek have always been basic to my thinking. I was enrolled in Unitarian Sunday school and in later adolescence attended Unitarian services periodically. At that time, New England Unitarian churches placed more emphasis on form and ritual than they do now and tended to provide a rather tepid Christianity. As I recall, there was a great deal more pressure for attendance and contributions than for acceptance of doctrine. These experiences increased my distrust of organizations and my independence in religious matters. My growing sense of reverence for life but suspicion of magic, myth, and dogma have kept me at a distance from mainline churches. On the other hand, over the years I have developed some commonalities with aspects of Unitarian Universalism, Quakerism, Reform Judaism, and Buddhism.

My classmates in the public schools of Weston and Cambridge, Massachusetts, were almost all white and middle or upper class, with just a few Irish Catholics. In contrast, during my two stints in the public grammar schools of New York City my classmates exposed me to variety in religion, class, and ethnic origin. At P.S. 6 near 86th Street and Madison Avenue, my friends tended to be Jewish. Although Mother took me aside to warn me that Jews were pushy and unattractive, I paid no attention. I encountered very few African Americans, but I was told that, genetically, they were intellectually inferior. I didn't believe that either. And I came to realize that much as Mother loved me (perhaps too much), her opinions on many subjects were not infallible. In her defense, Mother was merely voicing the conventional WASP wisdom of the time. She was courageous and tough enough to defy her own mother, to adopt liberal social behaviors, and to make her own way as a commercial artist, writer, and single parent during the worst of the depression.

When I was thirteen my mother and I lived in Cambridge, Massachusetts, as tenants in the home of Tab Smith, a manufacturer's representative and a democratic socialist. Smith had a substantial library, and I went on a reading binge: Mark Twain, O. Henry, Upton Sinclair, Ralph Bellamy, and Jack London, to name a few. As I felt drawn to unpopular social positions, I became an individualist and philosophical anarchist. At Peabody Grammar School each morning we pledged our allegiance to the flag. Curiously, nature called me to the boys lavatory at this very time until finally Miss Sullivan confronted me in my stall.

At fourteen, I attended a YMCA summer camp for disadvantaged youth on Cape Cod. During the day we earned our keep by caddying. One of our evening activities was military marching, which I loathed but could not avoid.

At about this time I gave up fishing because I began to empathize with the fish. I have never hunted, and I find the thought of killing an animal distasteful. Yet I think I understand how the thrill of the chase, the countryside, and the bonding with other sportsmen appeal to many men. Since I am partial to a sirloin steak or swordfish fillet, I realize now that long-held attitudes can be inconsistent. Logically, I should be a vegetarian!

When I entered Harvard College in the fall of 1936 as a commuter on scholarship, living with my mother, the country was slowly recovering from the Great Depression, Hitler was increasing in menace, and Japan was flexing its muscles in China. Professor Roger B. "Frisky" Merriman taught an enormously popular course on European history that featured gripping lectures, spirited discussion sections, and ample readings. Here I first encountered Erasmus of Rotterdam, the fifteenth-century humanist and pacifist.

That spring Mother remarried and, at nineteen, I was on my own. Arthur Blanchard, a bachelor in his early fifties, a Republican state senator, and an unproduced playwright, lived with his mother. He was not about to provide residence and college tuition to a stepson. Therefore, I dropped out of Harvard and, thanks to Mr. Blanchard's influence, took a full-time job as a coatroom attendant at the university library at fifty dollars per month. I did lots of reading and thinking that year. From an African American graduate student I learned about racism. Peggy and Sprague Curtis rented me a room in their Boston apartment and helped tutor me in the ways of adults. For instance, I learned to use alcohol moderately and responsibly.

When I transferred to Antioch College in Yellow Springs, Ohio, in the fall of 1938, I discovered a number of fellow students who shared my pacifist feelings and some of my more idiosyncratic attitudes toward authority and racial injustice. When my mother came to visit she was much distressed by my "pinko" pals and my romantic fixation on Marna, a Jewish leftist. Since Winifred and Horace Mann were paying my tuition, she could not do much about me. Except write letters. As the war and my incarceration came closer, those letters increased in frequency and vehemence: Antioch and those red Jews had corrupted and brainwashed me.

Mother was wrong about Antioch's influence. What the Antioch experience did was to prepare me well for World War II. Several of my placements under the cooperative work-study plan were especially relevant to my development as a conscientious objector. I took a co-op job as a counselor/teacher at the Norris Farm, a private institution for delinquent boys near Milwaukee, which took referrals of very tough kids from the courts. The staff, all of us untrained, was expected to use violence if the delinquents got out of hand, which they often did. As an enforcer, I was a dud, I lost a fist fight in my eighth-grade spelling class to a hulk of a youth. Another time the social worker arrived at the office in time to find me wrestling on the floor. She chided me. Most unprofessional! Child abuse!

Discouraged by my experiences at Norris Farm, I consulted Uncle Horace, as a former teacher. Yes, he told me, he had learned how to respond to young punks without violence. Collect relevant personal information about each one and identify his strong and weak spots in advance. Use this information to control, guide, or punish. If you are attacked physically or verbally, stay cool and friendly; don't respond aggressively, but know how to restrain the other person physically without hurting him. In the face of a verbal attack or obscenity, counter with humor and hint at certain inside, personal information that you may have to use: "If I tell Bob [the director] that you've been stealing pies from the kitchen, will he let you see your mother next Sunday?"

Back in Yellow Springs, Horace and Ava Champney, Bishop Paul Jones, Manmatha Chatterjee, and Arthur Morgan showed me that mature, thinking adults could reject war and conscription. Among my close friends were Paul "Happy" Smith, Max Ratner, and Bronson Clark, staunch pacifists all. In 1940–41 they invited me to share in the rental of a large apartment not far from the campus. Because Bronson owned a car, we were able to pick up visiting dignitaries at the train or bus station in Springfield and often invited them to our apartment for discussion after their lectures. Among such dignitaries I recall Evan Thomas, A. J. Muste, and Jim Farmer. An ongoing topic was what to do about the coming war and conscription.

Out of this ferment came Ahimsa Farm, an experimental pacifist community, in the spring of 1940. Our mission was to study war, war objection, alternatives to violence, peace, and justice making. Professor Chatterjee dug into his savings and provided faculty sponsorship. Bronson's mother loaned us a weatherbeaten farm near Cleveland. Early projects included making the farmhouse habitable, starting a vegetable garden, and building a small brick home for Bronson and his fiancee, Eleanor Meanor. As we worked on these projects we talked, and we read whenever we could: Thoreau, Gregg, Shridharani, Tolstoy, Gandhi, Kropotkin, and Schweitzer. We rehearsed our reactions to draft boards, Legionnaires, judges, and prison officials.

A steady stream of Antiochians received co-op plan credits for stints at Ahimsa; other objectors came for short or long visits. Women were accepted on an equal basis. The core group included the Neals, a thirtyish couple, and Lee Stern, who commuted by bike to a job in Cleveland, donating his earnings to the common good. In time we caught the interest of leaders of the Fellowship of Reconciliation and the War Resisters League.

Inspired by the concept of nonviolent direct action as a good means to a just end (Ahimsa means "without violence"), Ahimsa members helped to organize two marches to advocate feeding the hungry in Nazi-occupied Europe. In collaboration with local National Association for the Advancement of Colored People (NAACP) members, a group from Ahimsa entered a segregated Cleveland swimming pool on a very hot Sunday. When all other whites got out of the water and circled us menacingly, shouting obscenities, we stated in a calm and friendly manner the case for racial fairness. It was heartening that a few whites listened and then returned to the water. The following day the sheriff arrived at Ahimsa to check us out. Assured that we did not belong to the mob and had broken no Ohio laws, he departed. Unfortunately, World War II interrupted this project. However, several of the African American participants followed up later as leaders of the civil rights movement and CORE. I look back on my experiences at Ahimsa Farm—one six-week summer period for co-op credit and several brief visits—as invaluable preparation. Later, faced with hostile officials or angry psychotics, I had a rough idea of what to say and do. I had been through pacifist boot camp.

My work experience with the *CIO News* in Detroit was quite different from Norris Farm, but equally valuable. The spring of 1941 was a time of preparation for war and of major labor disputes. My friend, Bill Brett, who had completed his studies at Antioch the year before, was now editing the Michigan *CIO News*. Because of a strike against the Ford Motor Company, he suggested that as a co-op experience I work with him as a reporter; he would then have more time to put out special strike editions. While in Detroit I also worked as dishwasher in a boardinghouse for room and meals. Bill paid me pocket money.

The *CIO* occupied part of an old downtown office building. I saw the Ford strike in progress, thousands of men surrounding the plant in bitter-cold weather. I covered other labor situations. I listened as CIO Auto Workers executives argued strategy. How should they respond to Bill Bennett's thugs who were hired by Ford to break the strike? One faction said stay nonviolent; another said arm and, if necessary, retaliate in kind. I was especially impressed with the power of the strike as an industrial weapon. When ordinary workmen persisted in what they considered a just cause, in spite of threats, goon violence, and police harassment, they were able to shut down a giant industrial plant and often reached union recognition and a fair contract.

I also learned that the union was by no means as perfect as its publicity portrayed it. There were factions, and some organizers and officials were corrupt, Bill Brett told me. Although the labor news we published was by and large factual and accurate, it was one sided. I don't recall ever interviewing an employer for his point of view in a dispute. So far as the war in Europe was concerned, I was in the minority. Bill thought the United States should support the Allies in defending Russia. Most of my fellow boarders had moved up from the South for those good defense jobs and were ready to enlist if the country was attacked. I met one CIO organizer who had been jailed during World War I. Yes, prison was very tough, but he would do it again rather than fight for those war profiteers.

When I returned to Antioch after the Detroit experience, I was so stimulated by Horace Champney's course in social psychology that I switched majors from political science to psychology and dropped journalism as a career objective. In the fall of 1941, I became Champney's research assistant, compensated with National Youth Administration funds and free room. One of my assignments was to assemble a body of abstracts concerned with the topics of war, pacifism, and violence. Although I am not aware that Champney ever used these abstracts in any scholarly publications, compiling them most certainly deepened my pacifism from the vantage of a behavioral scientist.

In 1941, when I received "greetings" from President Roosevelt, I registered and applied for 4-E status as a conscientious objector. My "friends and neighbors" at the draft board in Xenia, Ohio, did not know me personally and had had no experience with COs. The fact that I did not belong to a recognized church was not helpful. They classified me 1-AO, assigned to noncombatant military duty. I respectfully failed to report but notified them of my whereabouts. In the face of a great deal of pressure from many quarters during 1941 and 1942, I remained consistent. I would not kill. I would not serve in the military, but I was willing to do work of national importance as a civilian. I thought such effort should be overseas and physically dangerous. And I hoped the newly created Civilian Public Service would be an effective undertaking under the leadership of the three peace churches, Mennonite, Friends, and Brethren. Unlike my friends Bill Richards, Bronson Clark, and Max Ratner, I was not ready to oppose all conscription, the absolutist position.

One member of the Xenia draft board, a Catholic priest, asked me to go for a drive. We parked. He spouted Catholic and patriotic doctrine. For more than debating emphasis, he put his hand on my thigh. I suspect that my rejection of his advances did not strengthen my case.

President Algo Henderson of Antioch called me into his office. Patiently and pleasantly he made the case for noncombatant service. Respectfully, I said, "no, thank you." At the college's request, I then consulted a lawyer in Dayton, a large, middle-aged man with an imposing manner and deep, booming voice crusted with certitude. He mentioned his service in the Spanish-American War and the importance of defending one's country. He described the horrors I would encounter in prison. I would be shunned, beaten up, raped. "If you do time," he asked, "what will be the effect on your later career? What will you tell your children when they ask, 'Daddy, what did you do during the war?'" I tried to answer calmly, respectfully, and pleasantly.

As my trial neared, my extended family was divided as to what I should do. The Manns communicated their support, whatever I decided. My father and my uncles Ralph and Bob Duncan wrote of their disagreement and hoped I would consider enlisting. My mother and Cousin Jim expressed their patriotic zeal. Not only did they urge me to do my duty, but they wrote the college and influential congressmen. Their message was clear, "Antioch has corrupted this fine idealistic youth."

On campus some faculty and students were supportive; others, not sharing my views, expressed tolerance. Lots of guys were enlisting or responding to their draft board's call. Perhaps I was insensitive, but I felt little or no pressure from those who were taking the military route.

I do not recall that I ever agonized over my position on war. I had no doubts because my beliefs were rooted in an emotional, religious foundation. In contrast, people who at some point decided on a logical basis that war was wrong often shifted their views under changing circumstances. Thus, American Communists turned from antiwar to ardent patriots as soon as Hitler invaded Russia. The very strong isolationist movement disappeared after Pearl Harbor. A number of COs altered their convictions because prison was unpleasant, CPS was stultifying, or the Holocaust was intolerable.

What I did find difficult to work through was how best to relate to those who did not share my views. Before Pearl Harbor I was a college activist. I participated in the War Resisters League and Fellowship of Reconciliation. Occasionally I attended Friends Meeting. I dissented. I argued against conscription and violence. Once the "good war" began, I reasoned that I would not interfere, would not oppose it, would respect the overwhelming majority's commitment to victory, and would not express my opinion unless asked directly. My objections to conscription and killing were primarily personal and private. I had to figure out satisfactory reactions to certain situations: stand for national anthem (yes), buy war bonds (no), pay war taxes (yes), hang out with guys in uniform (sure), volunteer to test diets and extreme heat and cold with results that may benefit our military (yes), express opinion on bombing of Dresden (not unless asked), and so on. I had special, positive feelings for those who served in the armed forces. Although I was glad to counsel young civilians about the draft, I would not try to persuade them to my point of view.

In July 1942, with the war well under way, Judge Robert R. Nevin sentenced me, my good friend Bill Richards, and three Jehovah's Witnesses to five years in federal prison. I entered the Preble County,

Ohio, jail on a sweltering July afternoon to await transportation to the Federal Correctional Institution at Ashland, Kentucky. That jail was dirty, crowded, noisy, dark, and hot. Unappetizing food was shoved at us on metal plates. There were only three wooden chairs. Our first night we were bitten by bedbugs. Our consciences did not include these creatures. When we realized that they lived in the cracks of our metal bunks, we lit wadded newspapers and immolated them. The other inmates were mostly petty thieves and drunks who were either friendly or kept to themselves. I don't recall any unpleasantness with them or the sheriff's personnel during the twelve days we awaited transportation to Ashland.

In sharp contrast to the county jail, Ashland was sparkling clean and relatively quiet. During our first month, when we were kept in the quarantine cell block, I soon discovered why Ashland looked so unsullied. Except for time spent in interviews with various officials, physical exams, and psychological tests, we spent much of the daytime mopping, dusting, and cleaning.

When, at age twenty-four, I became Inmate AK 1915 with a commitment to oppose violence and conscription, I had to decide what sort of prisoner to be. There was no party line for COs, no set of clear principles. Other things being equal, I adopted the strategy of the good convict. I would follow reasonable orders, keep my cell clean, and accept my work assignments. I would appear to follow the rules to the letter; but if they were silly or harmful, I would undercut them. I would be polite to the various prison officials who tried to persuade me to join the military, even though my answer was "no." In my relations with other prisoners, I would try to be helpful and would avoid patronizing them if I could. I would follow the convict's code: don't squeal on another inmate. Especially, if I were in a position to help another inmate, providing no harm was done, I would help him—write a letter for an illiterate, tip off my neighbor that "the man" would be around in a few minutes to search his cell for contraband, or pass on news of parole board decisions.

At Ashland I was assigned to the hospital as a clerk. My fellow worker, a man named Osborne Wilson, was also doing time for a Selective Service violation. He had failed to register for the draft. Although he had a bachelor's degree in chemistry, the only work he, an African American, could find on the outside was as a common laborer. He was extremely resentful about discrimination: "Why should I fight those Germans?" he asked. At Ashland, as a leader of the African American inmates, he made friends with white inmate leaders and quietly worked for racial harmony. Convicts with black skin were segregated in the dining hall. I asked Wilson about protesting. If we worked together, why couldn't we eat together? "Not now," he advised me. "They will crush you." Later, after I had been paroled, COs were successful in desegregating Ashland.

My work assignment provided advantages. Wilson tutored me in doing easy time. "Keep busy and avoid brooding about the past or worrying about the future. Stay away from 'the man.' Never snitch. Never get a fellow felon into trouble. Don't pry into another convict's affairs. If he wants to tell you his troubles and what he's in for, listen, but keep what he tells you to yourself." Wilson and I, in effect, were medical records specialists. After Dr. F. J. Krueger examined each new convict or patient, he dictated his findings on a wax cylinder that we then transcribed. Thus, we knew everyone's medical history and personal information. I found that this information was power, which I resolved to use for good, as Wilson did, with nothing expected in return. For example, I could reassure a prisoner that his record did not indicate cancer, or that he was scheduled for an operation to remove his bunions.

Although Dr. Krueger treated his inmate assistants fairly, he was generally feared and was considered mean and vengeful. He regarded any crime as evidence of psychosis or neurosis. He diagnosed one CO, whom I had known in college, as a latent homosexual. (Nonsense!) I tipped off my friend, whose friends and relatives made a fuss on the outside. Eventually there were enough other complaints that Dr. Krueger left Ashland.

Assigned to a single cell with welcome privacy, I was able to do an enormous amount of reading, despite the library's limited holdings, and to complete a college credit course in child psychology. I experimented with fasting, finding I could withstand a foodless regimen if I wished. For a month I read from the Bible and consulted with an absolutist war resister who was an evangelical preacher. Prizing its lessons but rejecting its magical thinking and monarchist structure, I decided the unquestioned Bible was not for me.

The five of us Selective Service violators were among the first COs to enter Ashland. The population then consisted mostly of petty thieves, forgers, moonshiners, pimps, car thieves, corrupt business-men and politicians, and a few other nonviolent offenders. About a third were African Americans. The average IQ on standardized paper and pencil tests was about eighty, and the average grade completed was about third. Many claimed to be devout Christians and innocent of their crimes. They used the m——f— word in every other sentence and argued constantly, often about events in the softball league, placing bets for cigarettes on each night's games. I learned a useful lesson for later life: often the most ferocious controversies are closely linked to ignorance, stupidity, selfishness, and distrust. I have confirmed this generalization in couples counseling and faculty meetings.

Big Lou La Fever was a handsome, bright, and charming but unschooled confidence man with an infectious laugh. He became my friend and advocate. He claimed he was doing well as a hustler until he was "framed" on a Selective Service rap. "Red," he said one night during recreation, "what say we become partners when we get out? We can work the rackets and live high on the hog." I politely declined. I never encountered a CO who was lured into a life of crime.

Other inmates were unsure at first about the war resisters, but leaders like Wilson and Big Lou gave their approval. When several of us (Bill Richards in particular) turned out to be excellent athletes and incorruptible on the softball diamond, we were accepted. Never in my months at Ashland did I experience any unpleasantries with other inmates—no physical assaults, no propositions, and no rapes.

Ashland was the model of a police state. We were controlled by clanging cell doors, whistles, and calls for "count" (when we were supposed to stand at the doors of our cells). Dressed in blue denims, we marched to meals or recreation. Much depended on the warden, whether he was benevolent or tough. Officers took their cues accordingly; a write-up for a trivial offense could lead to the Hole. Spies or finks would rat on their fellow inmates in return for favors. Tension was always just under the surface.

All of our mail, in and out, was censored, and we were permitted only seven correspondents. A year after I left Ashland, I wrote the following in response to a questionnaire:

> One c.o. (over 21 years of age) was unfortunate enough to have an emotional mother who was not sympathetic to his ideals. Her letters during his trial had upset him considerably. Accordingly, he omitted her name on his proposed mailing list. However, she headed the list of approved correspondents. When he objected to Mr. Yeagley, the censor, he not only failed to have his mother removed from his list but also learned that she had written to the warden listing those of his friends who had "subverted" him and should be prevented from writing or visiting him. This man then refused to open any of his mother's letters. Occasionally Warden Watson or Mr. Yeagley would read him her letters.

After the war my mother and I reconciled. She was especially pleased about my marriage in 1949. My wife's parents were Republicans and Unitarians.

At one meal I was served inedible mashed potatoes. A tough lieutenant indicated I should clean my tray. "Eat what you take" was the rule. "Lieutenant, would you like to try them?" He wrote me up. Warden "Jive Papa" Watson heard the evidence at my disciplinary hearing. "I'm letting you off, Dole," he said. "And tell me when our food is bad." Usually I thought the food was barely satisfactory, and starchy.

Larry Gara was a twenty-year-old red-haired kid whom we liked to tease. I picked up a rubber stamp on my desk and stamped on the back of his shirt "Syphilis." Someone else used the "Warden" stamp, and a third wrote "HAS" in red. Larry giggled and said, "Hey, cut it out!" But he did not know what we had put on his back. He found out when a guard wrote him up for defacing government property and insulting the warden. At his hearing he pled ignorance and refused to name the perpetrators. They let him off with a warning. Our respect for Larry's courage under fire increased.

At first there were too few COs to do much of anything about the prison system. Later, after I left Ashland, the proportion of war objectors became high enough to bring about substantial changes through such nonviolent strategies as strikes, boycotts, and fasts. A number of COs at Ashland and elsewhere later became leaders in the civil rights and anti–Vietnam War movements.

Looking back, I think my time at Ashland increased my self-control. I found that with a strong belief in pacifism and in myself I could take pressure and adversity. I matured. I have noticed that some in prison, including those who admit their crimes and those who do not, emerge stronger and undergo a kind of transformation, frequently accompanied by a religious conversion. Specialists call this phenomenon reform or rehabilitation. Other felons are either crushed or hardened by a prison term. They may suffer a form of post-traumatic stress disorder like veterans after combat, or they change from wild kids to professional criminals.

In August 1943 the draft board at Ashland reclassified me from 1-AO to 4-E, conscientious objector, and under Executive Order 8641 I was ordered to report to Civilian Public Service Camp No. 52 in Powellsville, Maryland. The unit was housed in what had been Civilian Conservation Corps barracks, and its assignment was to continue the CCC project of cutting trees and draining land for farming. Administratively, the Society of Friends provided leadership, service assignments, and a stipend of $2.50 per month. The work was supervised by the U.S. Department of Agriculture, but ultimate control rested in the Selective Service system.

The conscientious objectors I met at Powellsville were remarkably diverse in religion, occupation, social class, education, politics, and reasons for resisting military service. There were not only Friends, but also Methodists, Baptists, Fundamentalists, Catholics, Unitarians, Universalists, and atheists; there were farmers, mechanics, doctors, lawyers, professors, students, businessmen; some were illiterate and others were preparing dissertations or finishing novels; there were Republicans, Democrats, Socialists, and Communists. Some were Bible-quoting pacifists but others opposed this particular war because it was a product of a corrupt capitalist system. Some worked very hard at their assignments without complaint, while a minority loafed, bitched, complained, and conspired to make things difficult for their supervisors. A number responded to the daily work routines with a variety of physical and psychiatric ailments.

Some took or taught educational courses, read omnivorously, and argued, while others did little more than pray, eat, and sleep. A few men were married and had found apartments for their families. Many COs at Powellsville saw CPS as an opportunity, while a small minority likened it to an internment system that enslaved its victims.

Shortly after I arrived at Powellsville, an administrator approached me about asking my rich relatives to pay for my expenses. (I imagine Cousin Jim Dole, the pineapple king, would have exploded if asked to support me!) I was strapped financially. With no bank account and no other income than $2.50 a month, I had to scrounge and scrape. When I prepared to go to Philadelphia to be best man at my cousin's wedding, I obtained a fine, cast-off tweed suit from the camp clothing room. Apparently the suit had belonged to a thin Quaker about six-and-a-half-feet tall, so I found a tailor to alter it. It served as my best suit for the next three years.

Our work group consisted of three liberal Quakers and myself. We decided to work hard rather than goof off and became proficient at felling and stripping trees with two-man handsaws and axes. We considered ourselves the best team in camp. Conversations covered religion, politics, philosophy, and humor. Our supportive team spirit and fellowship made much more palatable the smothering hot summer days and the chilling late fall and winter that followed.

Although, in retrospect, there may have been some hope that Powellsville could have become a staging area for significant projects—overseas assignments, for instance—I consider it to have been a sidetrack. Dozens of gifted young men's skills were underutilized. Their resistance to war was largely unrecognized by the average citizen and their potential in developing alternatives to violence largely untapped. Among these men, for example, were a future foreign policy adviser to the president and a Nobel Prize winner.

From a pool of applicants, four of us were selected for reassignment to the Vital Economics Department, Strong Memorial Hospital, University of Rochester Medical School. Vital Economics, chaired by Dr. Murlin, an eminent and autocratic physiologist, had government contracts to study the effects on human subjects of extreme heat and cold, high-altitude pressures, and yeast and other diets. The results were expected to be invaluable in improving the chances for survival in extreme conditions and in preventing starvation. We were the human guinea pigs. At that time we signed no permission and there were no human subjects committees. When not participating in an experiment, we were employed as laboratory assistants to the scientific team. In return we were housed with the medical students, ate in the hospital cafeteria, and received fifteen dollars per month. We were issued white coats and called "Doctor" by the cleaning people. We were encouraged to learn the physiology related to the research and to attend medical school lectures. The Manhattan Project was down the hall, very hush-hush. It was exhilarating to be a small part of a major research university.

The medical school researchers were very supportive, treating us like graduate students. One of us, Ray Stanley, an Ohio Quaker farm youth, learned quickly and became adept with lab equipment. The department faculty strongly encouraged him to attend college after the war and continue on to the doctorate. They offered to arrange financial aid. He preferred to return to the family farm where today he is a respected senior member of his small Quaker community.

I responded eagerly to the many delights of a great university in a large city. I used the library, heard the Rochester Symphony, cheered Red Schoendiest as he played infield for the Rochester Red Wings, watched the ballet, attended a Unitarian church, dated a lovely research assistant, partied with some of the medical students, and played tennis each morning before breakfast. The Methodist Church and its pastor, the Reverend Robert Horton, and his wife, Kay, were exceptionally welcoming.

The experiments were demanding. I pumped a stationary bike in 120-degree heat or ate yeast for two weeks. A steak dinner after days of those unpalatable yeast meals was a treat. Lab work involved routine titrating of urine. Dr. Murlin and his colleagues later published the results in refereed journals.

After several months the CPS unit began to expand. The Friends CPS office in Philadelphia worked out an arrangement with Colgate-Rochester Divinity School to open some of its courses to unit members. A contingent of COs who were planning to become ministers arrived. Dr. Murlin became controlling and hostile with the group. I decided to apply for a new assignment at a mental hospital unit. This would be consistent with my interest in psychology rather than theology or medicine.

CPS Unit 41 at Eastern State Hospital in Williamsburg, Virginia, was intended to alleviate the severe shortage of mental hospital attendants. En route from Rochester I boarded a southbound train in Washington. As I walked through the coaches I found every seat occupied, until I reached the car reserved for African Americans. "Does anyone mind if I sit here?" Nods of guarded approval. But the conductor did not approve. "You'll have to move. It's the law."

"Does anyone object to my sitting here?" I asked. Again, nods of guarded approval. The conductor threatened to call the police. I stayed in my seat until I left the train at Richmond. He never returned.

Located in the center of the city, Eastern State, the oldest state mental hospital in the country, looked medieval. I was assigned to admissions in one of the few newer buildings. The two lower floors were for incoming patients and the top two floors were for the CPS unit. Although I had not yet had courses in abnormal psychology and was given no orientation or training, I started immediately as a charge attendant. On the night shift I was sometimes on duty alone, responsible for the welfare of thirty to fifty men ranging in age from twelve to ninety. Recalling my Uncle Horace's advice after my experience at Norris Farm, on my first day I went to the records and wrote each patient's name on a three-by-five card along with a few facts about him. I discovered that if I addressed a belligerent and wildly disturbed person by name and with a smile, he often responded cooperatively.

One night I ran to quell a commotion in the day room. Harold, a burly and senile fisherman, was cursing and swinging a chair at fellow patients. He came for me, cursing and insisting I was the devil and it was his Christian duty to kill me. Although he was bigger and stronger, I restrained him by throwing a blanket over his head and then pinning his arms from behind. I moved him to his room and locked the door.

This episode and hundreds like it experienced by other CO attendants in mental hospitals illustrated a revolution in the treatment of the mentally ill. They could be restrained without harm. COs in World War II permanently influenced the treatment of mental patients.

After a year I felt dissatisfied, even though the Williamsburg experience was valuable in regard to my later career as a professional psychologist. The war had ended. We were not part of postwar reconstruction. It was clear that official policy prevented overseas assignments for CPS units. Yet somehow my good friend, Bronson Clark, after his parole from Ashland, had been able to join a China ambulance unit. Meanwhile, relations between Dr. Barrett, the hospital superintendent, and the unit were worsening. In other CPS units morale was deteriorating in the face of what many COs considered oppressive Selective Service policies. After two years of giving the system every opportunity to justify itself, I concluded that conscription was wrong and that I could no longer continue in CPS. I asked the camp director to send me back to prison, which he could not do without cause. To get out of the CPS system I would have to break parole. That would mean returning to prison to complete my five-year sentence, because the time I had spent in CPS would not count.

In July 1945, after consultation and meditation, I walked out of CPS. I notified the hospital, Selective Service, and my parole officer of my intentions and left for Philadelphia. Pending my reincarceration I stayed with my cousin, Kay Briner, and her husband, Jack, and took a job in the clothing room of the American Friends Service Committee where I helped sort donated clothing for shipment to CPS camps and impoverished people at home and abroad.

After a few weeks the Justice Department instructed me to report to the Lewisburg Federal Penitentiary in Pennsylvania. On a cold morning I boarded a train at the Broad Street Station for Lewisburg, where I took a taxi to my new home—huge gray walls surmounted with guard towers and protecting gloomy, gray buildings. For a while after my arrival at Lewisburg I was famous as "the crazy guy who knocked on the door." Years later the Reverend Robert Horton, co-founder of the Prison Visitation Service, loved to rib me about this when introducing me. He realized, I'm sure, that this act represented a responsible method of violating a law with which one disagreed.

I was waiting in line at the Lewisburg hospital for my routine physical when a young man in a white coat approached me. "You're Dole?"

"Yeah."

"I'm Gurvitz, assistant to Dr. Lindner."

"Nice to see ya."

"Would you like to work here?"

"Sure."

After the usual quarantine I was called in by an assignment officer. "Dole," he said, "We have two openings which might fit you."
One was in the psychiatry/psychology department and the second
was the editorship of the prison periodical. Al Hassler, the previous
incumbent, who had just been paroled, went on to a distinguished
career as a pacifist editor. I chose the hospital.

The psychology/psychiatry department was impressively progressive. I reported to work as chief psychologist Robert Lindner
was leaving. Lindner, author of *Rebel Without a Cause* (Hollywood
bought the title but not the plot), was a pioneer in the diagnosis and
treatment of psychopathy. The psychiatrist was Dr. Marris Peck, a
young specialist in group psychotherapy and a staunch advocate of
inmate rights. The three inmate assistants were given a great deal
of responsibility for group and individual testing and for the treatment of patients. One assistant, Milton Gurvitz, a principal and
teacher who had burned down his school, was a master scrounger
and prison politician. As my mentor and sponsor, he taught me how
to administer various diagnostic tests and schooled me in the ways
of the institution. While still in prison he co-authored an intelligence
test and several publications in refereed journals. Julian Jaynes, also
a CO, was young and very bright, a good companion.

Dr. Peck, who was experimenting with innovative group treat-
ments, was frequently at odds with prison personnel over the han-
dling of inmates. All three of us assistants were able to use our
experience in Lewisburg as a springboard to careers after the war.
The former principal became a clinical psychologist with a flourish-
ing private practice. He attributes his rehabilitation to Robert Lindner. Julian Jaynes became a professor at Princeton, a specialist in
physiological psychology, and an author of influential books. Antioch College gave me course credit for my experience, and eventually
the Lewisburg experience helped me in graduate study at Ohio State
University and in my subsequent career as a professional psychologist and educator. I encountered Dr. Peck a few years ago when he
was featured speaker at an antinuclear meeting. Is it possible, as he
had influenced us, so too we had influenced him?

At this time I felt as close to the war as I ever had. Dr. Richard Sears, Lindner's replacement as clinical psychologist, was called to Washington to evaluate a special prisoner. When he returned, he asked me to help transcribe his report. The prisoner in question was Ezra Pound. I now realize that the report was used to justify Pound's commitment to St. Elizabeth's Hospital, where this poet, accused of treason, would be safer than in a federal prison, where he might have been murdered.

A substantial proportion of the inmate population were veterans who had been convicted of serious, violent crimes. Some were suffering from what is now called post-traumatic stress disorder, a psychiatric condition not yet in the textbooks at that time. Little was known about how to treat such individuals, and I was impressed with the concern that the medical professionals showed them.

As at Ashland, I encountered no difficulties with other inmates at Lewisburg. I was cautioned to avoid a number of men who were said to be members of the Al Capone gang. I was never approached sexually or abused, nor did anyone confront me about my war resistance. This is in sharp contrast to the experiences of my cousin Richa Chandler, who was an objector at Lewisburg during the Vietnam War. Richa was raped.

Unlike my experience at Ashland, I encountered no organized group of COs at Lewisburg. Several, including Larry Gara, were in segregation at Lewisburg, but it was very difficult to communicate with people in other parts of the institution unless they fell ill. As at Ashland, it was a challenge to combat feelings of intense loneliness. I much appreciated a visit from the Reverend Robert Horton, who was developing the Prisoners Visitation Service. Lewisburg was by no means a country club, and I had much less physical freedom than I had had in CPS. Yet I felt psychologically freer, more efficacious. Using a path of cooperation and self-improvement, I was making a statement: "No to war and conscription."

In March 1946 I was released from Lewisburg on regular parole. I went back to work in the AFSC clothing room, where I was offered a promotion to administrator of the AFSC travel service. But Dean Basil Pillard had written from Antioch that if I returned to college for the spring quarter, I could probably graduate in June. Rejecting a possible career as a professional pacifist, I decided to return to college as a much-delayed senior majoring in psychology. Because of my work in psychological testing at Lewisburg, upon my graduation Antioch officials offered me the position of director of the testing office with the rank of assistant instructor. (With my first paycheck I bought a new suit.)

The war was over, but not my continuing commitment to pacifism.

Fifty years later the world of the 1990s differs substantially from that of the 1940s. And so, too, the retired Arthur Dole differs from the young adult version of the same person. The "good war" against an evil empire was fairly simple to comprehend. Recent American engagements in Panama, Granada, Somalia, Haiti, Bosnia, Korea, Iraq, Cuba, and Libya, though limited in size, are complex and difficult to resolve, while relations with the United Nations, NATO, and the other nuclear powers tangle the situation. A grandfather living pleasantly in rural Maine and now in his ninth decade with attendant physical limitations is unlikely to be touched directly by America's small international interventions, by conscription, or by enemy attack.

Perhaps because it is religious in character and essentially non-rational, my commitment to the sacredness of life continues; it undergirds my beliefs as it has since childhood. Thou shalt not kill. Do no harm. The Golden Rule. For me, religion, both in the formal, organizational sense and in respect to the individual's basic ethical system, is a private matter. I respect others' religious beliefs, however bizarre or wrong they may seem to me. I expect others to treat me in the same way, and I will counter what I consider intolerance.

For me now, conscientious objection requires little or no cost. Since I prefer to live within the system, I grudgingly pay my full share of taxes. On the other hand, I have lobbied my congressman for a CO war tax, and I speak out against defense expenditures and strong-arm foreign policies. I belong to the Fellowship of Reconciliation and the War Resisters League, and I send contributions to the American Friends Service Committee and more than a dozen other peace-oriented organizations. I am prepared to protest. However, peace activism is not my highest priority.

Warnings during World War II that I would be shunned and discriminated against after the war have never come true. In fact, in the middle- and upper-class circles in which I have moved, pacifism is politically correct for some. For long periods the topic just has not come up with friends and associates. For various reasons I do not impose my views on others, confront militarists, or volunteer my World War II experiences under typical circumstances. I suspect that this strategy is in part a carry-over from my prison days. On the other hand, I do speak out publicly against American military excursions, and I do not hesitate to oppose our inflated defense budget.

Many of my friends are veterans, and I respect them. I find it psychologically difficult, if not impossible, to avoid some share in America's military exploits. I think I understand the feelings of patriotism, the reflexive dedication to a just cause. As a resident, some of the arrogance of our country's power, especially before Vietnam, has rubbed off on me. Recently, at the fiftieth reunion of graduation from Antioch College, I participated in a panel discussion of alumni experiences during World War II. I shared some events leading up to my incarceration. Fellow participants included a war widow, a war wife, and two former Air Force officers. After the panel a tablet was dedicated to the thirty-two Antiochians who gave their lives. My emotions were mixed. Could actions like mine prevent or diminish future casualties? Should I feel guilty that I had missed combat and the risk of death?

During a "good" war I like to think that COs serve an important function in mitigating the very real risk that our side may become like the enemy. Perhaps we offset somewhat the "bad" means directed at a noble end. We may remind our side that some of the enemy are innocent. For example, when my late friend and professional colleague, Dr. Eric Coche, was five years old, he somehow survived the bombing of Cologne. I am sure that few American bomber pilots thought about small children in the heat of combat. Two fine men of my acquaintance, now American citizens, were conscripts in the Nazi army. In war, young men on both sides, who must do atrocious things as they are ordered, may later become exemplary citizens. As COs we can remind the combatants of the human factor and can counter the demonization of the enemy.

A heartening development is the growing interest in understanding and preventing violence. What causes wars? What are alternatives to violence and how effective are they? Many colleges and universities offer programs in peace studies. Under the sponsorship of the International Association of University Presidents, more than 130 peace studies courses have been established at fifty-one universities in twenty-six countries. Books and academic papers proliferate, as do scholarly organizations and periodicals.

If, as I have argued, war is likely to create more problems than it solves, what are the alternatives? When a country or a group within a country feels it is oppressed, many nonviolent strategies are available. Gandhi's successful campaign to liberate India from the United Kingdom and Martin Luther King's effective civil rights movements are well-known examples. The potential power of nonviolent strategies is suggested by the example of Susan Mayberry in Guatemala, one person with a just cause whose courage to fast and deliberately violate a law influenced an entire country. And mediation by a disinterested player can be effective in resolving conflict. For example, small United Nations task forces helped to end civil wars in El Salvador and Guatemala. It is essential that the mediator be invited by all combatants and that they agree in advance to accept the mediator's findings.

Prevention of war, it seems to me, has real possibilities. Invented structures such as the United Nations, international law, the Marshall and Fulbright Plans, disarmament treaties, and the World Court—though often flawed—do suggest that humankind has the capacity to forestall and reduce many conflicts before shots are fired.

When I was a child, I came to reject war. When I was a young, draft-age adult, my religious, emotional beliefs served as a foundation for my conscientious objection to World War II. Over the past half-century, beginning in college, I have tried to understand the dynamics of human warfare and to identify possible alternatives. Despite the many terrible wars now raging around the world, I am heartened that so many thousands of people are working for peace in a variety of ways. I am therefore hopeful that war and conscription, like slavery and the duel before them, eventually will become obsolete.

My War on War

I am convinced that part-time activism is possible and can be effective.

As a CHILD and youth growing up in the 1920s and 1930s, I thought war and militarism had become obsolete. The possibility of a military draft seemed preposterous. Reaction against World War I had contributed to a strong isolationist sentiment that was reflected in Congress. Americans resented the refusal or inability of European nations to pay their war debts, and many vowed that never again should the United States be drawn into a European war. The 1928 Pact of Paris eventually included sixty-three signatories to an agreement to outlaw war as a matter of national policy. Loopholes in wording and its failure to address the basic causes of war meant that the pact was doomed. Meantime, millions of young men took the Oxford Pledge never to participate in war. Clerics, novelists, playwrights, and columnists all helped create an antiwar climate of opinion. Popular sentiment against war went far beyond the influence of a small band of pacifists.

Such views began to change with the Spanish Civil War and the rise of fascism and Nazi brutality in Europe. In the United States isolationist sentiment remained strong until the Japanese attack on Pearl Harbor. But by that time my personal pacifist convictions had formed to the point where military service was, for me, unthinkable. Reading, Pennsylvania, my hometown, was strongly socialist, and my family members not only voted for Norman Thomas but actually believed he had a chance to win the White House. They admired Eugene Debs and continued to hold to socialist opposition to war. Because my parents separated when I was very young, I never knew

LARRY GARA (b. 1922)
Larry Gara, a historian, teacher, and part-time activist, lives with his wife,
Lenna Mae Gara, a freelance writer and community activist, in Wilmington, Ohio,
where he retired from Wilmington College after forty years in the classroom.
He is concerned that the record of active nonviolence become more visible as
an important part of U.S. history.

my father. My mother and maternal grandparents raised me in a strong antiwar environment. My mother, a skilled dressmaker, had some wealthy Quakers among her clients. Through their encouragement I attended Quaker First Day (Sunday) School, where pacifist views were routinely taught as a part of Christian doctrine. When I was eighteen I joined the Society of Friends.

After graduating from Reading High School, I attended Kutztown State Teachers College as a commuting student, hitchhiking daily the eighteen miles from Reading. Even in high school I had joined a small Fellowship of Reconciliation group and had participated in a number of antiwar and antidraft actions. Reading Richard Gregg's *The Power of Nonviolence* revealed to me the possibilities of Gandhian nonviolence as an alternative to military defense. Two summers of volunteer work camps exposed me to Quaker service projects and pacifism and to books about World War I resisters. It also provided plenty of opportunities for serious discussions of peace and war, violence and nonviolence. My pacifist convictions deepened further during Christmas vacation of 1940 when I joined a walk from Lancaster, Pennsylvania, to New York City. Called the Food for Europe Pilgrimage, the walk urged the United States to send food to starving civilians in parts of Europe then occupied by Germany. During the following Easter break I joined a second pilgrimage, that time walking from Wilmington, Delaware, to Washington, D.C. The two demonstrations took my pacifist ideals from the intellectual and abstract to personal action. Moreover, the walk brought me into contact with several nonregistrants and with A. J. Muste and other national leaders in the peace movement.

Government officials and leaders in the peace movement were in agreement in hoping to avoid the sorry record of brutal treatment accorded conscientious objectors in World War I who were involuntarily inducted into the army, court martialed, and then confined in military prisons. Consequently the Selective Service Act of 1940 provided for special civilian work camps for those conscientious objectors who would not perform any kind of military service. Although funded by the traditional peace churches, the camps were under the strict control of Selective Service. Each draftee in the camps was obligated to pay thirty-five dollars a month for board and room, or find another person or agency to pay it. To me this smacked of the three-hundred-dollar commutation fee used in the Civil War draft.

In 1940 I learned of eight Union Theological Seminary students who openly refused to register, and I knew immediately that that would also be my position. Had they registered, the seminarians would have had automatic exemption. Similarly, if I chose to register I would almost surely have received classification as a conscientious objector, not to mention the fact that my slight build and low weight would probably have made me unacceptable to the military. The law required me to register on May 16, 1942, my twentieth birthday. Instead, I wrote the nearest federal district attorney explaining why, in good conscience, I could not register. My explanation was couched in such traditional religious terms as "God's will," which I would not use today. Two months later a pair of FBI agents came to my home, arrested me, and took me to the Berks County Jail where I was fingerprinted, booked, and involuntarily registered. After only a few hours a friend posted the two thousand dollars bail and I went home.

Having absolutely no money, I was fortunate to know Darlington Hoopes, a Quaker attorney and socialist who volunteered to represent me. In federal court in Philadelphia, the judge postponed my trial date because, according to the government, I had already been registered by jail officials. Soon afterward I received a Selective Service questionnaire that I refused to complete. Another court date followed. Darlington suggested that I enter a plea of nolo contendere rather than force the government to grant me a jury trial. Federal Judge J. Cullen Ganey would not allow me to read my statement explaining my reasons for refusing to register. Instead he thundered: "You set up your puny will against the great will of Congress. You are one of those who think you should have your own way. If we all had your views chaos would result in a short time." He then sentenced me to three years in federal prison. In that moment I had no awareness or concern for how much my stand on the draft would change my life.

Within hours after sentencing, I was sent to Philadelphia's Moyamensing Prison, a place best described as the "Jail from Hell." Built before the Civil War in the style of a medieval castle, Moyamensing had once held Passmore Williamson, an abolitionist accused of aiding a slave escape. The cells were small and beehive-shaped, with heavy iron bars on each door. Constant, nearly unbearable noise mixed with sounds from a blaring radio with the clanking of metal doors and the profane shouts of prisoners. Each night I greeted as a blessing the enforced silence after lights-out. Tasteless food arrived in containers that seemed to be left over from nineteenth-century supplies. I survived on the quart of milk I purchased daily from the commissary. For a twenty year old who had rarely been away from home, it was a painful ordeal.

The only officially permitted reading material in the jail was the Bible. While there I read the entire New Testament twice. Some magazines were also available, and with the cooperation of another prisoner I smuggled in several novels, which I had to read inside magazine covers. We had one hour a day in the yard for exercise; the other twenty-three I spent locked in my cell. My first cellmate was another nonregistrant who quickly decided that he had made a mistake and agreed to serve in the army. For more than a week he argued with me, and by the time he left I had refined every point in favor of my position. Next I shared the cell with a young Mennonite who had not been permitted to smoke at home on the farm so he seized the chance to enjoy strong cigars all day and most of the evening. Soon the smoke in such a confined space took its toll and I developed a severe sore throat and cold. When I reported sick, the jail doctor yelled at me and refused to provide medication. In desperation I told Amos his smoking was making me seriously ill. Though he could not understand my problem, he agreed to smoke only during outdoor exercise. He was a simple, highly moral young man who should not have been sent to jail; he was rearrested upon his release.

Confinement of federal prisoners in local jails usually lasts a week or two at the most before they are moved to federal prisons. Yet I was in Moyamensing two long months before my transfer to the Federal Prison Camp at Mill Point, West Virginia. My transfer occured only then because my mother had written repeatedly to the Justice Department and our local congressman. The excuse was that an official had misplaced my file, but many years later I learned that some other resisters had had much the same experience, suggesting that it may have been a deliberate attempt to break our will to resist.

Mill Point was a minimum-custody prison without walls, bars, or a fence. We were told, however, that "an invisible fence" was five years high—the penalty for escape. The population at Mill Point included other resisters, Jehovah's Witnesses, and Kentucky moonshiners. All prisoners lived in dormitories. After a short period of orientation I was assigned to the prison library where part of my work was editing the prison paper. That comfortable job had a big drawback: there could be no criticism of the prison or of the criminal justice system. When I complained to prison officials, pronouncing such censorship intolerable, I was reassigned to outdoor work, shoveling dirt and breaking up rocks in the cold West Virginia mountains. Though the product of our labor was to be used for covering roadbeds, the work seemed of little value. Several other resisters had already notified the warden that they would no longer perform such labor or keep themselves voluntarily in prison. They were immediately taken to the closest county jail, then transferred to more secure institutions.

After several months in Mill Point, I joined two others in taking the same stand. We were taken by car during a snowstorm to Marlinton, where we waited a week for transfer. It was a small jail with few prisoners. The sheriff was friendly and the food was home cooking. Though it was dirty and there were cockroaches, that jail was not a bad place to do time. I still remember watching cardinals in the snow outside the jail window. Had our families lived nearby, we could have had food and books brought in to us. The Marlinton jail also lacked the numerous annoying counts and constant noise that is so much a part of jail life. We three war resisters—Joe Alter, Straughn Gettier, and I—had many serious discussions and some good laughs while in Marlinton.

After about a week two federal marshals drove us to the federal prison at Ashland, Kentucky, handcuffing us only when we left the car. Before reaching Ashland we spent a night in a larger county jail in Huntington, West Virginia, where a kindly deputy told us we were still young and had time to "go straight." His fatherly advice, though well intentioned, gave us something to chuckle about.

The Federal Correctional ("corruptional," as we called it) Institution at Ashland, Kentucky, was a medium-custody prison. Its buildings formed a square around a courtyard, thus functioning as a wall without giving the appearance of a walled institution. New inmates underwent several weeks of orientation that began with a thorough physical examination. On that February day I stood with other prisoners stark naked in a chilly room. Nervously, I cleared my throat, whereupon Dr. F. J. Kreuger, the chief medical officer, yelled that I had deliberately coughed in his face and warned that I would be punished if it happened again. I had not coughed at all, but at that point it was inevitable that I would again clear my throat. Immediately I was taken to "the Hole," a completely bare, isolated cell with only a floor drain for a toilet. I was permitted no reading or writing material and had neither a bed nor a mattress. Each evening a guard brought a blanket and took it away in the morning. Food arrived in very small amounts, rinsed under cold water to render it tasteless. The associate warden arrived to warn me that the Hole could drive a person insane, promising to release me as soon as I apologized to the doctor. But I would not apologize for something I had not done, and after a few days officials recognized the absurdity of the charge and released me. I've always felt that the real reason for my punishment was to demonstrate the power of prison officials and to discourage me from getting out of line. Yet even the hole had its bright side. Bill Roberts, another resister, was in a nearby cell at the same time and our conversations, though we could not see each other, laid the basis for a lifelong friendship.

I was in total isolation only one other time. While living in the dormitory, I developed the habit of rising early to sit on my cot and meditate. A rule-conscious lieutenant, always looking for infractions against resisters, ordered me to stop the practice. If I wanted to meditate, he said, I should go to the recreation room. I made the mistake of questioning the logic of his order and refused to move. That offense was insubordination, something I could not deny. I resented being punished for such a foolish rule, and after one cold meal I ate nothing more until I was released from the Hole about four days later.

After quarantine, I was surprised to learn that I had been assigned to work in the prison clinic under the same Dr. Krueger who had reported me for coughing in his face. He turned out to be a decent supervisor, though I suspected that he wanted me there for further observation. Dr. Kreuger was a skilled surgeon who also acted as the prison psychiatrist. After a five-minute interview with each prisoner, he wrote up a profile, frequently consulting a psychiatric dictionary since he had no training in that field. His reports were so obviously biased against resisters and some other prisoners that eventually the Bureau of Prisons sent a well-known criminologist to Ashland to question us about the doctor's behavior. This led to Dr. Krueger's transfer to another institution, where he practiced surgery, his specialty. In the clinic I worked as a clerk, an uncomplicated job that allowed time for discussion with other resisters who were assigned there.

Once again a matter of conscience influenced my situation. It was the case of the "Barefoot Boy," so well described by Bronson Clark in his reminiscence. Though no formal disciplinary action ensued against me for going several days without shoes to support the barefoot prisoner, I was transferred from the clinic to work in the machine shop. In the shop, where we worked on various aspects of maintenance, I learned some useful skills and had the added pleasure of working with my friend Bill Roberts. In our spare time we made chess sets for the other inmates. Later I was assigned to teach other prisoners the fundamentals of reading and writing. I was astonished at the number of my fellow inmates who lacked even rudimentary reading skills, and I found this work very rewarding.

In Ashland the days crept by with dreary monotony, and the weekends were especially difficult. Yet for the most part my morale was high and I adjusted well to the prisoner's creed of doing one day at a time, blocking out the weeks, months, and years still to be served. For the twenty-six months I spent in Ashland, prison was my entire world. About a third of the inmates were either war resisters or Jehovah's Witnesses. Most resisters had had some college training, some of them at the country's leading colleges and universities.

In the prison yard during exercise time, we discussed all aspects of war, peace, racism, and social justice. As prisoners of conscience we faced a dilemma, since we did not wish to set ourselves apart or to request special privileges. We had now joined what Eugene Debs called the "criminal class" and we accepted that category. When we protested censorship of mail and other oppressive regulations, it was with the expectation that any change we might effect would benefit all prisoners. I never observed any homosexual activity in Ashland and only once witnessed a violent incident, the attack on Bayard Rustin described by Bronson Clark.

As time passed, more and more of the Ashland population consisted of Selective Service violators. A few, like me, had refused to register. Most were there because their draft boards had not recognized their sincerity as pacifists. Since these men had followed the law and should have been classified as conscientious objectors, it was the boards that had violated the regulations—but it was the objector who landed in prison. A handful accepted parole to the military as noncombatants. The regular parole available to federal prisoners was almost always denied to resisters, though the Justice Department eventually offered a special parole to civilian public service camps.

Before entering prison I was considering a career in art, so I studied art history from standard works eventually permitted to me, and I used any available time to draw and paint watercolors. I also read widely, even using the time waiting to be counted for reading. Indeed, I read all of *Moby-Dick* while "standing for count," a ritual that occurred many times daily. The prison library contained many good books, but the education officer censored anything he personally disapproved of. A request for Walt Whitman's poetry was denied because, said the officer, Whitman was a homosexual. Yet one of the works I most enjoyed was a selection of writings by Oscar Wilde. Apparently the education officer did not know about him.

Considerations of criminal justice issues seldom recognize the psychological impact of long prison sentences. Deadly boredom marks every day, while living only with persons of the same gender makes thinking and talking about sex a major preoccupation. When I entered prison I was young and prudish, uncomfortable with my own sexuality and embarrassed by such discussions. Prison rules forbade even masturbation, though it was a restriction largely ignored. Although movies were carefully screened for sexual content, some of the resisters liked to taunt me by playing a game they called "Knockers and Buns" in which they kept score of sexy scenes that had slipped past the censors. I thought their humor was in very poor taste.

There were few African Americans among the resisters, but one who later became a major figure in the civil rights movement was

Bayard Rustin. Bayard had to live in a segregated cell block and in the dining hall he had to eat at tables set aside for African American inmates. We found this intolerable and took our grievance to the warden. When it was obvious there would be no change, we began organizing for nonviolent action. We planned to sit wherever we chose in the dining hall, and if we should be physically prevented from doing so we would go on work strike. Even the majority of Jehovah's Witnesses agreed to the plan. But the night before it was to be implemented Bayard was placed in the Hole for alleged homosexual activity. I knew that, should the charge be valid, I would be disillusioned with Bayard for carelessly putting our action in jeopardy. If, however, it was not true, I would no longer cooperate with prison authorities. To learn the truth, I bolted past a startled guard who was posted at a stairway leading to the Hole, ran down the steps, and asked Bayard if there were any truth to the charge. He denied it, and that was good enough for me. From that day until my release, I refused to work at Ashland.

Several others joined the strike, and officials put us all in administrative segregation. We were confined to our cells all day except for a brief period of exercise and for taking showers. We could communicate through cell doors but could not see each other. We were allowed books and writing materials, and regular prison food was brought to our cells. How we did our time was now completely up to us. We had discussion times and tried some classes. I continued to work on a correspondence course in small community from Antioch College. Bayard even had a mandolin sent in and learned to play it despite our pleadings that he limit his practice times. Somehow we continued to get word of what was going on with resisters in other prisons. We were encouraged by the total noncooperation of Corbett Bishop and the prison strikes in which other resisters were involved. Despite the close confinement, I did very easy time in the Ashland segregation unit.

Before my refusal to cooperate with the prison system I had decided to reject parole or conditional release, since either would require my promise to obey all laws, including the Selective Service Law. I preferred to serve my entire sentence and leave prison a free man. My original release date under good time was January 18, 1945, but on that day I was informed that the date had been pushed

back twenty-nine days because of my noncooperation. When news
of this reached the general prison population more resisters joined
the segregation unit in protest. They saw the warden's decision as
double punishment, even though I had not asked for conditional release. When my new release date arrived, I was offered a draft card,
which I refused, and papers to sign, which I also refused. Despite
my unequivocal position, the officials released me, and I accepted
the release on my own terms. How the Justice Department would
react remained to be seen.

When I returned to Reading to visit my family, I learned that an
FBI agent had already scoured the neighborhood looking in vain
for angry residents who did not want me to be released. Finally, in
frustration, he asked a neighbor, "Doesn't anyone around here dislike this guy?" My experience was not unique. Many resisters were
viewed sympathetically even by those with family members in the
military. During my brief period of freedom during the war, I met no
personal antagonism except from draft board members or other officials. Most of my contemporaries who were in the armed forces were
there involuntarily, having seen no alternative to enlisting or being
drafted. I sensed that they viewed the war as a nasty job that had to
be done. Many of my generation also found defense jobs to avoid
serving in the military. Early in the war fathers were deferred from
the draft, a policy that led to a rash of early marriages and babies.

Before my release from Ashland, I had arranged to work for the
Fellowship of Reconciliation in New York City as a shipping clerk. I
lived with a group of pacifists in a small Christian community at
Fifth Avenue and 125th Street known as the Harlem Ashram. It was
wonderful to be free. Just walking to work was a joy, as were dates
with girls, riding the Staten Island Ferry, seeing Paul Robeson in
Othello, and working with A. J. Muste and the rest of the FOR staff.
Soon, however, a visit from a federal parole officer brought the threat
of rearrest if I would not fill out monthly forms and obey parole conditions to which I had never agreed. I was not surprised, therefore,
when two FBI agents came to the office on June 15 to arrest me for
parole violation.

After a short period in the Federal Detention Headquarters, known
also as West Street, I was transported to the Federal Penitentiary
near Lewisburg, Pennsylvania. At that point I felt no hesitation—

I would not cooperate with prison rules. When I made that clear by refusing to stand by the cell door for count, the guard replied, "Oh, you're one of those." That first evening I managed to contact the others who were noncooperating by shouting through a window directly beneath the large dormitory room where they were being held. By next morning I was there, too. It was as if I had been taken to another world, a world vaguely familiar from past dreams. At Lewisburg I had no contact with any prisoners who were in the general population. My entire world was in that dormitory room, which we did not leave even for exercise. My only contact with family was through a monthly visit with my mother, since I had refused to sign a form to permit censorship of my mail and could neither send nor receive letters.

Our "Enormous Room" housed a strange mix of persons. Living with a dozen or more war resisters twenty-four hours a day was sometimes difficult. Close proximity exaggerated differences in personalities and life-styles. Some men refused to talk to one another. Our group included a New York lawyer, a cartoonist who was a member of the Industrial Workers of the World, several socialists, a few devoutly religious men, and a few avowed anarchists. Also present were my good friends from Ashland, Bill Roberts and Bayard Rustin, as well as Lawrence Templin, who had been the only nonregistrant student at Bethel College, a Mennonite institution in Kansas. We had several "troublemakers" who had been transferred from Danbury to Lewisburg, a maximum-custody institution surrounded by a high concrete wall. Probably Bureau of Prisons officials considered us all incorrigible. I, for example, had graduated from Mill Point to Ashland to Lewisburg. Still, there were moments of pleasure even in that setting. We enjoyed watching the changing seasons from our prison windows, which overlooked Pennsylvania farm country and the Allegheny Mountains in the distance. One evening we heard a lilting melody played on a flute. Next day we learned that Bill Roberts had constructed the instrument from homemade papier mache by mixing crumpled newspapers with leftover oatmeal, then molding it around a mop handle. Bill's formal training in music combined with perfect pitch to produce a result that was enchanting.

It was in Lewisburg that we learned of the atomic bombing of Hiroshima and Nagasaki and the abrupt end of the war. Bill Roberts responded to the news by immediately holding a one-week fast in penance and protest. It was one of several early actions that led the world in a half-century campaign against atomic and nuclear weapons.

As the war wound down our little community of resisters at Lewisburg began to shrink, and when we were down to about six or seven we were moved to a cell block. It was from there I would be released when I had served the entire three-year sentence. I looked forward to it and to the party some New York friends had planned for me. However, prison regulations required my return to Reading, where I had lived at the time of sentencing. A prison official visited my cell to convince me that I should accept a railroad ticket to Reading. I listened politely but declined. When I had served my time, I said, I would go wherever I wished. On my release day I barricaded myself in the cell with a mop handle barring the door, refusing to leave unless I could travel freely. Two burly guards quickly removed the mop handle and tried to force me to walk by twisting my arm. When that failed they placed me in a large wire laundry basket. Two resisters, Bayard Rustin and Rodney Owen, lay down in the path of the guards, who then walked on their backs. As we proceeded down several flights of stairs, I told the guards the whole thing was silly. I would not go to Reading, and if they insisted I would remove my clothing when they put me down. On the other hand, I was eager to cooperate if they would only let me choose my own destination. Weary of the whole episode, they accepted my offer and took me to the station, where once more they offered me a ticket to Reading. When I refused it they both left, stranding me with no ticket and no money. When the stationmaster paged me for a telephone call, I thought it must be Justice Department officials ready to rearrest me. But the call was from my mother, who had somehow learned of my location.

Having served every day of my sentence, I felt I had a perfect right to join my New York friends for a party. I decided to hitchhike to the town of Lewisburg and somehow get the money to travel to New York. Knowing there was a pacifist minister in town, I stopped at the first parsonage I saw. Amazingly, it was the right one, though the pastor was not at home. His wife, a baby on her arm, listened to my story. She would be glad to lend me the money, she said, if I would hold the baby while she went to the bank. With her help and trust, I bought a ticket for New York and enjoyed a wonderful party with friends. That event was planned by Julius and Esther Eichel, whose staunch support of imprisoned war resisters had cheered us through some difficult times. Julius, an older nonregistrant, was the only World War II resister to have been arrested in both world wars.

My release from Lewisburg occurred on January 24, 1946. The war was over and I was at last free. After a brief visit with my family in Reading, I returned the borrowed money to my benefactors in Lewisburg and traveled westward for the next chapter in my life's adventure. My immediate plan was to complete my undergraduate degree, and for this I enrolled at William Penn College in Oskaloosa, Iowa. Cecil Hinshaw, the president, was a strong Quaker pacifist who went out of his way to invite prison resisters and former Civilian Public Service participants to the college. For a few years, William Penn College became a kind of halfway house for those of us recently released from prison. We were again in the company of a support group and were able to enjoy such simple pleasures as a walk in the woods, seeing a movie of one's choice, living without being counted every day, and, of course, communicating with women as well as men. Penn College had no fraternities or sororities, but we formed a small group of like-minded friends that was very special. In December 1946 Lenna Mae Goodson, a member of that group, became my wife.

After graduation and one semester teaching social studies in a small Iowa high school, I enrolled in graduate school at Pennsylvania State College (later University). There I combined academic studies with peace activism while working as a part-time secretary for the State College Friends (Quaker) Meeting. We were in State College when Congress enacted the Selective Service Act of 1948, relieved that my age, twenty-six, put me beyond the law's registration requirement. Things were looking up when I received a master's degree and got a one-year appointment to teach history at Bluffton College, a Mennonite school in Ohio.

Soon after our arrival, I learned that a Bluffton student had recently refused to register. When marshals came to arrest him, I was present and said he should not let them coerce him into changing his conscience. For that sentence, along with public statements I had made in philosophical support of nonregistration, I was charged

with "counseling" him to refuse to register. In March 1949 I had a
jury trial in the federal court in Toledo. Bluffton faculty and adminis-
trators and many students attended the sessions daily. Dr. Lloyd L.
Ramseyer, president of Bluffton College, protested my arrest and
continued to support me even after I was convicted and sentenced to
eighteen months in prison.

The government's case rested on an interpretation of the law that
made the registration requirement a continuing obligation. Thus,
even though I had not known the young man when he refused to
register, my having done the same thing and the fact that I did not
try to dissuade him from his action made me guilty of "counseling"
him to continue his refusal. It was twisted logic that in 1970 would
be thrown out by the Supreme Court. But that did me no good in
1949. My attorneys filed notice of appeal, but the judge refused to
grant me bail and I was immediately remanded to jail.

My new prison home was the Federal Correctional Institution
at Milan, Michigan. Everything about my third imprisonment was
different and much more difficult. The war was over, removing the
feeling that I was part of a noble crusade to uphold the principles
of nonviolence. I missed the support of other resisters; the student
I was accused of counseling was the only other objector at Milan,
and he was soon paroled. I knew, as did my friends at Bluffton, that
I would never advise anyone to register or to refuse to register for
the draft, a decision I have always believed is highly personal. I felt
myself caught in a nightmare in which my chief worry was that I
would never teach again.

To protect my emotional stability, I decided to cooperate with
prison regulations if I could possibly do so. My work assignment
was in the front office, keeping books for the prison purchasing department. It was a task for which I was poorly qualified, having no
accounting skills whatsoever. I have often wondered if those books
were ever straightened out!

Each day in Milan seemed an eternity. When ragweed season
arrived, I had a serious attack of asthma that put me in the prison
hospital for more than a week. I learned to know several German
prisoners, who were intelligent but openly anti-Semitic, and two
rather conservative Toledo businessmen who were in prison on a tax

charge. My solace was in reading, the few visits I had with Lenna Mae, and one visit from my mother.

Some of my pacifist friends could not understand my willingness to cooperate in prison. When they planned to picket outside the institution to protest my incarceration, I asked them to demonstrate in Washington instead. My concern was that if such an action took place in Milan I would be transferred, making visits impossible for Lenna Mae and my mother. Perhaps I was unduly worried, but my experience on the receiving end of a cat-and-mouse game with the Justice Department had heightened my anxiety. Since I was no longer liable for draft registration, I decided to apply for parole. Because of the large amount of publicity about my case, the Department of Justice was probably glad to get rid of me. In any case, I was paroled in December 1949, finally able to move on with my marriage and my life.

Meantime, my legal case was moving slowly through the courts. The Central Committee for Conscientious Objectors in Philadelphia led the charge, with pro bono legal help and funds from Quakers and other religious groups as well as civil libertarians. In October 1950 the Supreme Court returned a split decision, with Tom Clark abstaining because he had been attorney general when the prosecution began. That meant that the court issued no formal ruling, in effect confirming the lower court's decision, and we never knew which justices voted to support me. It was disappointing, but it did not affect me personally because I had served my time and was in no danger of being returned to prison.

When I left Milan I had to decide whether to continue my pursuit of a teaching career or become a full-time professional pacifist. Several factors influenced me to follow the example of Dr. Evan Thomas, a World War I resister who became a medical practitioner but continued peace activism on a part-time basis. My interest in scholarship and my love of teaching were foremost. It was also clear from my recent trial that some government officials were trying to keep me out of the teaching profession. "Gara," said U.S. Attorney Gerald Openlander, "was a rotten apple in the barrel." That only increased my determination to stay in academe. So it was on to the University of Wisconsin for a Ph.D. in American History.

Two members of the Wisconsin history department were pacifists, and the others were fair-minded and tolerant. In 1950 almost all male graduate students were veterans on the GI Bill. Some were wholly disillusioned with the war. None was antagonistic to me because of my stand on the war. Wisconsin was an intellectually stimulating environment, and the history department was one of its best. But when I got my degree in 1953, the market for historians was overcrowded and, with my record, finding a teaching post was not going to be easy.

In the summer of 1953, with the doctorate in hand, I accepted a position as lecturer in U.S. History at Mexico City College. Although I spoke no Spanish, my classes were all in English, and Lenna Mae and I were able to study the language as we spent a pleasant year in that beautiful country. Anxious to increase my professional contacts in the United States, I took a position at Eureka College in Illinois where I taught history for three years. While we were living in Eureka our daughter, Robin, was born.

In 1957 we moved to Grove City, Pennsylvania, where I was to teach U.S. History at Grove City College. It was to be the one job in my teaching career of forty years that turned sour. In 1962, after five years of teaching and chairing the history department, with annual pay increases and encouraging notes from the dean, I was suddenly fired without a clearly stated reason or an opportunity to defend myself. In order to clear my name and continue in the profession, I asked the American Association of University Professors to investigate my dismissal. It did so, eventually placing the college on its list of censured institutions. More than thirty-four years later it remains on that list. While I had no desire to hurt the college, I was determined to save my professional career. As we were preparing to leave Grove City, Wilmington College in Ohio was looking for a history teacher. President James Read, a Quaker pacifist who had spent ten years as deputy high commissioner for refugees with the United Nations, made Wilmington College a unique institution. He not only supported my research and writing but also encouraged me to be more active in the peace movement. During the Vietnam War a college trustee even suggested that I go to Washington for civil disobedience. Where else could that happen? I had finally found a place where I could work professionally and also work for peace. Soon after we moved to Wilmington our son, Brian, was born.

Following the trustee's suggestion, I went to Washington, where I spent a few hours in a local jail for a demonstration at the Capitol. It was the only time since the 1949 counseling case that I have been arrested. While some may romanticize going to jail for peace, I have studiously avoided arrest. Three and a half years in prison had its price, but it in no way diminished my commitment to work for peace and to help build a more just society.

What have I concluded from all this? First of all I am convinced that part-time activism is possible and can be effective. Because he was a respected medical professional, Evan Thomas's peace actions carried more weight. He was contributing something important to society as well as protesting war and militarism. Medical research was the positive side of his witness. Combining teaching and activism can be more difficult, as my experience at Grove City College proved. Moreover, the demands of each activity compete relentlessly for one's time. The responsibilities of teaching limited my peace activity, but it was possible to work around them and continue in the struggle without sacrificing the demands of the profession. Besides teaching, I have managed to write five books plus dozens of articles and book reviews.

Second, over the years my commitment to nonviolence has deepened. I have questioned many of my beliefs and actions but have never once doubted that refusal to register for Selective Service was the correct path for me to follow. It was the strongest stand a male youth could take against war in 1942, and I instinctively knew it was what I had to do.

In a world where wars still rage, in which violence escalates in our national life with rapes and murders, spousal abuse, and the sexual abuse of children—not to mention the horrifying reality of a bombed-out federal building in Oklahoma—it is easy to dismiss nonviolence as irrelevant. But this is to accept the twisted views of tabloid journalism and the entertainment industry. Violence is big business today, while random acts of kindness often go unnoticed. Yet there is a long history of nonviolence that is often overlooked. In our own country most of the abolition movement was nonviolent, as were the movements for women's suffrage and civil rights. More recently we have observed the near-miracle of nonviolent change as one after another of the totalitarian regimes in the Soviet Union and eastern Europe have toppled bloodlessly. During World War II pacifists in occupied France succeeded in smuggling hundreds of Jews to safety, while Norwegian teachers waged a successful nonviolent campaign against Nazi indoctrination. In fact there is a long history of nonviolent action, including, of course, the heroic struggle against British imperialism led by Gandhi. We are only beginning to study the potential of nonviolent power.

My study of history has been a continuing source of inspiration. It is tempting to feel discouraged when those in power dismiss nonviolence as unrealistic and irrelevant. Yet William Lloyd Garrison and a handful of followers provoked the same reaction when they began a crusade that was to help end chattel slavery in the United States. The same is true for that small group of courageous women who met in Seneca Falls, New York, in 1848 to demand social, economic, and political rights for women. And who could have predicted that powerful segregationists in the South would be forced to accept open accommodations in public places because of the nonviolent crusade led by Dr. Martin Luther King, Jr.? While it is not a guarantee of success, nonviolence has a good track record. The stakes for humanity are too high to ignore its possibilities for resolving conflict at all levels.

Another conclusion I have reached is that individuals can make a difference. A few protestors who tried to sail into the Pacific nuclear test zone in the yacht *Golden Rule* helped expose the hazards of atmospheric nuclear testing and spark a movement that led to the limited test ban treaty of 1963. Henry David Thoreau's one night in jail led him to write "Civil Disobedience," an essay that is now a guide for nonviolent activists everywhere. When the Swiss government, during World War II, required all homes to participate in blackouts, Pierre Ceresole placed a lighted candle in his window. For that action he was jailed, but his candle has become a symbol for the many who are trying to prevent the darkness of hate and war from becoming total.

Indeed, that was the major contribution of those who resisted World War II. We knew our actions would not stop the war. Though the bombings of London, Dresden, and Hiroshima horrified us, and we saw nothing but terrible evil in the Nazi regime, we did not think that killing German and Japanese civilians was the answer. In truth, we had no answers, though we knew that much earlier there had been opportunities for governments to prevent the war. Our friends were being drafted for military service, and some of them died. My own brother-in-law was shot down over Germany and became a prisoner of war. We felt part of the struggle for a better world. Our witness was against conscription and war itself, not against members of the armed forces. What we did was to light a few candles in the darkness, to keep the ideal of nonviolence alive for use when the world came to its senses.

JOHN H. GRIFFITH

War Resistance in World War II

*I felt a need to say as emphatically as I could that
war is insane and that conscription is the first step
in that insanity.*

AN AMENDMENT TO the Selective Training and Service Act of 1940,
approved December 20, 1941, required the registration of all male
citizens of the United States of America between the ages of eighteen and sixty-five. Nineteen years old at the time, with a registration date of June 30, 1942, I wrote a registered letter on June 29, 1942,
to Gen. H. B. Springs, head of Selective Service in South Carolina.
In this letter I wrote, "I take this opportunity to inform you of my
position. I am conscientiously opposed to war, for any cause whatever, and shall refuse to comply with this act, or any act in the future
which I feel to be a contradiction of Christian teachings, democratic
liberty and individual freedom."

In rereading this letter fifty-four years later, I am surprised to note
that I did not plainly say that I intended to refuse to register. There
is no question, however, that General Springs was aware of this by
the following day, when my father wrote, "My son knows about the
law concerning registration. He feels that here is the place to take
his stand against war, and I must take my stand with him where he
thinks best. I tried to show him that he would not be compromising
to register, but he thinks otherwise."

Since the age of seven I have been aware of a spiritual dimension
to life. A few years later the awareness that one can have guidance
from this spiritual side of life became a reality to me. A few more
years and I came to appreciate that each of us is also the product of

JOHN HARVEY GRIFFITH (b. 1922)
John Griffith devoted much of his life after prison to the cooperative movement, including his ten years spent administering a program to train managers for farmer cooperatives. In 1948 he refused a second time to register for the draft, but his action was ignored by the Department of Justice. He and his wife, Reva, live in Kansas City, Missouri, where he remains a participant in numerous peace activities.

cultural conditioning and that spiritual guidance is usually affected by one's cultural conditioning.

My mother died when I was twelve years old. That event had a profound effect on me. I saw how precious life is and how horrible the suffering is when a loved one suddenly dies. I developed a comfort in being alone and practiced rudimentary levels of contemplation. I am sure this confession would amaze my high school classmates. To them I was a regular guy—outgoing, active in sports. I was usually class president in public school. But this other contemplative side, this being aware of how precious life is, was very much a part of who I was. And it was a contributing factor to my abhorrence of war.

I was also influenced by my father's ministry in the Methodist Church. Even though my father could have been deferred as a minister, he volunteered for service in World War I. The war ended within just a few months of his enlistment and he did not see service overseas. But the war was a significant experience for him, and he was quite aware of the maiming and killing that went on in "the war to end all wars."

My father was studious. History was his favorite field of study. Within a few years after the war, his study of history led to disillusionment with war. He came to view the demonizing of the German people during World War I as a lie. He became convinced that the war was about lust for power and economic advantage for a few political and industrial leaders. He believed that innocent young men on both sides were deceived into killing each other on behalf of those few. And he came to see that war is incompatible with the teachings of Jesus.

My earliest memory of the antimilitary focus of my father's ministry is a reference he made to the National Anthem when it was adopted by the U.S. Congress in 1931. He complained that the "Star Spangled Banner" glorified war and that a much better national anthem would be "America the Beautiful." Why this would impress a nine year old, I do not know. But it is part of my cultural conditioning.

I assume my father was consistent in preaching against war, although I confess I was only dimly aware of this until sometime after 1939, when Germany invaded Poland. That message then became part of world reality. It was no longer just a "feel-good" message to deliver to a contented congregation on a pleasant Sunday morning.

I remember, at the time of the invasion of Poland, that in discussions with my friends I was firmly opposed to going overseas to kill young men who would be there only because their government had conscripted them. As I recall, I said I would reluctantly agree to Coast Guard service, which I perceived to be purely defensive. I think my father's conviction that young men had been misled in World War I was embedded in my consciousness.

As the war expanded and became more threatening during the next couple years, I became concerned about what I should do if and when our government decided to conscript American youth. I read a great deal. Reading the Methodist youth magazine *Motive*, the writings of A. J. Muste of the Fellowship of Reconciliation, accounts of the nonviolent struggle for independence in India under the leadership of Gandhi, the teachings of Jesus, and, in addition, the practice of meditative prayer were all important aspects of this search for a right course of action.

My position gradually shifted from a willingness to serve in the Coast Guard (killing for defense) to service in the medical corps (no killing). I then became troubled that serving in the medical corps was an integral part of the war process and that my serving there would only release someone else to do the killing.

I next considered applying for conscientious objector status, which would involve doing work of national importance within the conscription system. I soon came to believe this action presented the same dilemma for me as serving in the medical corps.

Perhaps it was early in 1942 that I experienced a drastic shift in my thinking. Up until then I had been thinking of how best to accommodate the legal requirements of the Selective Service System. But now it seemed to me that the whole world was going insane. And rather than seeking accommodation, I felt a need to say as emphatically as I could that war is insane and that conscription is the first step in that insanity. I decided to refuse to register.

At the time I was supposed to register, I was a counselor at a YMCA camp near Columbia, South Carolina. A few days after I mailed my letter to General Springs, YMCA officials came to camp to visit me. The FBI had informed them of my pending arrest. The YMCA officials urged me to register for the draft and apply for conscientious objector classification. When they became convinced that I was firm in my intention not to register, they suggested that I go home to be arrested. They wanted to avoid embarrassment for the YMCA.

My first experience of verbal abuse as a nonregistrant occurred July 9, 1942—the day I was arrested by the FBI and taken to the U.S. district attorney's office. Claude Sapp, the district attorney, came barging into the office, his face flushed with anger. My diary entry of this incident reads: "I managed to keep cool and refused to answer any of his questions until he would talk like a gentleman but Dad got hot and told him off." All of my diary entries are very concise. My memory of the details runs more like this.

Mr. Sapp entered the office and said, "Listen here, boy, just who in the hell do you think you are? I want you to know that I am the United States District Attorney and I am not going to put up with this shit. I am telling you right now to get your ass down to the draft board and register like you are supposed to."

I responded, "Mr. Sapp, if you want me to talk with you about my position, the first thing you have to do is to stop cussing and talk like a gentleman."

Mr. Sapp answered, "You listen here, you unpatriotic slacker. . . ."

Then my father interrupted and said, "Now wait a minute, Mr. Sapp, I want you to listen to me." (This account is based on a newspaper item covering the event.) He continued, "I served in World War I because I believed in the American cause. After the war I became disillusioned and ever since then I have opposed war. I love my country, but you don't have to go to war to show your patriotism. I have another son in the navy. I think he is sincerely trying to do the right thing and I will stand by him. But John is also trying to do the right thing. I can assure you he is not unpatriotic, and I will stand by him as he tries to be true to his religion and to his conscience."

A short time later Mr. Sapp exclaimed that he was finished trying to reason with this "idiot." My father was unable to meet bail requirements of $7,500, so Mr. Sapp ordered the FBI agents to take me to jail. When the steel doors clanged shut behind me, I felt peaceful and happy.

The jail was the Richland County jail. In my diary I noted: "For the noon day meal I had a cinnamon roll and a cup of buttermilk. For supper I had seven slices of bread and a cup of stale syrup. I couldn't stomach the syrup. . . . Last night wasn't very peaceful. Bedbugs feasted on Griffith flesh for the first time and seemed to enjoy it immensely." Not included in the diary entry was note of the presence of foot-long rats which seemed to have little fear of humans. In desperation I made a torch out of a newspaper in an effort to kill the bedbugs in the cracks of the solid steel bed—no mattress—I was to sleep on. I slept very little.

The next afternoon I was transferred to Sumter County Jail. I learned from the U.S. marshals that the Richland County Jail was condemned by federal officials and that a federal prisoner could be held there for no longer than twenty-four hours before being transferred to an approved jail. I had another twenty-four-hour stay in the Richland County Jail after my trial in November 1942.

The Sumter County Jail was a big improvement over Richland County—no bedbugs, no rats, and the food was okay. There were six other federal prisoners. We all shared one big cage-type room. My diary notes "175 bars to insure my safekeeping." I quickly made friends with the other prisoners.

On July 16, 1942, I noted in my diary that I "spent most of the day reading and answering letters. . . . I have gained a lot in the way of new friends in comparison to enemies. The friends I have now are ones you can count on no matter what comes. . . . I hope that I will have the chance to make the others understand. Today I nearly cried when I read my letters. I didn't have one criticizing me. They were all from fine, free thinking people who can never know how happy they have made me. . . . I have felt happiness many times before, but it is seldom that it touches so deeply in my soul as it did today. I actually felt like turning 'Holy Roller' and shouting in praise to God—'in bonds yet freer than the free.'"

On July 17 I had my second experience of verbal abuse. My diary reports, "A prominent Sumter doctor came up to see me today and for the first time I was called a son of a bitch through bars. . . . I must be more Christian now for I felt no anger but only sympathy for the old gentleman." Not mentioned in the diary is my memory that the doctor also accused me of being a coward. Several of my cellmates came to my defense and told the doctor, with equally profane eloquence, that he didn't know what he was talking about if he thought that I was a coward.

The other noteworthy thing about my experience in Sumter was that we had a spell of unseasonably hot weather. The cell was on the second floor of the jail next to a flat roof. The radio reported temperatures of 103 degrees in Sumter. My jail buddies and I were estimating temperatures of at least 115 to 120 degrees in our cell, and it may well have been higher. I literally lay in a puddle of my own sweat when trying to sleep at night. This lasted several days. A couple of my cellmates were elderly (probably sixty years old) and were having a rough time with the heat. I, on the other hand, was in excellent physical condition. During the early hours of the night, I would fan these older gentlemen until they dropped off to sleep. They appreciated it, and I felt good knowing that one could be of service to humanity even in jail.

July 23—two weeks after being jailed—my dad came to take me home. Two courageous families in his church had put up their homes with a combined value of $16,000 as security for my bond. To convey some sense of relative money values between 1942 and 1997, those two homes in Columbia today would, I am sure, have a combined market value of well over $200,000! My bond had been set at $7,500 cash or $15,000 property. That was a lot of money in 1942. Both of these families stated for the press that they were not supporting my position but were rather assisting their pastor.

Several incidents are noteworthy during the time that I was out on bond, July 23 and before my trial, November 2, 1942.

First, I discovered when I got home that my father now wanted me to register. He was under intense pressure to get me to register and was having trouble sleeping at night. He told me that I had made my witness. He even said that my stand (in terms of making people face the morality of conscription and war) had been the best thing for South Carolina he had witnessed. There had been extensive press and radio coverage. But he now thought I should register. But I felt that to register would be a betrayal of what my conscience was telling me I needed to do.

We agreed that I would go to the Methodist Conference Center in the mountains at Lake Junaluska, North Carolina, to have time to reflect and reevaluate my position. We both knew that the noted Methodist missionary to India, Dr. E. Stanley Jones, was at Junaluska. Dad thought it would be good if I discussed the situation with Dr. Jones.

I took this very seriously and was considerably troubled that my father was suffering. I had a conference with Dr. Jones. We talked for perhaps a couple hours and his final advice was, according to my diary, "that I should view my actions not for success, or failure, but to do only as a Higher Intelligence directs me." I am sure my father had hoped Dr. Jones would encourage me to register. Dr. Jones had not done this, but I still was not sure what I was supposed to do in terms of his "Higher Intelligence" advice.

A couple of days later I had a very moving experience that I did not record in my diary. In reading my diary as information for this essay, I noticed an entry on August 1, 1942 (seven days after the experience): "Told Dad that I would not register. Hope I can make him see that I am doing the right thing. *It is a fact for me now.* So many things happened to me at Junaluska concerning this that I am afraid to write them down in my diary, much less tell Dad about them." I did write my father about this experience in a letter dated August 6, 1943, from federal prison at Petersburg, Virginia. This letter was in response to his question about a hymn that he had noticed I had handwritten in the front of my New Testament: "Jesus, I my cross have taken. All to leave and follow thee. Destitute, despised, forsaken, Thou from hence my all shall be."

In the letter of August 6 I wrote,

The evening before I left Junaluska I was by myself in the open air auditorium in prayer. Perhaps meditation is a better word for I really wasn't saying anything in my mind. After a while of such meditation I happened to glance at the hymnal in my hand and at the same time felt a strong urge to open it. It opened to page 92. [This was the hymn mentioned above; I think I referred to the page number, as I didn't want the prison censor to know what I was talking about.] The words shocked me a bit, but I closed the hymnal with the word "accident" in my mind. But, Dad, the experience was repeated several times! I realize the danger involved in inferring revelation. I only know that something let loose inside me and that for the first time in months I knew what Peace was. I wrote "hymn 92" in my New Testament (at that time).

I did not tell my father how different and profound the *instruction* was to open the hymnal. Nor did I share with him that I also knew then that I would not register under any imaginable circumstance. I felt then that I was at the place of personal commitment Gandhi asked of his followers, "When using non-violent resistance, state the minimum objective of your resistance and be prepared to die for it."

The experience at Junaluska would have to be considered a Christ-centered experience. In honesty, I should record here that since that time my religious thought has shifted from being Christ-centered Methodist to Quaker Universalist. The subtleties of the differences between these two are far beyond the scope of this paper. While I now think the Junaluska experience would have been different for a Quaker Universalist, I acknowledge that the Junaluska experience, whatever the explanation, completely resolved any doubts that I had about what I was supposed to do.

The second experience of note during the time between my arrest and being sentenced has to do with my relationship with my closest high school friends. According to my diary, on August 16, 1942, my younger brother, Bill, and I decided to visit our friends in Easley, South Carolina (115 miles from Columbia). We had moved to Easley when I was in the seventh grade. I had remained there to finish high school with my friends even though my family moved to Lancaster, South Carolina, midway through my senior year. During several months of this time, I lived with one of my best friends, Dupree Sitton.

When I arrived at the house where six of my friends, including Dupree, were sitting on the porch, I went over to shake hands with Dupree. Without a word, he got up and left, obviously angry and indignant. No one said a word about why Dupree had acted this way. According to my diary, only one of my six friends seemed to be relaxed in my presence. The other four, after Dupree left, were civil, but I had the feeling that they were noticeably reserved. Perhaps they were startled by Dupree's behavior. Perhaps each of them wondered if any of the others felt like Dupree. I noted in my diary that even though they tried to act as if they were glad to see me, "it was that certain artificial gladness that I am becoming used to." I had planned to stay in Easley overnight to visit with my friends, but after a short time with them I decided to spend the night with relatives in Greenville. I was very disappointed.

The third experience relates to my relationship with Emily Hinnant, a young girl in our church. We both thought we were very much in love. As soon as I was arrested, Emily's parents angrily told her never to date me again. We did manage to see each other at church youth functions, but dates were almost out of the question. On one occasion when Emily was returning from an evening church program, Emily's stepmother thought she had secretly dated me. She slapped Emily hard. Emily smiled and her stepmother slapped her again. Emily smiled again and was slapped a third time. Her stepmother then stormed out of the room threatening to disown her. Interestingly, Emily never professed pacifism during our relationship.

Emily moved out of her family home and for a short time stayed with an older, married sister who was friendly toward me. Shortly after that, Emily signed up for a nurse's training program at the medical school in Charleston. A short time after I had been sentenced and was in Sumter County Jail (awaiting transfer to a federal prison), Emily wrote that she was questioning her love for me and said she thought she should date other boys. I wrote and encouraged her in this. We continued to correspond for a short time, but within a few months Emily married a military person stationed in Charleston. She died of cancer while I was still in prison.

The fourth experience is related to my trial. At first both my father and I agreed that there was no point in having an attorney. I knew that I was guilty of violating the law and planned to plead guilty. However, while out on bond, we visited Sky Valley, a retreat center near Hendersonville, North Carolina, that was owned and managed by a retired lawyer (also a pacifist) from Columbia, James Perry. Mr. Perry thought that it was advisable to have a lawyer represent me in court. I cannot remember why Mr. Perry did not volunteer to do that himself. Perhaps he had let his license expire.

When we returned to Columbia I contacted several lawyers Mr. Perry had mentioned. Only one of them, Mr. Hubert, showed any inclination to accept me as a client. It became clear after several sessions with Mr. Hubert that he also was very reluctant to be associated with the case. I remember he asked me to read the account of the trial and death of Socrates in Plato's "Apology." I think Mr. Hubert thought the lesson to learn from Socrates was that Socrates was willing to die in acknowledging the authority of the state. What I saw in the story was that Socrates was willing to die rather than stop his search for Truth. In any event, Mr. Hubert's reluctance to represent me reflected the intense patriotism in Columbia at that time.

When I was arrested, a Quaker by the name of Wilmer Young read of my arrest in the newspaper and came to see if he could be of any assistance and to give moral support to my family. He and his wife were operating an American Friends Service Committee project near Abbeville, South Carolina (eighty-five miles from Columbia), designed to help sharecropper families become landowners. After this initial visit, we continued to be in touch with Wilmer Young and advised him of our experience in trying, unsuccessfully, to get legal assistance. A few days later we had a phone call from Walter Longstreth, an elderly Quaker lawyer from Philadelphia. Longstreth said that Wilmer Young had informed him of the situation and he would consider it a privilege to come to Columbia and represent me in court. He assured us that there would be no charge for his services.

When Walter Longstreth arrived at our home a day or two before my trial, I shared with him the statement I wished to make in court. He liked the statement. He felt fairly certain, however, that with the strong feeling in Columbia regarding my case that the judge would not allow me to make the statement. He advised that we make five hundred copies of the statement. Then, in the event the judge disallowed the statement in court, my father, my stepmother, and a courageous young Methodist minister, Claude Evans, would hand out the statements in the courtroom to the general public as well as the news media. Mr. Longstreth thought there was some risk of being held in contempt of court, but it was agreed that an attempt would be made to distribute the printed statements.

As it turned out, when Walter Longstreth asked the judge if I might plead guilty and then make a statement to the court, the judge

agreed to this. I made the statement without incident. In my statement I said I could not reconcile war with the teachings of Jesus.
I said Gandhi's struggle in India was showing humankind an alternative to war. I said that by refusing to register, I considered I
was making one more protest against man's inhumanity to man and
for that I would cheerfully accept any penalty handed down by
the court.

Another part of Walter Longstreth's service as my legal representative was to give a brief biographical account of my life. He told the
court of my popularity in school, my leadership in Methodist youth
programs, my volunteer work in a Methodist "settlement house"
serving the poorest people in Columbia, and my volunteer service
as a counselor at YMCA camp. He finally pleaded with the judge to
sentence me to a year and a day in prison, which, we understood,
was the minimum sentence the judge would consider.

Although Walter Longstreth represented me as well as I could
have been represented, federal judge G. B. Timmerman sentenced
me to thirty months in prison and a fine of two hundred dollars. In
explaining why he could not impose the minimum sentence, Judge
Timmerman said, "It seems to me that by his example he is, in reality,
urging others to do just as he has done, because we can teach quite as
forcefully by example as by word of mouth." Given the framework
of the law, the level of nationalistic feeling in South Carolina and the
directness with which conscription was being challenged, I believe
Judge Timmerman would have been well within the scope of his
responsibility if he had given the maximum penalty prescribed by
law—five years in prison and a ten thousand dollar fine. I never
learned if or how the two hundred dollar fine was paid.

At the time I refused to register my father was pastor of Main
Street Methodist Church in Columbia, the largest Methodist church
in South Carolina at that time. In the two years he had ministered to
this church, it had experienced unusual growth, and Dad was enjoy-
ing considerable popularity with the main body of church members
and attenders. The church was usually well filled on Sunday morning. There were, however, a few men—a couple on the church board
of stewards—who considered themselves to be powers behind the
scene and who were not happy with the social gospel my father was
preaching. I am sure they thought it lacked patriotic fervor. As soon

as I was arrested, these few men mounted a campaign to have my father removed from Main Street Church. Lies about my father were fed into the rumor mill and a delegation went to see the bishop. The bishop had his district superintendent visit my father. The bishop's message, via the district superintendent, was, "If you care about your ministry, you had better make that boy register." My father did not mention this incident to me. I learned about it much later. But I realize now that it was part of the pressure he was under when he asked me, just after I got out of Sumter County Jail, to register.

I was sentenced on November 2, 1942. Within several weeks my father was notified by the bishop that he was being transferred to a much smaller church about as far away from Columbia as is possible and still remain within the geographical boundaries of the conference.

As it turned out, this was a major turning point in my father's ministry in South Carolina Methodism. Other ministers came to admire my father for his courage in standing behind a nonconformist son and for not compromising his own ministry during a time of intense nationalism. He became the acknowledged leader of reform-minded ministers in South Carolina Methodism. In the years following the war, the church in South Carolina underwent significant changes toward being more democratic under the persistent lobbying of my father and the reform-minded ministers who followed his leadership.

When I began serving my sentence at the federal prison near Petersburg, Virginia, I was committed to follow another of Gandhi's instructions to his nonviolent followers: "When in prison as a nonviolent resister, be a model prisoner."

When I arrived at Petersburg there was one other nonregistrant there, David Morgan, son of a Baptist minister in North Carolina. There were probably a dozen Jehovah's Witness inmates who, when denied ministerial exemption, had refused induction. The rest of the prison population (several hundred) was largely made up of uneducated men who were caught making or transporting whiskey. A minority were in for such things as driving stolen cars across state lines, transporting prostitutes across state lines, sending pornography through the mail, etc. A few had been arrested while in the military. Over the next year and a half, the number of COs gradually increased to perhaps two dozen and the Jehovah's Witnesses increased to over one hundred.

I quickly settled into a routine of work, study, exercise, meditation, and trying to be as helpful as possible to my fellow inmates. Some of them were illiterate. I wrote many letters for these men and read their incoming family mail to them. One especially tender memory I have is concerned with an illiterate inmate the same age as my father. This man's son, my age, was operating a "moonshine" still on the father's property. When federal law officers discovered the still, the father claimed ownership to keep his son out of prison. I believe that the father's sentence was eighteen months. After several months of being this man's letter-writer and letter-reader, I was especially saddened when he received a letter from his wife informing him that their son had been arrested for rape. The poor man was devastated. My memory is that the son was sentenced to fifteen years in the state penitentiary.

Although there were opportunities at Petersburg for recreational sports, I felt that, with the war on, sports were frivolous. I did occasionally play checkers with some of the men after the library had closed for the day, but my main endeavor during "free time" was serious reading. I eagerly tackled books on religion, philosophy, history, economics, and sociology. I also took several university-level correspondence courses.

I think that, on the whole, I developed a good rapport with most of the other inmates as well as with most of the guards. However, there were a few inmates, probably no more than six, and perhaps three or four guards who seemed to feel it their patriotic duty to harass "draft dodgers."

The closest I came to physical attack by an inmate was by a man named Clive. Clive was perhaps twenty-five to thirty years old and about my size. He was also the leader of the few inmates who disliked draft violators. He constantly made derogatory comments about "draft dodgers." I, just as habitually, tried to respond with humor and goodwill. As I recall this incident, Clive was seated at the table across from me during the evening meal. He started in on his draft dodger thing with me and I reminded him that he also was avoiding the army by being in prison. I think Clive thought I was calling him a "draft dodger" and he became very angry. He jumped to his feet, grabbed a table knife, and threatened, "I'll kill you, you bastard, if you call me a draft dodger."

I replied, "You know, Clive, you have been cussing and threatening me for a long time now. I have tried to be friendly with you but it seems to do no good. Now if you would like to go out behind the mess hall [normally out-of-view of the guards] and get this out of our systems, it's OK with me." Clive looked perplexed. He finally stammered something to the effect, "I ain't going to the Hole for fighting you. You ain't worth it." What Clive didn't know was that I fully intended to respond nonviolently to his aggression. As it worked out, Clive didn't harass me after that. Sometime later he even asked me to write a couple of letters for him.

There were also several guards who, like Clive, had an intense dislike for "draft dodgers." A couple of experiences with these guards will serve as examples.

I was working on the prison dairy operation. The guard, Mr. Shepherd, in charge of the dairy, was one of the few guards with a college education. He had a habit of making derogatory comments about draft dodging to other men working at the dairy. These comments were not made directly to me but were made in my presence so that I could hear them. One day a cow bolted from her milking stall and started galloping toward the door. I happened to be near the door. Mr. Shepherd yelled at me, "Shut that door, you son of a bitch." I got the door shut and caught the cow by her halter. I then told Mr. Shepherd that I would like to talk with him. I said something like, "Mr. Shepherd, I have never spoken to you with disrespect. I cannot believe that you would like for someone to speak to you as you just did to me. I would like to ask, in the future, that you speak to me with the same respect that you expect when I speak with you. That's really the only way I can work for you." Mr. Shepherd was apologetic. He may have thought that the warden would not be pleased with an account of the incident if he wrote me up for insubordination. Or he may have simply been ashamed of his behavior.

Interestingly, Mr. Shepherd did stop his harassing. I remember that we later had serious discussions together. One in particular was about an article I had read in the *Christian Century* magazine written by Dr. Hornell Hart of Duke University Divinity School titled "Perfect Christ, Imperfect Jesus." Mr. Shepherd even asked to borrow the magazine.

When I first went to prison I fully intended, someday, to follow my father in the Methodist ministry. But my prison experience began to change this. The experience of discussing Hart's ideas with Mr. Shepherd reflects these early changes that were going on in my thinking. On May 27, 1943, I wrote to my father, "I have read quite a few books [since being in prison]—both by religious writers and by historians. I have read several histories about other great religious movements that did not grow out of the writings of the Hebrews. I must confess that my mind has been unsettled more concerning religious belief than at any time in my life."

I had been reared in a racist culture in South Carolina. From a young age I think I knew in my heart that the white supremacy ideology was wrong. It never occurred to me, however, that there was anything one young white person could do about it. This problem weighed on my mind as the prison was segregated and I had developed close friendships with several African Americans.

On February 7, 1944, I wrote my dad, "The matter of going to church is becoming quite a problem to me, I fear. We go in, the whites on the right, the Negroes on the left. I have a good Negro friend. . . . We meet each other on the way to church and begin a friendly chat. We come to the chapel and pass through the door. I look at Joe. Joe looks at me. Then we part—'or else'—in a Christian church! . . . I am not certain what action I should take—whether (1) to grin and bear it; (2) to simply stop going to church or (3) should a Christian first protest and then act accordingly?" I did not mention it in my letter, but the protest I was considering was to sit with Joe and refuse to move to the white side. A later letter indicated that I made the decision to discontinue attending segregated church services.

On March 22, 1944, in a letter to my father, I was reflecting on my study of "Types of Religious Philosophy" by Dr. E. A. Burt. I said, "I have necessarily—and this is the only place where you may be a bit hurt—left the highway of orthodox Christianity in its doctrines and creeds about Jesus. . . . involving belief in the virgin birth, supernatural states, resurrection from the dead, the Trinity, etc." I then complained that traditional Christianity had become sidetracked by emphasizing *belief about Jesus* and was neglecting what *Jesus taught* about how we should live our lives.

During this time of my incarceration, I confronted other guards on several occasions as I had Mr. Shepherd. I gradually became convinced that several of the guards had made a decision to try to make me more subservient in the guard/inmate relationship and that our relationship had now reached an impasse.

An encounter with one of these guards, whose name I no longer remember, occurred in early April 1944. At this time I was working on the farm detail. On this particular day the inmates were spreading fertilizer by hand. There were perhaps fifteen inmates in this operation. Each inmate had a five-gallon bucket with fertilizer in it. We would broadcast the fertilizer by hand as we moved across the field in a straight line. The inmates normally carried on an animated conversation with each other as they performed this task. As near as I could tell, the only limit to free speech would be critical remarks about the prison administration. Certainly profanity and lewd jokes were standard fare.

Charlie Walker, a fellow conscientious objector, and I were in the middle of this line and were talking to each other. The guard, who would fit the general description of a bigoted, redneck Southerner, suddenly called the line to halt. He came over and told me to get my "ass to the far end of the line." I asked, "Why are you asking me to move?" As I remember his answer was that he was tired of hearing about "poets and authors and all that god damn draft-dodging crap." I told him that I was sorry but I didn't feel our conversation warranted that kind of behavior on his part and that I would not move to the end of the line. He ordered the line to proceed with the broadcasting. But when we reached the edge of the field where the prison truck was parked, he took me to the main office and charged me with insubordination. I was sentenced to either ten or fourteen days (I can't remember which for sure) in solitary confinement on bread and water.

With this experience, I reevaluated my seventeen-month experiment of following Gandhi's advice to be a model prisoner. I decided that I could no longer function under supervision of guards who were intent on trying to humiliate me.

I will try to describe solitary confinement as I remember it. In prison vernacular, a solitary confinement cell is referred to as "the Hole." Confinement in the Hole is considered the ultimate form of prison punishment, at least legally. At Petersburg there were perhaps five solitary confinement cells joining one another. Each cell was about six feet by ten feet. These cells were located in the basement level of one of the buildings. There were no windows to these cells. Each cell had a steel bar door plus a solid steel door with a small window so that guards could check on the occupant of the cell periodically. There was also a small opening through which food could be passed to the inmate. There was no stool, only a small round hole in the floor, perhaps six inches in diameter. I do not remember how body wastes were flushed down this hole. There was a cold-water faucet. And there was one small light bulb in the ceiling, perhaps ten feet from floor level. Otherwise, the room was completely bare.

For eight hours at night the occupant of a solitary confinement cell was given a filthy, urine-stinking mattress along with a dirty army blanket. Clothing consisted of a coverall. I believe that socks were allowed but not shoes. During the time that I was in the Hole, the daily food allotment was two slices of white bread. No reading material was permitted. Sitting on the cold concrete floor soon became quite uncomfortable. Prison lore had it that sitting on the concrete floor caused "piles" (hemorrhoid problems). My diagnosis was that the bread and water diet caused constipation. I started eating the bread during this stay in the Hole, but before my time was up I had decided that it was better not to eat the bread but to drink a lot of water.

It was not unusual for inmates to suffer minor nervous breakdowns while in solitary confinement. While I was at Petersburg one inmate committed suicide while being confined to the Hole. The prison grapevine reported that this inmate had used his coverall to hang himself, using a bar in the door to anchor one leg of the coverall and the other leg around his neck.

I used my time in solitary confinement to exercise, recite Bible verses, sing songs, and meditate. I remember one time in the middle of the night the guard shone his flashlight into my cell. I was sitting cross-legged on the mattress meditating. He played the light on me for several seconds. I tried to ignore the light and continue with my meditation. Perhaps half an hour later the guard came back with his flashlight and found me in the same position. He opened the steel door and with obvious anxiety said, "Hey, John, are you okay?" I think his concern was genuine. I told him that I was meditating and assured him I was okay.

I think I was blessed with a temperament that handled the solitary confinement experience with a minimum of mental anxiety. The physical aspect was a bit more stressful.

It just happened that about this time, my brother, Bob, returned home for a short visit while his ship was in port for repairs or some similar circumstance. The family decided to visit me while Bob was home. I think my apprehension was shared by other family members that we might never be together again. Bob was an officer on a troop transport ship and commanded a group of beach landing boats whenever they were trying to establish a beachhead.

Bob had also visited me shortly after the allied invasion of North Africa in November 1942. He told me then that if he had to go through many more operations like that he thought his chance of survival was quite low. I worried a great deal about his welfare.

Even though Bob and I chose different paths during the war, we always respected each other's convictions and never let our differences block our love for each other. A typical example of this is a quote from a letter I wrote my dad on January 31, 1944: "Had a note from Bob last night. . . . The last paragraph of his letter reads, 'I was thinking that if you wanted to take a correspondence course or two from some university it might be very practical. It would give me worlds of pleasure to foot the bill.' Sure is swell to have a brother like that, isn't it?"

At any rate, the family showed up for this visit just a few days after I had been released from solitary confinement. I felt I was in great spirits, but my father's diary reads, "Saw John after rude treatment by officials and it was shocking. Looked like a ghost. The warden threw him in 'the hole' on bread and water just after a spell of flu and he has lost a lot of weight. Lips thin and bloodless. Did not want me to protest because it would only make it harder for him. I must find a way to do it. They have other ways to kill besides shooting it seems. I felt as if I was attending a funeral." I should say here that my memory is that I asked my father not to interfere as I wanted to "fight my own battle" with the prison system. In some way that message must have gotten garbled.

In reading my father's diaries after his death, I found that he had several communications with Walter Longstreth about my treatment. Walter apparently made contacts with some official in Washington. My father's diary of April 27, 1944, reads, "Letter from Longstreth. Seems Washington has put a bit of pressure in John's case by asking report of warden. Expect warden to make a fair case for himself."

In December 1996 Bob mailed me a box of letters that he had retrieved from our father's attic after his death. He had discovered that these letters to Dad were written by people who had taken an interest in my case, especially following my experience of being sentenced to solitary confinement.

There are numerous copies of letters addressed to James Bennett, director of the Bureau of Prisons, that are critical of the solitary confinement conditions at Petersburg and of the treatment I had received for "discussing pacifism with a fellow CO." These letters are from prominent citizens: A. J. Muste, executive secretary of the Fellowship of Reconciliation; Rev. Charles Boss, executive secretary of the Commission on World Peace of the Methodist Church; James Mullen, authorized prison visitor for the American Friends Service Committee; Dr. Evan Thomas, a noted physician and brother of Norman Thomas; Walter Longstreth and his wife, Emily. A number of these people sent multiple letters to Mr. Bennett.

Three of the more interesting letters from this period of time include:

A report of a personal visit by James Mullen to the office of Howard Gill, Assistant Director of the Bureau of Prisons. During this visit James Mullin listened as Gill called the warden at Petersburg and questioned him about solitary confinement conditions and told him that, given the circumstances of my case, the punishment was too severe.

An amazing letter from Mr. Bennett to Emily Longstreth, dated June 15, 1944, responding to her protest over solitary confinement conditions at Petersburg and my treatment. Bennett writes: "I think you should know that we do not have any 'of those ugly, uncomfortable, and in some cases ill smelling cells' in the Federal Prison System. Such isolation cells as we have are all above ground with plenty of light and air and sunshine. Some of them are furnished with a bed and other conveniences, while others are devoid of any furnishings. These latter are for disturbed men or men for whom it seems better that they shall be deprived of all of the comforts of life except the bare necessities until they are willing to cooperate." One is left wondering if Mr. Bennett was totally ignorant of what solitary confinement was like at Petersburg or if he was being deliberately deceptive.

A letter from the prison chaplain, an Episcopalian by the name of Sydnor, in response to a letter from my father seeking his assistance as a fellow minister. My father had apparently written to Sydnor that it was discriminatory to punish me for talking about pacifism while ignoring discussion by other inmates of "liquor and women." Sydnor wrote: "Unbridled discussions of liquor and women do not cause riots. . . . But discussion of pacifism in the presence of men who have sons or brothers in uniform are very likely to result in fights. . . . It is for that reason that the men are not allowed to discuss pacifism." Sydnor then went on to tell my father that I understood this as well as the consequences. (For the record, I have absolutely no memory of ever being told that there was a rule against talking about pacifism. And if there had been one, I am confident that I and most of the other COs at Petersburg would never have cooperated with such a rule. Needless to say, my estimation of Sydnor as the "Good Shepherd" was never very high.)

Due to prison censorship, I was completely unaware of these actions on my behalf. But there was an interesting development shortly after this. At the time I suspected that there might be a connection with what happened but had no way to know for sure. What happened was that an official from the Bureau of Prisons visited Petersburg to check out the conditions in solitary confinement. As a result of this visit, a change was made in the food allotment for inmates in solitary confinement. My memory is that each inmate was now to receive a minimum of fifteen hundred calories a day, including bread and vegetables with meat at least once daily.

I am now satisfied that there is a direct relationship between my being in solitary confinement, my father's visit, and the subsequent protests from respected citizens. Fifteen hundred calories was a big improvement over two slices of white bread! A small dent in the inhumanity of the Hole system!

Following my first solitary confinement experience I had several discussions with the warden, Mr. Nicholson, at his request. My memory is that Nicholson had a degree in penology. I had studied some articles and perhaps a book or two on penology, so our discussions were, at least to some degree, about problems connected with operating a prison. I had the feeling that Mr. Nicholson had taken a personal interest in me and was sincerely trying to figure out some way to keep me out of solitary confinement while at the same time not being openly critical of his guard staff when I objected to their behavior. He frankly discussed with me the problem of staffing the prison with the manpower shortage caused by the war and admitted that there were guards who were seriously lacking in both education and professional training.

After being released from solitary confinement, I returned to the farm detail for a short period of time. I am unable to reconstruct the actual time sequence, but I believe that shortly after the solitary confinement experience in April I was again sentenced to either a five-day or a seven-day period in the Hole for refusing to work. Although I now have no clear memory of the specific incident of work refusal, I believe this was related to the introduction of a war-related industry into the prison—the manufacture of cargo nets to be used on troop transport ships.

My letters to my father reveal a concern I had because the prison was being drawn into mobilization for the war effort with some men working in the war industry and the other men working the farm and dairy to feed them. In one letter I explained that I could not cooperate with a totalitarian society—prison—geared to war.

I remember that Mr. Nicholson came to visit me during this second solitary confinement experience. I doubt that he had ever visited an inmate in the Hole before. When the door was opened and I saw Mr. Nicholson standing there, I remember saying, "Oh, it's good to see you Mr. Nicholson. Did you bring your buggy whip along?"

Mr. Nicholson was friendly, but his primary objective was to try to figure some solution to the impasse between me and his "draft dodger"–prejudiced guards.

While these events were happening in my prison life, I was also struggling with what to do about my relationship to the Methodist Church. The church, at its General Conference, had rescinded its long-standing statement against war and its equally strong support of conscientious objection. A number of Methodist COs, including some of my good friends, left the church, and I was troubled. On May 22, 1944, I wrote my friend and fellow pacifist, Dot Kirkley, with whom I corresponded: "But if you believe as I do now that there is still a strong anti-war movement stirring in the Methodist conscious-ness, then it seems to me that it is wise to hold out until you are pretty sure there are no possibilities left [to work within the church]." On May 15, 1944, I had written my dad, "I read 'Who Are The Friends' by William Hubben. I find that I come closer to being a Friend [Quaker] in spirit than I am to being a Methodist. However, like you, for the time being, I intend to work within the Methodist Church."

I believe that following my second solitary confinement experi-ence, I was confined to administrative segregation for thirty days. I suspect that I continued to refuse to work because of the war indus-try. (I am unable to reconstruct this from my letters and am making some logical guesses.) When I returned to population from segrega-tion, I apparently was still determined not to cooperate.

This time I was surprised by a strategic move on the part of Mr. Nicholson. It was obvious that all of the guards had instructions to ignore me. For at least several days I refused to stand by my bed for "body counts." I refused to line up for body count at meal time. I refused to report to my farm detail for work. In fact, I refused to ob-serve any prison rule. The amazing thing was that I had a free run of the prison compound and all the guards totally ignored my nonco-operation. A letter to my father from the wife of another CO reported that Nicholson had said that "he was going to tear a page out of John's book and use a non-violent strategy on him."

Within a few days the prison grapevine had it that the prison ad-ministration was giving me special treatment. There was the grow-ing suspicion—planted, I think, by an inmate "stooge"—that I was being groomed to be a "stooge," if indeed the agreements had not already been made. (A "stooge" is an inmate who provides the prison administration with inside information about prison population in return for special favors. Stooges are not popular with the rest of the prison population.)

To counter this misconception I printed a number of signs on regular typewriting paper. The signs read: "BUCK THE WHOLE SYSTEM." The printed signs looked, at first glance, as though they said "Buck the Hole System," but I inserted the small w in front of "hole" to reflect my unhappiness with the "whole system." I put these signs up on the bulletin board of the building where we slept, on the mess hall bulletin board, and in other strategic places throughout the prison compound. When a guard would tear a sign down, I would ·post another at the next opportunity. My fellow inmates, of course, were completely aware of what was going on and were quickly convinced that I was no stooge.

One evening when the men gathered in the dormitory "social room" for "mail call," I made a speech in which I pointed out to the other inmates that there were only five "Hole" cells in the prison, and that if every inmate would refuse to work as long as any other inmate was in solitary confinement, we could break the "Hole" system. The guard looked perplexed but did nothing to interrupt my message. Mr. Nicholson's instructions to the guards not to harass me must have been pretty clear!

While this minor battle was going on between Mr. Nicholson and me, Mr. Nicholson called me to his office. He had an unusual offer. He told me he had been wanting a rock wall around his home, which was just a few hundred yards outside the prison compound. He said that if I would report to his house each morning, I could work around his house without having any guard supervision. He would arrange to have rocks and mortar available in case I might like to build a rock wall. It was during this visit that Mr. Nicholson told me, "You know, John, I would like to have a prison full of inmates like you. But just one of you is causing me pure hell." At the time I thought he was referring to my protest activities in prison. I was unaware of all the flak he was getting from interested friends in the "free world."

I believe Mr. Nicholson was sincere in believing his offer was a way out of the impasse we had reached and that it was in my best interest. But anyone who has been an inmate and knows the resentment with which "stooges" are held, would recognize that the plan was pregnant with problems. Anyway, I didn't want special treatment.

It was during this same period of time I was approached by two of my CO friends, Bob Swink and Billy Holderith, who had decided to go on work strike. They invited me to join them in preparing a joint work strike statement. I had already decided I could no longer work in prison under prevailing conditions, so I agreed to join them in the strike. We prepared a statement detailing the various reasons for the work strike. As I recall, we mentioned the war industry, racial segregation, the inhumanity of solitary confinement, the unprofessional behavior of certain guards, and probably several other issues, which have since left my memory.

On June 14, 1944, we mailed a copy of the statement to James Bennett, director of the Bureau of Prisons. We also provided the Petersburg administration with a copy. We were to begin our work strike on June 15. The prison censors returned—undelivered—the copy we tried to mail to Bennett.

On June 15 Bob and Billy were placed in isolation cells, but Mr. Nicholson chose to let me remain in population. I immediately began a hunger strike insisting that I would not eat until either Bob and Billy were released from isolation or I was also put in isolation. I believe it was at this point that Mr. Nicholson decided to conclude his efforts to change my mind. Bob, Billy, and I fasted for ten days in protest against the manipulative way we were treated.

Billy and I were placed in adjoining isolation cells in the administration building. Bob was placed in an isolation cell in another building, the same building where the solitary confinement cells were located. We were given adequate food. I was allowed a Bible for reading material. I memorized the fifth, sixth, and seventh chapters of Matthew, the thirteenth chapter of First Corinthians, and various other parts of the Bible. Billy and I could communicate with each other by shouting through a thick wall that separated our cells. I thought it especially interesting that we seemed to develop a level of telepathic communication—one of us would shout something that the other had on his mind—not an uncommon occurrence. But we had no way of communicating with Bob.

Apparently I wrote my father about this time that I had decided to become a socialist. He had written a letter back questioning whether I was making this decision with insufficient study. I wrote him on August 1, 1944: "About socialism—sorry I gave you the impression that I had read only one book on the subject. What I intended to say was 'The Case For Socialism' has contributed most to my becoming a socialist. As a matter of fact, I have put in quite a few hours in the study of economic systems since my incarceration. . . . I certainly intend to continue an unbiased study of economics. If I find a system which meets contemporary demands more effectively than socialism, believe me, I will waste no time in changing." (Years later I concluded that what is in people's hearts—their awareness of the fundamental kinship of all humankind—is much more important for world peace than is any particular economic system).

I noted in a letter to my father dated August 7 that I saw Bob Swink through my cell window. I was surprised that Bob was now in population with the other inmates. I knew that Bob was having a rough time in isolation. His wife was expecting a baby about this time, which, I am sure, was a worry. Mr. Nicholson visited me and explained that Bob had "sort of gone berserk." He had blocked his cell door with his bunk, stuffed a roll of toilet paper in the stool in his cell, had opened the flush valve and flooded a whole floor of the building before anyone figured how to turn the water off. Following this episode, Bob was convinced to discontinue the strike. My guess was that it was related in some way to his expectant family situation. But I never knew for sure.

When Mr. Nicholson was visiting with me about Bob I told him that the building flooding incident would not have happened if they had not separated Bob from Billy and me. He agreed and said he figured if Billy and I were separated that Billy would also discontinue the strike. I think Mr. Nicholson thought that I had persuaded Bob and Billy to go on strike with me, which was not the case at all.

Early in August I was transferred from Petersburg to Ashland, Kentucky. I later learned that Billy had agreed to end the work strike. I was told that an agreement had been reached in which both Bob and Billy would be transferred to another institution. My memory is that the other institution had no war industry and was for juvenile offenders. Bob and Billy were to be counselors or "big brothers" to the young offenders. I do not remember ever confirming these details with either Bob or Billy after I got out of prison. The facts may be a bit muddled.

I suspect that my transfer to Ashland was due to a couple of calculated guesses on the part of Mr. Nicholson. I think he really cared about me and was concerned about having me locked up in an isolation cell. Perhaps he thought a change in environment would provide me an opportunity to go off the work strike without "losing face." But I also remembered his statement that if Billy and I were separated that Billy would probably discontinue his work strike. I didn't like that kind of psychological manipulation.

I was disappointed to learn when I recently read my father's diaries that Director Bennett had also suggested to my father that Ashland was a prison for mentally disturbed inmates. While it is possible that the chief medical officer at Ashland may have been a psychiatrist, I have no memory of any psychiatric-type of discussion with him. And it was simply not true that Ashland was a prison for "mentally disturbed inmates." I feel that Bennett's insinuation that I was being sent to Ashland for psychiatric reasons was most unkind. My father was worried enough about my physical well-being without worrying that I might be becoming mentally unbalanced.

When I was transferred to Ashland, we arrived in the late evening. I was placed in a segregation cell. Early the next morning a guard opened the gate to the tier of cells where I was and blew his whistle. This was the signal for each inmate to stand at attention beside his bunk while the guard completed a body count. When the guard reached my cell I was seated on my bunk. The guard said, "Griffith, don't you know you are supposed to be at attention for body count?" I replied, "Yes, I am aware of the rules and I don't mean any disrespect to you, but I have been refusing to cooperate with the penal system for several months and have no intention of cooperating now." Normally this response would result in the inmate being sentenced to solitary confinement. But the guard made no issue of my noncooperation and proceeded with his body count. I soon discovered that the Ashland administration had decided not to try to force me to conform.

Although I was confined to a segregated cell, I was taken to the mess hall for meals and was able to visit other COs during meal time. Not long after my arrival at Ashland, I suddenly was joined by four or five other COs who had gone on a work strike to protest treatment of Bayard Rustin, a well known African American peace activist who was an inmate in the Ashland prison. Bayard had been sentenced to solitary confinement for some alleged infraction of prison rules. When these men were placed in the same cell tier, my recollection is that our meals were brought to us and that I no longer went to the mess hall for meals. Before long, we were allowed, as a group, to go to an outside segregated area for perhaps thirty minutes of exercise each day. On the whole I found the environment at Ashland to be a considerable improvement over Petersburg.

Some months before, while still at Petersburg, I had refused to apply for parole. The parole papers stated, among other things, that the parolee would not break any laws while on parole. As a nonregistrant I fully expected when I left prison to leave without a draft card, thus breaking the existing draft law. I had no intention of signing a paper that would bind me to obeying that law. So I had been through the process of explaining all this to Petersburg prison officials.

But now my "conditional release" date was coming up on November 2, 1944—two years after being sentenced. When asked about requesting "conditional release," I explained to the Ashland officials my objections to the terms of the release. I figured the matter was settled and that I would remain at Ashland until my thirty-month sentence was up on May 2, 1945.

However, the morning of November 2 a burly guard came for me. He took me to a small room with table and chair; there were papers on the table. I do not remember the exact conversation, but it was obvious that this guard had orders to try to bully me into signing the conditional release papers. He swore at me, made threatening remarks, and told me to "sign those goddamn papers." I told him, as politely as I could, that I had no intention of signing the papers. I said that if the prison officials wanted to get rid of me all they had to do was open the front door and let me out. But I would not agree to any conditions for my release.

The guard took me to the clothing room where I was given a cheap suit of clothes. My personal belongings were given to me in a cloth bag. The guard then took me to the train station and handed me a ticket to Gaffney, South Carolina, where my family now lived. He told me that he hoped to never see me again. I told him the feeling was mutual.

A few days after I arrived home, a parole officer showed up at the house with a draft card and a sheet of instructions on the conditions of my release. I told him I had just served two years in prison for not registering and would not accept the draft card. I also told him I had refused to sign any conditional release papers at Ashland and would not be bound by any conditions that might be on the sheet of instructions he wanted to give me. The parole officer then said I would be arrested for breaking conditional release. I answered that if he would just give me a few minutes to pack my toothbrush, razor, and a few personal belongings, I would be ready to go. My poor dad and mom were silently observing this exchange with considerable anxiety. But then the parole officer left. I never heard from another parole official.

There is one final ironic twist to my story. I believe I first voted when Adlai Stevenson was running for president in 1952. After that I voted regularly in all elections. I was also quite active, politically, in efforts to elect several peace-type candidates.

I think it must have been in the summer of 1978 that I was called for jury duty in Kansas City, Missouri, where I now live. This is a rather large court system and there must have been a couple hundred prospective jurors in the large courtroom used for initial screening. The judge asked those in the room to raise their hand if the answer to any question he asked was affirmative. One of the questions he asked was, "Have you ever been convicted of a felony?" I raised my hand and was called to the bench. I explained my felony conviction and the judge said, "Mr. Griffith, I don't understand why you are here. Our jury selection is taken from voter registration records and if you are a felon you cannot legally vote and therefore should not be on the voter registration record." I told the judge I had been voting for many years and had never had any trouble in being able to vote. He told me he didn't know what he would have to do about my situation and for me to take my seat again.

I was actually called to serve on a jury the next day. (A friend of mine who was a judge—now deceased—said he couldn't understand a judge allowing me to serve on a jury when I had not been pardoned for a felony.) But the judge warned me, "Mr. Griffith, I have informed you that you cannot legally vote and if, in the future, I discover you have continued to vote I will have to press charges against you."

Jimmy Carter was president. I knew he had friendly connections with Koinonia Farm people in Georgia and was likely sympathetic to individual pacifists even if he did not hold the pacifist position himself. I wanted to continue to participate in the political process, so I decided to apply to President Carter for a presidential pardon. I applied for the pardon on July 8, 1978.

Months passed and the only word I heard about my application were random reports from professional associates from previous years in Iowa. These people had been visited by the FBI for character reference checks on me. Typically my former business associates would ask, "What's up, John? Are you applying for a job with the FBI?" Or, "Are you applying for a job with the government that requires a security clearance?" The FBI also contacted some of my neighbors, as well as officials of the company where I worked. And then another dry spell followed with no word on my pardon application.

Ronald Reagan defeated Carter in the election of November 1980. And still no word on my application. With the turn in events at the political level, I decided that I might as well put the application out of my mind. Then late in December 1981, I received in the mail a presidential pardon from President Reagan—the crown prince of the military-industrial complex—the old Gipper himself! Such is life! And I have been voting ever since.

When first asked to submit my story about war resistance during World War II, I was reluctant to do it. Censorship, particularly at Petersburg, was very strict. It was impossible to write letters about what was going on in prison. As one example, after the work strike statement addressed to the director of the Bureau of Prisons was returned by the Petersburg censor, I tried to hide a copy behind the leather binding of my Bible. I thought perhaps the censor would not check my Bible closely when I left prison. No such luck. When I was transferred to Ashland, the Petersburg prison censor went through my belongings and removed the statement. So, because of the lack of good data, I thought I might not be able to reconstruct events in proper sequence with historical accuracy.

Fortunately both my father and my friend, Dot Kirkley, saved the letters I had written from prison. After rereading these letters, as well as my father's diary entries, my own diary for the period July 7 to November 17, 1942, as well as the letters discovered by my brother in December 1996, I have felt some confidence in telling the story with at least an impressionistic resemblance to history. (My diary and New Testament were taken from me when I entered Petersburg. At a later date, approval was obtained for a new Bible, which my father mailed to me.)

The other cause of apprehension is that I felt it would be almost impossible to tell the story so briefly and maintain a good balance between accounts of the good times and the bad times. I think this apprehension has been validated. I am sure the story seems more dramatic, even confrontational, than it actually was. There were months of normal relationships, mostly good, some quite tender, which are not adequately reflected in this account. Also, I am well aware that what little I may have suffered in prison is totally insignificant compared to the fifteen million military fatalities, the twenty-five million civilian fatalities, and the unknown additional millions who survived but were permanently scarred by the horrible conflict of World War II. It was a terribly tragic time when most people, regardless of nationality, did what they thought they had to do.

If the reader keeps this in mind, this essay may have value in conveying something of what one war resister experienced during World War II. I hope this is the case.

Perhaps a closing word is warranted about how, in retrospect, I see my act of noncooperation during World War II. I now believe that it was just one response to the promptings of human consciousness that we all share. I have deliberately not used the phrase "*my* consciousness." With the passing of years the distinction between my consciousness and human consciousness has become more and more elusive. We are all connected. I believe that human consciousness intuitively knows that it is wrong for human beings to kill each other. At this stage in the human story, the cultural conditioning of most humans is such that the apparent necessity to kill sometimes overrides the intuitive feeling that it is wrong. Due to a complex combination of circumstances, my own cultural conditioning was slightly different, and human consciousness, as expressed through my perception, had to protest the rush to worldwide slaughter. My faith is that human consciousness is becoming more and more aware of the kinship of all humankind and that someday this awareness will, for most people, be stronger than the feeling that circumstances may require killing. We, together, will then develop an alternative to war.

After prison I attended and graduated from William Penn College in Oskaloosa, Iowa. Cecil Hinshaw, a radical young Quaker educator, was president. Cecil promoted an interracial faculty and student body, democratic community government, simplicity, and the Quaker peace testimony. I was happy there. It was good to have a respite from protesting.

While at Penn, Reva Standing, a birthright Friend (and now my beloved companion for fifty years), and I exchanged marriage vows. Our most noteworthy achievement has been to raise four sons, each in his own way becoming a productive and caring member of the human family. Professionally, I was involved in the cooperative movement—which I consider the most peace-oriented of the various economic systems—until my retirement in 1985. As of the winter of 1997, Reva and I continue to be active in our Quaker community. And we continue to work for peace and justice in the world community.

George M. Houser

Reflections of a Religious War Objector
(Half a Century Later)

Our action . . . did not create a massive movement
[but] was a witness to the possibility of helping to
create a peaceful world.

THE DATE WAS September 14, 1940. I was in the small town of Norwood on the western slope of the Rockies in Colorado, only a few miles east of the Utah border. I had been there for about three months on a temporary summer job pastoring a Methodist church. I was scheduled to return in a few days to New York City to begin my senior year at Union Theological Seminary. I had been pretty well cut off from the goings-on of the world in this out-of-the-way part of the country. But the news came to me over the radio. Congress had passed the Selective Training and Service Act of 1940 requiring every young man on October 16, only a little over a month hence, to register for military service. This was the first-ever peacetime conscription act adopted in the United States. I wondered what I ought to do to protest this action by the government.

There was no one in this rural village of fewer than four hundred people with whom I could discuss the issue. Although the United States was not yet in the war in Europe, a military psychology prevailed in the area where I was. All over town placards were appearing in store windows distributed by the American Legion and the Lions Club with such cryptic phrases as "If you don't like America, you can always get a passport to the land of your choice," or "millions for battleships but not one cent for tribute." Virtually all the townspeople and the ranchers in the outlying areas accepted conscription with little thought. Many of the young fellows in town, who had nothing exciting to look forward to, were joining the navy.

GEORGE M. HOUSER (b. 1916)
George Houser, one of the original Union Theological Seminary nonregistrants, has dedicated his life to working for peace and justice. Until his retirement in 1981, he had worked with the Fellowship of Reconciliation and served as executive secretary of the Congress of Racial Equality before becoming executive director of the American Committee on Africa. He and his wife, Jean, now live in Pomona, New York, where he continues to do freelance writing and organizational work.

I was deeply disturbed by the thought of having to register under the Selective Service Act. True, I would be given an automatic exemption as a theological student, but this seemed like an evasion of responsibility somehow. I was a Christian pacifist. I had been brought up in the Methodist youth movement and had been active in the Student Christian Movement in college. I was a product of the idealism, optimism, and social activism of the 1930s. World War I was in the dim past for me, and it had failed miserably to save the world for democracy. It was unthinkable that the United States could be involved in another world war.

When World War II started in Europe in September 1939, I was attending a national Methodist youth conference in Missouri. Hitler's aggression and the beginning of the war had a sobering effect on the gathering. We utterly rejected the totalitarianism, the militarism, the anti-Semitism of the Nazis, but most of us were convinced that a massive war was not the way to resist this evil. Christians should not go to war; to do so was a violation of Christian love as taught by Jesus. Our creed was the love ethic of the New Testament, and non-violent resistance in the Gandhi tradition. But our faith had never really been tested.

Toward the end of September 1940, I left the isolation of western Colorado and returned to New York for the beginning of the school year at Union. Of course the passage of the draft law was of major concern. Most of my fellow students accepted the necessity of registration, some with misgivings, but most with a conviction that this was an inevitable part of the strategy to defeat Hitler. However, there was a significant minority who were deeply troubled. I was one of them.

Serious discussion began almost immediately among a group of us and an idea took shape. It came to a head about a week before registration day. I was awakened late one night by one of my close student friends with the news that a statement was in the process of being written announcing that a number of us would refuse to register on October 16. I joined in the discussion and the drafting of the statement. We entitled it "A Christian Conviction on Conscription and Registration."

Twenty students originally signed the document. In it we set forth our position that "it is impossible to think of the conscription law without thinking of the whole war system"; that "if we register, even as conscientious objectors, we are becoming part of the Act"; that "war is an evil because it is in violation of the way of love as seen in God through Christ"; that "we do not expect to stem the war forces today, but we are helping to build the movement that will conquer in the future."

This statement was released to the press and sent to about fifteen hundred family, friends, government and church leaders on October 12. Then our real crisis began. Young and inexperienced, we had not anticipated (at least I hadn't) the overwhelming reaction to our announcement. Up to this point we were exhilarated by a group process and the excitement of charting a new path of resistance with the comradeship of twenty fellow divinity students. But a new reality set in. Our intended action became a major news story: headlines in the press, top billing in the movie house news reels, massive radio coverage. One of my aunts was shocked to learn of our action when the news came on at a theater in Florida.

The *New York Times* headlined its story "Divinity Students Face Jail in Draft." The *Herald Tribune* headed the announcement "10 Theological Students Unite To Defy Draft." The *New York World Telegram* covered the story with "Bible Students Defying Draft Will Be Jailed." Because I was from Denver, both the *Denver Post* and the *Rocky Mountain News* carried my picture and a front-page article.

Then the reaction set in. Col. Arthur McDermott, director of Selective Service in New York, said authorities would "crack down without delay" on the twenty students. He added, "I hope these young men will not be as foolish as their statement indicates them to be." The penalties under the law called for five years in prison and a fine of ten thousand dollars.

The publicity given to our intended action and the threats of fine and imprisonment were sobering to say the least. But this was only the beginning of the pressure. The administration of the seminary was considerably agitated by our action and the resulting publicity. It did reflect on the institution. Enraged seminary supporters called and in some cases demanded our expulsion, so we were told. Henry Sloane Coffin, the seminary president, refused such recourse, but telegraphed each of our families. In my case the telegram went to my father, a prominent Methodist clergyman in Denver, saying,

"Your son George has signed a statement that he will not register next Wednesday under the Selective Service Act. The penalty for such offense may be five years in prison. I have been unable to deter him. Can you prevent this tragedy?" I had, of course, already informed my folks of our action, so the telegram came as no surprise.

The seminary faculty as a whole adopted a statement recognizing that there are circumstances in which "individuals or groups may deem it necessary to refuse to follow the will of government because to do so would be to deny their religious convictions." But they concluded that this principle did not apply in our case because the Selective Service Act recognized the right of conscientious objection. The seminary's most influential professor, Reinhold Niebuhr, expressed "thorough disagreement" and said our stand "goes beyond any valid pacifism."

Added to the public pressure was family response. Some of us had parental support, and I was fortunate in this. My parents wrote and telegraphed me expressing anguish, but also pride. My father faced criticism from some of his parishioners, but supported my action from the pulpit. Others in our group were not all so fortunate. Mothers were concerned that fathers would have heart attacks. Some parents came to the scene to engage in anguished discussion with their sons. We feared that we were causing suffering worse than our own. Our faith was really being put to a test.

All of this prompted serious reevaluation in our group of twenty. On October 14, just two days before registration day, our whole group spent hours rethinking, arguing, praying. I subsequently wrote an article in diary form for the seminary student quarterly, the *Union Review*. "We have had the most real heart-searching and the most sincere consecration to what we conceive our Christian faith to be that any of us have ever known." Finally, twelve of our group changed their position and decided to register. Some of them later left the seminary to volunteer for alternative service as conscientious objectors. Eight of us reaffirmed our position. I remember the peace I felt after making this decision.

In our group was Don Benedict, later a founder of the East Harlem Protestant Parish and for years executive director of the Community Renewal Society in Chicago; Joe Bevilacqua, who was later with the Colorado Council of Churches and director of Denver's War on Poverty; Meredith Dallas, who served on the faculty of Antioch College as director of the drama department; Dave Dellinger, who is well known for his leadership in nonviolent action for peace and justice over the years; Bill Lovell, who spent many years with the National Council of Churches, and subsequently was stated clerk of the Presbytery of Chicago; Howard Spragg, who was for many years executive vice-president of the Board for Homeland Ministries of the United Church of Christ; and Dick Wichlei, who was association minister of the Wisconsin Conference of the United Church of Christ.

On the eve of registration almost all the seminary faculty and students took part in a powerful worship experience of reconciliation in the chapel. I wrote in my diary article that "the worship was not just a gesture to affirm our basic Christian unity; it was a testimony to the fact of its existence." James Russell Lowell's hymn (poem) "Once to Every Man and Nation Comes the Moment to Decide" was never sung more meaningfully.

The next day eight of us filed into the place of registration where members of the draft board were present and also a representative from the office of the U.S. attorney. It was set up right in one of the rooms of the seminary. I always felt that this was done not really for our convenience, but to minimize publicity. No photographers or news reporters were present. We handed in our joint statement and immediately were given subpoenas to appear before a grand jury. We were also told that if at any point we changed our minds, registration was still open.

In spite of the fact that the decision was made and the nonregistration action had been taken, the pressure did not cease. The executive secretary of the American Friends Service Committee called on us to talk about the vision he had for the "work of national importance" that would be available for conscientious objectors under the alternative service provisions of the act. A representative of the American Civil Liberties Union met with us to discuss the civil liberties aspect of our action, given the option for CO status. Other such prominent people as Harry Emerson Fosdick of New York's Riverside Church met with us. These meetings and others were not necessarily designed to urge us to change our positon, but were a subtle pressure in that direction nevertheless.

In addition there was continued newspaper publicity and hundreds of letters and telegrams. Most of the newspaper items reported the facts. Many of the letters were supportive of our right to take the position we did, without necessarily agreeing with us. John Haynes Holmes of the Community Church of New York wrote: "I wish you could find it in your hearts to register. . . . However if you are finally resolved to stand by your conviction you will have the sympathy of all those who recognize the sanctity of conscience." One young woman wrote: "I hope you and your fellow war resisters will be firm and let no one dissuade you from the stand you have taken."

Among the letters received, two were especially noteworthy. One was from A. J. Muste, newly appointed executive secretary of the Fellowship of Reconciliation. The other was from Dr. Evan Thomas, imprisoned as a CO in World War I. Muste wrote: "We believe the time has come when it will be recognized that this [nonregistration] has been a genuine service to the well-being of the nation and of the church, and to the cause of peace, democracy and true religion." He explicitly said that he had come to the conclusion that nonregistration "was the patriotic and Christian thing to do." Evan Thomas, a venerable leader in the antiwar movement, met with us personally and expressed himself in writing as "united to you in strong bonds of kinship." He caught some of my feelings when he wrote: "to go to prison and know that the overwhelming majority of your fellows cannot understand it is perhaps the loneliest task of all. . . . If you chaps share any of my weaknesses you will wonder whether it is worthwhile. . . . But you will be blazing your trail through the thickest and blackest part of the wilderness and the light must come from within you and through great faith." These communications strengthened us immensely.

Our group honored the subpoena to appear before the grand jury, although all of us did not appear personally. I was one who did and I remember how daunted I felt as I tried to explain my position and to answer questions. The issue they were dealing with was whether we were guilty of violating the law, and of course we admitted this. The jury did not seem hostile. They seemed to try to understand the position and some of the jurors tried to influence me to change my mind. "Do you realize a prison sentence will be a black mark against you for the rest of your life, that you will be turned down for jobs because of your record?" some asked.

A "true bill" came in the form of an indictment in the U.S. Court for the Southern District of New York, saying that the "defendant unlawfully, willfully and knowingly failed and neglected to present himself for and submit to registration . . . against the peace of the United States."

The date set for trial was November 14, which gave us time to get ready for a probable jail sentence. I decided the best thing to do was to go home to Denver, primarily to see my parents and to make everything as easy as possible for them. My mother especially was suffering, but she never altered her support for me. I was required to report to the probation officer while in Denver because our whole group was out—not on bail, but on our own recognizance—while we awaited trial.

The probation officer was sympathetic to me personally while in strong disagreement with my action. He could not understand why I took the position I did, both because I had an automatic theological exemption and because I could claim a conscientious objector status under the law. On my part I tried to explain the rationale for non-violent civil disobedience in protest against an act of government, a position as old as the Bible and as current as the movement for independence led by Gandhi in India.

I returned to New York shortly before the date for trial. Because our case had attracted such massive public attention, there was a lot of activity around the U.S. District courtroom on November 14. A supportive picket line was in place outside the federal courthouse in lower Manhattan, and opponents were there too. A few of them shouted insults and one spit in Benedict's face. Inside, the courtroom was overcrowded with the curious, as well as reporters, friends, and supporters. Many could not get in and milled around in the hallway.

Our attorney, Kenneth Walser, volunteered his services. He was a fatherly figure. We had several meetings with him and he never tried to influence us to change our position, and in court he made a statement that presented our position as sympathetically as possible. "My position is perhaps unusual," he began, "as the whole matter is unusual, because my clients have not asked me to urge clemency." But he put before the judge certain considerations, such as the character of the defendants. He pointed out that the attorney general and the probation officer "have had hundreds of letters attesting, first to these defendants' characters, and second to their sincerity in the stand which they take." Referring to Dellinger, Dallas, and Benedict, he said, "A number of them work in the slums of Newark and live there with the people to whom they minister while pursuing their theological studies." He went on to say: "The trouble is that some time ago there came to them a call to the ministry—a call to spread the teaching of Jesus—and they find in those teachings an instruction to have nothing to do with mass killing which we call war."

The U.S. attorney, John Cahill, presented his case succinctly, that the defendants "right up until the last minute before they were indicted were offered the opportunity of complying with the law and they have persisted and continue to persist in their refusal to register." Then he recommended the judge give each of us a sentence of a year and a day in a federal penitentiary.

Before the judge sentenced us, each of our group made a statement to the court. The press particularly noted what Joe Bevilacqua said: "Because we are theological students does not mean that we should have privileges which other people do not have. We want to identify ourselves, not with a selected group of men or class of people, but with the vast majority of people . . . and it is for this reason that I would like to say that I do not expect any leniency." We all agreed with this.

We understand that the judge, Samuel Mandelbaum, wrestled long and hard on what kind of sentence to give us. At one point we had heard that we might be convicted on a conspiracy charge which could bring at least fifteen years in prison. But our attorney reported that in discussion with him and with government officials, the judge considered everything from probation to five-year terms. In spite of our theological status, the vast publicity we had received and the hundreds of communications for clemency, the government could not let us off without a sentence. Clemency would only be a signal for more challenges to this peacetime conscription. Judge Mandelbaum stated: "I believe this is the first case of its type and I am constrained to follow the Government's recommendation and impose

the sentence of one year and one day on each of the defendants."
This made our action a felony rather than a misdemeanor. Then in a
gesture of goodwill the judge concluded, "I shall, nevertheless, keep
the term of the court open . . . in order to give these eight divinity
students a chance during any time of this sentence to comply with
the law."

We were immediately taken into custody without even a moment to say farewell to many of our friends in an aroused courtroom. Handcuffed, each with one of our companions, we were led to
a waiting paddy wagon. A picture in one of the newspapers shows
Joe Bevilacqua and me securely handcuffed. Again, this sentencing
received widespread news coverage with headlines such as "Eight
Divinity Students Who Defied Draft Get One Year in Prison." The
Denver papers gave the story front-page attention. "Denverite Sentenced with Seven Others for Refusal to Register in Draft" was the
lead story in the *Rocky Mountain News*. Under an editorial entitled
"Too Proud to Register," this newspaper wrote unsympathetically,
"Try as we may, we can muster up no sympathy for those eight
divinity students, including one Denver youth. . . . The pulpits of the
country can probably struggle along for a year without the services
of these young men in their self-imposed hair shirts."

A good many angry letters to the editor came in response to this
editorial. Some of the public comments, especially in the religious
press, were humbling. The *Rocky Mountain Churchman* headed its article "Students Reproduce New Acts of Apostles." My feelings at the
moment of incarceration were far from what I conceived an apostle
might feel. I felt relieved that it was all over, and expectant about a
new phase of my life that was to begin, and a bit apprehensive.

The paddy wagon went a short distance through the crowded
streets of lower Manhattan to the federal detention headquarters
called simply West Street, for that was where it was located near
the Hudson River. We were to stay there for a week waiting to be
shipped off to a new federal correctional institution at Danbury,
Connecticut. For some reason I was reminded of the famous quote
from Eugene Debs: "While there is a lower class, I am in it, while
there is a criminal element I am of it, while there is a soul in prison,
I am not free." I felt a certain exhilaration that I had stuck with my

position which I considered a Christian witness and had withstood the pressure to give in to the power of the state.

Prison was a new experience. Those incarcerated form a community. There was a certain curiosity among our fellow prisoners and probably among the guards as well about the "divinity students," as we were called. Publicity about our case had reached behind the bars. The week in West Street was a good transition from civilian to prison life as we experienced the impersonality of a system in which inmates were objects to the administration, and we were separated from loved ones outside. We almost grew accustomed to the frequent count of prisoners several times a day and during the night; the frisking by guards to detect any possible contraband material hidden in shirts or pant legs; the clang of gates being unlocked, opened, and closed.

The routine of sameness set in: being in a communal cell with others at West Street, a bunk of our own, meals at stated hours, prison clothes, an hour's recreation on the fenced-in roof overlooking the Hudson, lights-out and sleep, only to wake up and feel the unreality of it all.

We were transported to Danbury by car. I was in the same car with Mr. Edgar Gerlach, the warden at this new correctional institution. I remember being in the back seat on a cold November 20 with two others of our group, handcuffed, and the warden and a guard up front. The front window was open part way, sending an unpleasant chill in the back. We asked for the window to be closed but the warden ignored the request. And so we were introduced to the authoritarianism that is at the heart of the prison system.

As I write this piece, my Danbury experience is fifty-six years in the past. Yet it made an indelible impression on me. I remember some aspects freshly. Over the years I have been arrested on quite a few occasions and have spent a limited time in custody. The Danbury episode lasted only nine months and twenty days of our year-and-a-day sentence, with time off for good behavior called "good time." This has been the longest of my imprisonments. Certain things stand out about the experience. Most important was that my companions and I rebelled inwardly and sometimes outwardly against the authoritarianism and the punishment aspect of the prison system. Perhaps prisoners were supposed to have a sense of guilt and shame about the "crimes" that landed them in jail. We looked upon ourselves as political prisoners, prisoners of conscience, and we felt more pride than guilt. We rejected the idea that punishment was in any sense justified.

We felt the attempt of the prison system to take our individual personalities away immediately upon arrival at the institution. Danbury was a new federal prison. The inmate number given to me was 280. The prison had been opened in August, really only a few weeks before we got there, and I was the 280th prisoner to be registered. From the moment of entrance I was either "Houser" or "280." For the first thirty days in Danbury (a period which was called quarantine), our group of eight was in a cell block of individual cells separate from other sections of the prison. We were locked up except for meals in the mess hall or for individual interviews by prison officials or for periods of recreation.

At the end of our building there was space for a ping-pong table and we were given limited time for playing. I was one of the members of our group that liked ping-pong and was pretty good at it, along with Benedict and Lovell. I think the warden was curious about our group and tried to understand us in those early days of our imprisonment. Because he was warden, he could set his own rules. On several occasions in those first days he would come into our cell block after lights were out, when it was supposed to be quiet, and ask me to play ping-pong with him. He wasn't very good.

Once the warden called me into his office to talk about what impelled me to take the nonregistration position. I think he tried in an amateurish way to psychoanalyze me. I recall his asking me once, "Houser, do you hate your father?" I laughed. It was so obvious that my "rebellious" action would be simple to understand if I was somehow resisting my father. Nothing could be further from the truth.

Although our group was separate during those early days except at meal time, we managed to establish ourselves in the life of the prison. I don't recall exactly how it developed, but our group challenged the Danbury softball team to a game, eight of us plus one other. We had a secret weapon. Don Benedict was an outstanding softball pitcher with at least semi-pro ability. Although, as a new prison, Danbury was not yet landscaped, there was plenty of space for a ball diamond in the yard completely surrounded by low-level prison buildings. The game in the cool of a late November Saturday was one-sided. We beat them something like fifteen to one. They couldn't hit Benedict and we had other competent athletes in our group as well. This helped to establish the "divinity students" as a force in inmate life.

After the first month our group was separated and we became an integral part of the general inmate community. We were assigned to such jobs as farm work, laundry, and library. The Protestant chaplain, who was a student at Yale Divinity School and came to Danbury three days a week, asked that I be his assistant. This meant that I had the use of his office and access to the typewriter even on the days he was not there. I think he felt a bit guilty in not being one of us and gave me little work to do, so I had considerable freedom.

What galled me, and I am sure the others, was the constant reminder that we were in a completely authoritarian environment. It was not just the major practices of censorship of mail and reading material which I suppose one expects in prison life, but the smaller incidents that were upsetting. An inmate who was a medical doctor on the outside was publicly chastised because on some occasion he had had the temerity to call himself "doctor" so and so, thus violating the anonymity of prisoners. A woman who came on visiting day to see her husband coughed while she was in the waiting room and was unceremoniously refused the visit in spite of her tears. I suppose the rationale was that she might spread infection, but this was not explained. The racial segregation in housing and in dining facilities was a constant issue with the prison authorities. Some of our group were disciplined for spontaneously sitting with our friends among black inmates at mealtime or at the weekly movie. I recall Dave Dellinger spending some time in the "bing" (isolation) for so doing. There was no segregation in the religious services.

There were times when challenging the authoritarianism of the institution just happened. On one of the chaplain's days away from Danbury, the warden dropped in unexpectedly while I was working at the desk. Whatever he had on his mind I never found out. I greeted him but remained seated. He upbraided me by saying: "Houser, when I come in the room, I want you to stand up." Whether my response was right or not, I am not sure, but I said, "Warden, I respect you as a man, but not as the warden." Perhaps this was not the best nonviolent way of reacting at the moment, but it was a protest against his imperious manner. He angrily wheeled around and left the room. I was called before the disciplinary committee for chastisement and immediately received a new work assignment, to the boiler room. There my assignment was to crawl into the large boilers and clean them by hand, an unpleasant task after the ease of the chaplain's office. I spent the winter months cleaning boilers in the furnace room, which gave me a constant cold because of the irritating dust invading my nostrils. In the spring I asked for transfer to the farm and it was granted.

During the time we were in Danbury, the number of war objectors grew. To our original eight another twelve or so were added before we left. Our fellow CO inmates were a mixture of religious and socialist-oriented men. Among them were Bill Clarke, Arle Brooks, Al Winslow, Ernie Kirkjian, Lowell Naeve, Charles Swift, Francis Hall, Jim Alter, Rob Rae, Stan Rappaport, Al Herling, and Howard Schoenfeld. Although we were well integrated into the prison population, there were times when we acted as a group. We protested racial segregation. We sent joint communications on occasion to the warden or to James V. Bennett, the head of the Bureau of Prisons in Washington, protesting prison policies. I sometimes typed our communiques on the chaplain's machine while I worked there. Perhaps the prime issue upon which we acted as a unit took place in April 1941 on the day of the annual Student Strike Against War.

Among my papers from the Danbury experience is a copy of a memo I addressed "To whom it may concern." It began: "Since 1934 there has been celebrated annually a National Student Strike Against War. For the young people throughout the nation who are intellectually and emotionally opposed to the war system as one of the greatest evils of our day, this has been an extremely important event. The event itself is significant because it is an expression of nonviolent opposition to the war policy of the U.S. It is especially significant this year because the nation is so close to actual armed intervention in a war which will bring only suffering and injustice to the world."

I went on to say in my statement, which was in line with a joint action of our group, that the fact that I was in prison should not deter me from cooperating in this annual event. I outlined what our group had agreed upon, that on April 23 we would not work and would spend the day fasting and in meditation. This action, I explained, was designed as a way of consecrating myself to building a warless world, and it should not be misinterpeted as opposition to the prison administration.

But from the warden's perspective, it was a challenge to the prison system and to his authority, and it could not go unanswered. Striking in an authoritarian environment is unthinkable. We announced our intention to the warden some days ahead of time. The warden met with a committee of us to let us know that the prison would crack down on us. I remember that when he came into the room to talk to us, he rather ostentatiously brushed off his knees and let us know that he had been praying. I am afraid we didn't take this gesture too seriously, simply because of the showmanship. In any event, we let him know we were committed to the day of solidarity with antiwar students around the world.

This was indeed a challenge to the prison system. The warden decided to make a speech to all the prisoners, and he did it outside the mess hall as the inmates gathered for dinner. His aim was to turn the inmates against us. It was a rabble-rousing speech in which he said we were disloyal to the government, that we were trying to get all the prisoners to strike, and that our intention was to take over the institution. In our previous meeting with the warden, we had specifically told him that none of these things were our intention. A couple of our group (Arle Brooks I remember especially) interrupted the provocative speech by shouting, "It's a lie, Warden." It seemed to us that the warden hoped our fellow prisoners would turn on us. It didn't work. I know I never received a threat from any inmate after the warden's speech. In fact, during the meal that followed this speech, several inmates went out of their way to show their support by bringing us extra coffee with encouraging words.

The institution itself took preventive action. The day before we were to strike, all of us, which included more than our "divinity student" group of eight, were taken to isolation cells and "sentenced" to thirty days by the prison disciplinary board. We weren't even offered food on the day of the strike and were separated from the prison population at mealtimes while on strike. We were taken to the mess hall as a group after other prisoners had left.

I smile even today, more than a half-century later, when I reflect on how this event ended. For two weeks, members of our striking group were in solitary. The softball season had started. The Danbury team, which was part of a regional league, was playing an outside team and was getting beat. The inmates began to chant, "We want Benedict." The warden's pride in his softball team was on the line. He sent the captain of the guards to get Don Benedict. It was the last of the fourth inning of a seven-inning game. Don answered the call and struck out the next nine batters who faced him. Danbury won. Then Benedict was brought back to isolation. A few days later another game was scheduled. Again Benedict was summoned by the captain. But this time he refused to go unless all of us were let out. The warden gave in and again Benedict was the hero, pitching a one-hitter and winning the game.

After the game we were all put in our solitary cells again, but at dinner time, after all the other inmates were at their places in the mess hall, the warden gave the signal for our release. It had been more than two weeks since we had eaten at the regular time with the other inmates. As we entered the hall the place broke out into wild applause and a standing ovation. How sweet it was, unexpected, spontaneous. I don't think the warden was pleased.

The hardest part of the prison experience was separation from outside contacts. After the newness of imprisonment wore off, I felt the isolation from other friends and loved ones. This was the area in which restriction in freedom of movement was felt most deeply. Visits were limited to one hour a month, which could be divided into two half-hour visits. There was also a limited correspondence list. My correspondence was limited to my parents, one of my special student friends at Union, Roger Shinn (later a distinguished faculty member at the seminary), with whom I had a warm relationship in spite of our great difference on the issue of war and pacifism. Shinn later gave up his theological exemption, joined the army and was captured during the Battle of the Bulge. He credited our example in following our convictions as a prime reason he gave up his exemption and joined the army.

My third correspondent was Jean Walline, who was also on my visiting list. I had met Jean only a few days before our crisis of nonregistration began. She was studying at the seminary and at Teachers

College of Columbia University. We had only a few days to get acquainted but rapidly developed a real interest in one another. How I looked forward to her visits! She came for half an hour twice a month, along with a car full of wives and sweethearts of our group from New York City. We literally got acquainted sitting across a table from one another in the visiting room, never being able to touch. Less than a year after my release we got married. Jean met my folks when they came east from Denver to visit me, in a rather emotional reunion.

There was a kind of aching in my soul by the separation from outside, in spite of the comradeship inside and the demands of prison life. When, for a time, I had a cell with a window looking out on the countryside, I would stand for long periods after lights-out watching the lights of passing cars a half-mile away, wondering where the people who could not see me were going. There were periods of isolation in the cell when I could do extensive writing, which the prison censor allowed me to take with me when I was released. I look at this material now and it brings back vivid memories of plans for an ex-prisoner association, an outline for what I called a new monasticism, and an outline for a nonviolent movement encompassing more than just an antiwar crusade. And there was time for prayer and meditation and Bible study.

This kind of work became more difficult when I was transferred from a private cell to a dormitory with the general prison population. At about the same time I got a reassignment in my work detail, from the boiler room to the farm, just in time for spring plowing. I felt almost free as I, along with others, went through the prison gates to the sound of their clang as they closed behind us and we walked to the farm area. Dick Wichlei of our group was among the farm workers. I developed a close relationship with Charlie Swift in the farm work. He had been a senior at Yale when he ran afoul of Selective Service and ended up at Danbury. Charlie later became a psychiatrist, working for many years in Tanzania. Our close relationship continues today. There were days of real freedom on the farm when the guards did not interfere with our roasting corn as it became ripe. And sometimes I would take a couple of pieces of bread from breakfast and carry them in my shirt to the farm, where I would make delicious tomato and lettuce sandwiches.

Individually and as a group of "divinity students," we had an un-usual relationship with our fellow inmates. We mixed well in the life of the prison community. We were pretty good athletes, with Bene-dict as the star of softball as already indicated. I was number one on the ping-pong team and represented the institution when we were challenged by outside teams. But our group was also sought out by prisoners who needed help in writing letters to wives or sweethearts, or applications for parole and the like. Never once was I threatened by another inmate, nor did any prisoner ever make anything that could be interpreted as a sexual advance. I must say that in the bull sessions in the dormitory, I learned a lot about the sexual exploits of some of my fellow inmates on the outside, but never a suggestion of anything toward me or any of our group so far as I know.

One incident haunts me as I think back on the period of June 1941. The prison population consisted of men from many walks of life: doctors, lawyers, and businessmen, in addition to more traditional prisoners, such as those who took stolen cars across state lines, com-mitted postal thefts, or violated the Mann Act or other federal stat-utes. Among those who were really political prisoners were some trade unionists found "guilty" of some kind of subversive activities. One was Joe Winogradsky, a vice-president of the Furriers Union. I became quite friendly with Joe. I am sure that Joe was a member of the Communist party, and I was with the Socialist party headed by Norman Thomas. The Communist line, when we entered Dan-bury during the Hitler-Stalin pact, was for the United States to stay out of the war. This all changed overnight when the Nazis attacked the Soviet Union on June 22, 1941. I can vividly recall walking toward the mess hall with Joe just after the news was released. He said to me very cryptically: "Well, I'm against you guys now." Shortly afterwards, Joe was released and went back to the Union, and I would read about him in the news from time to time.

In spite of the racial segregation in housing and at meals in the prison, there was plenty of opportunity for association with our fel-low black inmates in the yard, in athletic pursuits, on the job, and at religious services. Some of us developed very friendly relationships. This was strengthened because our group was known to oppose racial segregation by our actions and by petitions calling for an end to segregation in housing and dining. This carried over after we were released. I know that when Dellinger, Benedict, and Dallas went back to Newark, at least one black inmate joined their community. Another black inmate joined us for a while in Chicago.

As the time approached for our release from Danbury, we faced the question of what next? I know that in my own thinking I had assumed that I would return to Union Seminary. Doubts arose when President Henry Sloane Coffin came to visit us at Danbury. We began to realize that our return would not be uncomplicated. The seminary had apparently been under public pressure from contributors and supporters and there was uneasiness that our return might generate new unwanted publicity, especially in the period leading up to direct U.S. participation in the war. Other faculty members came to visit us, too. Finally, something came in writing, setting two conditions for our return:

> You will recall that the Seminary through the President made you an official request last autumn when you announced your determination not to register under the Selective Service Act, asking you to go to your own home and meet the Draft Board there. This request you and your associates ignored. It is impossible to carry on the Seminary as a fellowship unless students respond to the very rare requests of the administration. Therefore we wish to know whether, should you receive an official request, you are prepared to say that you would either comply or quietly withdraw from the Seminary.
>
> You and your associates brought the Seminary a great deal of publicity. If we allow you to return, will you give us assurance that you will give yourself wholly to your studies and to the position you may hold in a church or kindred institution by avoiding any course of action which would bring similar publicity?

Our group had some serious discussions in making our decision. We decided it would be impossible to accept Union's conditions. If we did, we would be constantly under pressure. The conditions made for conflict. The three who had formed the Newark Christian Colony decided to return to their community work. Five of us decided to go to Chicago Theological Seminary where the president, Albert W. Palmer, welcomed us.

Our date for release was September 3. I remember with what exhilaration I approached this day. The thought of freedom was sweet. I was excited by plans for the future, study in Chicago, the challenge of community action, and seeing Jean and finding out whether this relationship could develop into something more permanent. In preparation for release, I had begun a correspondence with A. J. Muste about the future of the pacifist movement and my own relation to it. This culminated in an offer for me to work part-time with the FOR as Chicago youth secretary as I completed my seminary work. This, in effect, would be my fieldwork. The prospect excited me. Little could I know that this would lead me into the struggle to oppose discrimination and subsequently to align myself with the forces for liberation of African countries from colonialism, even as I maintained my ties with the Methodist Church as a member of the Rocky Mountain Annual Conference.

The morning of our release from Danbury, we were called one by one into the warden's office. We had all been given a prison-made suit and ten dollars, as I recall. I thought this last trip to the warden's office was just a goodbye session. I had been through a lot with the warden in nearly a year of confinement. He was an authority figure to me, but not by any means a father figure. I sometimes felt sorry for him and had not always respected him because of his imperious manner. But I think it was with a certain feeling of nostalgia that I prepared to say farewell. At the close of our last few moments the warden thrust a card toward me and asked me to sign it. At first I thought it was a pro forma piece of paper that you sign having to do with release. I read it and was startled when I saw it was a registration form for Selective Service. I smiled and gave it back to him. "Warden, you know I'm not going to sign this. I just did my time in your prison because I refused to sign this." I found out later that others in our group went through the same routine, even being warned that it was a condition of release. No one signed, of course. Then we walked out of the prison gates, hearing the clang of the locked door behind us for the last time, and moved on to the next phase of life.

How do I size up this prison experience? It stands out as one of the unforgettable episodes of my life, which has included many thrilling moments. It made me plumb the depths of my faith. It taught me something about the importance of strength to be gained from an action with a committed group. Prison life opened up a world to me that I never would have known without becoming a part of it. It deepened my faith and set a direction for my life.

Our action no doubt did influence others to take the same position. It did not create a massive movement. Rather, it was a witness to the possibility of helping to create a peaceful world. I did, however, have a sense of guilt growing out of this nonregistration witness. I played no direct role in resisting the horror that was nazism. If I had been in Europe, I could have joined others in the underground to help rescue Jews and opponents of Hitler. But from my vantage point in the United States, this was impossible. It was in part this realization that motivated me to initiate nonviolent direct action against segregation that led to the formation of the Congress of Racial Equality, where I was executive secretary for ten years, and to organizing such campaigns as the Journey of Reconciliation (the first Freedom Ride) in 1947 to challenge Jim Crow seating on buses and trains in the south. CORE had its beginning in Chicago in 1942 and through the war years the young organization gained a significant following as it opposed segregation through sit-ins and other nonviolent direct action techniques in restaurants, theaters, and housing in many parts of the country. I wrote a pamphlet in 1945, published by the FOR, called *Erasing the Color Line*, which detailed many of these campaigns. And later, from the early 1950s into the 1980s, I aligned myself with the liberation movements in Africa struggling for independence from colonial domination as executive director of the American Committee on Africa.

I wrote an article about my nonregistration position in the *Christian Century* (August 16, 1995) in which I concluded: "I believe in the struggle for justice. I also believe that a Christian has a responsibility to support such struggle. However, I am still unwilling to take life in the pursuit of justice, and I am unwilling to condone the terrible destruction, the saturation bombing, the use of atomic weapons inevitably associated with war. So I am still a conscientious objector. I do not, however, wear rose-colored glasses. I make no easy assumptions about realizing a nonviolent world. Nevertheless, we do have the responsibility to struggle for such a world—and the struggle goes on."

Perhaps above everything else, the Union-Danbury experience taught me something about facing crises and making decisions. I learned that one often does not know where a road will lead when one starts out on a journey. The first step is of ultimate importance. Gandhi's favorite hymn (and my mother's as well) goes:

> Lead kindly light, amid the encircling gloom,
> Lead thou me on.
> The night is dark and I am far from home;
> Lead thou me on.
> Keep thou my feet;
> I do not ask to see the distant scene:
> One step enough for me.

Times have changed at Union Seminary. On October 16, 1990, the fiftieth anniversary of the date of our nonregistration, the seminary hosted a reunion of our group. The event was put together at the initiative of Bill Lovell and was enthusiastically backed by the seminary president, Donald Shriver.

Five of us were present: Benedict, Dellinger, Lovell, Spragg, and me. Dallas and Wichlei couldn't make it. Joe Bevilacqua had died in the early 1980s. We all participated in a panel discussion commemorating the event. Since this reunion one more of us has died, Howard Spragg.

After that occasion, Shriver wrote to all of us through Bill Lovell:

> That was a great event you all arranged for us on October 16. I am truly glad that we did it. It connected me with a vital strand of Union tradition and it reminded us all that Faulkner was right when he said that "the past is not over and done; it isn't even past."
>
> For the work you and your colleagues put into arranging the event, we are grateful. And Union is proud of the sum total of ministry and witness represented in that remarkable panel.

A further indication of changing times is that in April 1996, Don Benedict and I were honored by being chosen for "Distinguished Alumni Awards" by the seminary. I was particularly surprised because I didn't even get my degree from Union.

William P. Roberts, Jr.

Prison and Butterfly Wings

*We flapped our butterfly wings in prison. Who can
know their effect in our interconnected world?*

When Larry Gara suggested that I write a chapter for this compilation, I was not sure what I could add of interest, because Larry and I had remarkably similar prison experiences and much the same circuit of prisons: Mill Point in West Virginia to Marlinton County Jail to Ashland, Kentucky, and eventually to the Federal Penitentiary in Lewisburg, Pennsylvania. Perhaps if I shift the focus of my account away from the external experiences and struggles of a war resister in prison to the internal aspects of the experience, it will appropriately supplement what Larry and others describe so effectively.

Of course, when one deals with the mental, emotional, and spiritual aspects of such an intense situation, one can only speak for oneself without any attempt to extrapolate to others, no matter how similar may be the external prison experience and the witness against war.

In this endeavor I am extremely fortunate in having at my disposal all the letters I wrote from prison to my mother. More than a mother, she was my confidante to whom I could open my heart and who, as I discovered only after I had made my commitment, was fully sympathetic and supportive (even though her husband, my father, was at the same time a prisoner of the Japanese in a Shanghai internment camp). My mother saved all my letters and, shortly before her death, returned them to me. I shall use excerpts from them, with only a minimum of explanation of their context, for they are authentic and reliable in a way that my memory, fifty years later, cannot possibly be.

WILLIAM P. ROBERTS, JR. (b. 1922)
Bill Roberts was born in Shanghai, China, the son of Episcopalian missionaries. From 1947 to 1961 he was a contemplative monk in a Trappist monastery. Marriage and work as an insurance actuary followed. From 1967 until his semi-retirement in 1984, he was consulting actuary and principal of Peat, Marwick in Philadelphia. He and his wife, Maria, now live on Nantucket Island, where he continues to work for conservation agencies and causes.

But first let me give a few background notes. My parents were religious missionaries in China. I was born there in 1922 and lived in Shanghai and Nanking until I was thirteen years old. So I was privileged to have firsthand knowledge of another country and culture, in contrast to the provincial patriotism of so many who have never lived outside the bounds of their own culture. Also, I grew up in a strongly religious family; not until the prison experience did I begin to break away from the need of expressing my convictions and ideals in traditional religious terms.

It was only after the United States entered the war, while I was a sophomore at Yale University, that I thought seriously about my response to the demands and implications of the Selective Service System. One month after Pearl Harbor I wrote: "I have never done so much concentrated, constructive thinking in my life." But there was no internal struggle or agony of decision; I realized, almost as a matter of course, that I must follow the path of a conscientious objector. Inspired by the Yale graduates who had already taken the "absolutist" stand of refusing to register for Selective Service and who had served a year's prison sentence as a result, I knew that I too would say *No!* to military conscription, even to the relatively benign conscription to a Civilian Public Service camp.

As a nineteen year old, I was required to register on June 30, 1942. Shortly before that date I sent a lengthy letter to the attorney general in Washington explaining why I was refusing to register. To make the most of whatever time I had left before the inevitable arrest, I left Yale to be part of the Ashram in the Newark slums, where the ex-Yale nonregistrants and other war resisters were serving the community. They had acquired a small farm outside the city, and on weekends would take some of the slum children out to the farm for their first experience of green nature and animals. It was on the farm that I was arrested in August 1942. As I wrote my mother in my first letter from county jail:

> I was taken at the farm Monday evening after supper. I had spent such a grand last day! I helped clean up the house in Newark in the early morning, then hitch-hiked out to the farm. We spent most of the afternoon digging up potatoes way up in the fields. Then Dorothy [a fellow member of the Ashram] and I stayed in the field in the tall

grass and talked for a couple of beautiful hours, looking up to the white clouds and out to the hills. Then supper altogether, and after the dishes I went in to play the piano that is there—all out of tune and broken. I was playing when I was told the FBI was outside, wanting me. It seemed so natural for this to happen—so much a part of the whole picture—that I went out to greet them with no resentment or worry in my heart. The time had come, that was all, and I thanked God for the two months of growth and happiness I have had—two months that I did not think possible for me to so enjoy. A whole new life and a new meaning to life has opened up to me in that time, and it has given me the strength, I am sure, to go to prison singing. It was hard to say goodbye to all the gang at the farm—the best thing was to say nothing. Words were not needed, knowing that every one of them was with me heart and soul, ready at any time to follow the same road.

I was taken to the Hudson County Jail in Jersey City, where I was held for nearly three months while the whole trial process very slowly and very surely took place. I wrote from the jail on September 21, 1942:

> Tomorrow the United States is thoughtfully throwing me a little party over in Newark in commemoration of the completion of four weeks here. I am to be arraigned before the judge—that is the time when one is supposed to plead guilty or not guilty. By the time you receive this it will be a thing of the past. I see quite clearly what I feel is right for me to do, and I'll let you know about it when it is over. The heading of the notice said "United States vs. William P. Roberts"— and I thought for a moment of what a stone wall I was butting, with a whole country as my accuser, but then I realized that I was really the big bully in the case, with the whole "cloud of witnesses," past, present, and future, at my side!

Finally the date of the trial was set, and on the eve of the trial I wrote: "Since this is the last time that I can be absolutely certain of the chance of writing, I'm going to make use of it. . . . Please don't be worried, Mother, about what may happen—I assure you I am not. It all seems so clear and right and joyous to me."

At the arraignment in Newark's Federal Court I told the judge that I would not participate in the trial in any way. Because I refused to plead, the judge put in a plea of not guilty for me and insisted on a full jury trial. The prosecuting attorney read aloud my statement to the attorney general as proof of my willful refusal to register, and thus provided my defense. It took the jury only ten minutes to find me guilty. After sentencing me to three years in prison, Judge Meaney spoke to me privately in his chambers, telling me that this was the hardest sentence he had ever had to give, because in the first World War he had initially considered conscientious objection himself.

I was kept at the county jail for several more weeks, and of that time I wrote later from Ashland:

> Those 3 months in county jail I look back on with a really nostalgic feeling—I was so happy there and learned so much. And I was able to grow close to some fine characters there—in a way that is impossible here where every co-operative, sympathetic action is stifled. . . . One evening when I was in solitary in county jail, the guard relented a bit and handed me my book of Tagore's poems. And I spent a wonderful evening alone with the cockroaches and Tagore, reading by the light that came through the grating from a solitary electric bulb, looking through a window at the darkness over the city, and feeling the awesome beauty of the pulsing of rhythm within rhythm which pervades the universe.

Finally I was taken—in handcuffs—to the Mill Point minimum custody prison in the West Virginia mountains. It was almost comical to find myself with a sledgehammer on a rock pile "making little ones out of big ones"—the universal image of prison life. Actually, we were involved in the construction of a mountain road, but it was clearly "made" work, since machinery could have accomplished the result in a tiny fraction of the time we took. Mill Point had no fence or wall around it—nothing that would keep a determined prisoner from escaping. Only prisoners with short sentences and who were deemed not dangerous were sent there. It did not take me many days to realize that I was, in fact, staying there voluntarily. So I told the warden that I could not promise to continue as my own jailer and would feel free to walk away at any time. Within the hour I was being taken to nearby Marlinton County Jail, and then to the medium-custody federal prison at Ashland, Kentucky, where I was to stay for the next year.

Externally, life in the Ashland prison was a mix of regimentation and boredom, instructive work in the machine shop, close friendships with COs and non-COs, and through it all were the protests, fasts and hunger strikes (usually focused on some prison injustice such as racial segregation), acts of peaceful noncooperation and their inevitable punishment. Internally, there was always the unresolved (and unresolvable) tension between the merits of working within the system despite its evils and of refusing to accept those evils. I could not look to logic for a solution to the dilemma, for perfect consistency in noncooperation with the evils of the system meant refusing to eat or to be more than a limp rag doll, and I rebelled against that extreme. My reaction to the dilemma was like a pendulum, swinging from one side to the other, never achieving a stable resolution of the tension. As I wrote in April 1943 from Ashland: "My desire to act with complete honesty toward my feelings at the time, regardless of the act's consistency with the past, has led me a merry chase trying to keep up with myself."

This tension was expressed in the following excerpts from a letter written in May 1943 to Rev. John Magee, my father's very close friend in China and later a prominent pastor in Washington, D.C., who tried through visits and letters to get me to abandon my pacifist stand. Our families were so close that I called him "Uncle John." He must have sent this letter on to my mother.

Dear Uncle John,

I feel obliged to give something of a rebuttal to some parts of your letter—though not, of course, with argumentative intent. First, when you consider me a "young idealist" you are quite mistaken. Where you think in terms of the Kingdom of God (i.e., the ideal society), with its ideal ethics of the Sermon on the Mount, I am concerned with making life, as it is, worth-while, and cannot for the life of me see why such ethics as Jesus' should not be employed now. Where you are working for progress towards an ideal society, I must admit that I am

quite doubtful of the idea of continuous progress—feeling that progress is a purely relative affair—and am very certain that there will
never be an ideal society. You say "progress of human fellowship,"
while I say, "Let's not worry about progressing towards it, but rather,
let's experience the reality of it now." You say this is all "adolescent thinking" and "unrealistic dreaming." I cannot deny it, although
such an accusation cuts deeper than I can tell. Compared with other
youths my age, I have had my share, perhaps, of soul-searching problems and all-demanding decisions. I question whether it is possible
to enter solitary, not expecting to leave it until my mind cracked, and
wrestle there through two agonizing weeks with the problem of life
on prison terms vs. death, (finally changing my mind in favor of life)
and then come out still "thinking adolescently." I do not ask for agreement, nor do I desire a condescending sympathy, but I long for a sincere tolerance. I have been gladly amazed at the extent I have found it
among my "un-Christian" fellow-inmates here.

And in my comments to my mother at the same time:

If Uncle John had talked with me six months ago, I would have
given him a very confident, lofty-sounding answer in terms of ab-
solute principles to any question he would have asked. In the ensuing
months my answers have sunk from the intellectual, theological plane
to the depths of feelings. Words, alas, are fashioned for intellectual
use—and, not being a poet, I am unable to explain a matter of feeling
in thought-terms. Every time I would try to convey something of
what I felt to Uncle John, he would stop me with "But don't you see
that that is false thinking!" And he was right, for feelings cannot be
pressed into a logical, consistent thought-structure without one or
the other losing its form. Also, while Uncle John has—and believes it
is right to have—a confident (I feel like saying blind) faith, I feel the
need of a healthy doubt which says, "This seems to be right for me
now, though I can speak only for myself and only for the present."

But three months later, in August 1943, I wrote my mother:

It has been a gradual path, often rocky and rough, often dark, but
as I stand now on this endless path, I seem to have come out of a dark,

prison-like forest of a year ago, into an open field in the sunlight, and for the first time I seem to see the path ahead quite clearly, and my spirit seems more able than ever before to walk with confidence and joy along that path. Not that the path will help much to guide the lost world of humanity, but at least it is the path which calls this insignificant individual, and believe me, Mother, it is the call of joy and expansion of spirit.

And ten days later:

I'm writing this in bed at 6 A.M. We supposedly sleep here for 9 hours each night, and that is just plain too much for me. So after lights-out, I usually stay awake another hour—a good time to meditate and listen to the sounds of night. And when it is light enough, I sometimes start the day an hour ahead. By all convict standards, I am "building my time" in just the wrong way, but life, even in here, is too precious to waste in unnecessary unconsciousness.

I have waded through some marshy ground, but in the last week or two I feel as if I've found a more solid, more tempered happiness than ever before. Your letter, I think, had much to do with it—it came just when I most needed it. Mother, you are the only person in the whole wide world who always does the right thing at the right time.

In November 1943, just after my twenty-first birthday, I wrote:

My birthday celebration consisted of going to bed at the very ordinary hour of 10 o'clock. I composed this poem in honor of the occasion:
> Ain't it absurd
> Becoming of age
> While only a bird
> In a gilded cage!

Also that November I wrote about one of my closest prison friends:

Lew Aumack left here last Friday for the medical corps of the army—or navy—I'm not sure which. It's under non-combatant service. I don't need to tell you that I miss him; we have been through much together—Newark, Jersey City, Mill Point, Marlinton Jail, and here. We were so inseparable that we were almost considered twins by everyone. I am two days older, but we were just the same height and weight. He helped me a great deal through everything—it's so much easier and happier, when one must buck a mighty system, to have a real companion, one who truly understands and agrees when everyone else misinterprets. Even while our paths began to diverge as time progressed here, we knew each other so well that we could really talk from our hearts, and it was good. Lew feels as strongly against the war as ever, but he came to feel that the active and personally constructive life and training of the medical corps outweighed the value of this frustrating and stagnant existence here. Lew's integrity is tremendous, and it took great courage to obey his feelings in spite of the inevitable misunderstanding of CO's and administration alike. I wonder if I shall ever see him again. . . .

When one year of my sentence was up, I was in theory eligible for parole, and with considerable misgivings I had decided to apply for parole to a hospital, not really expecting anything to come of it since I had so many black marks on my prison record. But on December 1, 1943, I was able to write my mother:

I was called up this afternoon and told that I had been given parole!—to Massachusetts General Hospital. Oh, if you knew how complete was my lack of hope, you'd know what a stroke of lightning it was to me—in fact it was such a powerful bolt that it kind of stunned me, and I feel as if the whole thing has not fully sunk in yet. It just is too much for me to change—and fully grasp the change—from having a year and a half to stay here, to the position of leaving this prison in a few days. It's too big to be felt all at once—but O how good it feels, even while it is still sinking in. . . .

There is sorrow with joy—it hurts terribly to leave behind in this place so many people—when all within me cries out that they should be free—wonderful people who need to be outside and deserve to be outside far more than I. I feel shamefully lucky and very humble, and now that I have felt this place, happiness cannot be complete while one man remains behind bars. If I could help, believe me I would stay. Part of the humbling is that I know if I were the person I should be, I could help and so would stay. When the time comes to return to this kind of society—as I know the time will come—perhaps I will have grown nearer to being that person, and really can help. May the breathing spell outside help me to grow. I want to terribly.

As it turned out, the hospital changed its mind, considering me—wisely perhaps!—too poor a risk. So I spent a second Christmas at Ashland, after which I wrote:

> I feel that it has been good for me to have been here over Christmas. The two musical programs we put on were a big help to a lot of people and it would have been mighty tough without a piano. On Friday we mainly sang carols. The most enjoyed was Silent Night in all the different languages. Much applause after each language—even after German—it made me feel really good. Then last evening our chorus joined with the Ashland Episcopal Choir to sing Christmas anthems. There were solos, duets, trios, quartets and everybody. I sang some and accompanied some. It is like a long deep dive into a lake to hear female voices—to see their hair and their faces and the bright colors of their clothes.

Someone, possibly my mother, put in a good word for me, and the hospital once again decided to accept me. I left prison in January 1944 to work as an orderly in the operating rooms. While there, I wrote frequent letters to Larry Gara, who was still at Ashland. He has since returned them to me. This was my first letter to him, written a few days after arriving at the Boston hospital:

> There is such a flood in me that it is hard to control a trickle. I would prefer to play you something on the piano than to use words—I'm so terrible at this. It's not the big things that hollow me out—things like freedom or non-regimentation—they are too deep and formless to be taken ahold of in themselves, they are drifted into almost casually. It's girls' hair and the color in their dresses, the music in a negro lady's eyes, the rough, strong feel of a tree's bark. In my first ramble among snow and trees I had a long talk with a terribly wise and ancient maple druid and he asked especially about you, Larry, and wanted to know what this conscription thing is that has the

ghastly power to pin you to cement, where he can't talk with you. But druids know how to wait and I told him you do too.

Though I'm beginning to feel less of a stranger in this new world, I'm still just standing, letting all this symphony pour over me—listening, not talking—feeling, not thinking. Indeed, I am happiest when I do not think, for thoughts turn to all of you, and believe me, heaven cannot sleep with hell.

The best thing about living here is that it is beside the Charles River and in the evenings I can go out on the bridge over the river, with the singing stars above and warm darkness around. Truly the most precious thing in this outside world is the chance to be out in the darkness of night. Only in the darkness does the awesome oneness of all time and all space flood in through the senses without the effort of mind—at least in my weakness. It is in the dark that we know that stones and trees breathe and sing.

There is a certain amount of tension at the hospital about CO's but not too bad. It is a bit of a jolt to become a terrific minority again after being a virtual majority. I thought I knew what to expect, but the tidal wave of uniforms uniforms uniforms everywhere was a shock at first—now just a dull pain. Although there is much that hurts, there is so wonderfully much that sings—which, after all, is life.

To another friend I described the work in the operating rooms: "With many operations going on at once, the place is charged with a strong mental, almost spiritual, tension. There is something truly holy about the business of saving lives and curing suffering—each operation is far more of a religious experience for me than church." Two months later to Larry I wrote: "I think it will make you happy to hear, Larry, that the longer I am out here the more strongly do I know that I shall not compromise at all with Selective Service to stay out of jail. It is not on as idealistic a plane as it was before prison, but it is lots deeper and more a part of me."

In April 1944:

The best time is, as usual, the days when I wave the city goodbye and enter the land of trees again. Trees have come to epitomize all that is good to me—to be among them in the night when it is quiet and dark or when there is a faint breeze in the moonlight is an awesome thing—I feel so totally in the life—conscious life—all around, and it is such a pure and timeless life that I feel like an unholy intruder as well as a part of it. Last Sunday I had the best time yet, climbing way up into the top branches and sitting and watching the birds.

In May:

Yesterday I splurged and heard Koussevitsky conduct Bach's B Minor Mass. I wish I could describe what I feel in that music—ever since I sang in it in New Haven I have felt more and more strongly that it is the greatest work of art that I know. Last night it was a chorus of 150. With the first notes I broke out in a cold sweat. There is the sweep and flow of the ocean and the solid strength and agelessness of the mountain. A huge chant of joy and a cry to the heart of things for forgiveness. I'm tempted to call it an atonement for all the rottenness that man has caused. I spent a good part of the night afterwards walking along the river and the music seemed to fill everything.

I keep asking around to find out about my destination, but when I inquire of My Lord the Sun, he replies that whether I reach my goal or not, the world will continue to revolve on its axis, and he will continue to rise in the east and set in the west, and what do I matter. The clouds, when asked, reply "Never fear, for the winds will blow you where you are to go." The moon and the stars are foolish enough to whisper that my destination is where I am, if I but realize it. The trees give the best answer because they, too, are trying to reach something—only until I find a druid that speaks English all that I can gather is "Beauty comes out of Mother Earth, but slowly—inhumanly slowly—and meanwhile the feel of birds and the winds is a good feel." So you see Nature is playing some sort of game with me—and I am not much better off than I was to start with.

In July:

I have spent a wonderful and happy ten days in a pattern of living that I want to continue for quite a while. My evenings have consisted of one or two hours of Bach at the piano, then perhaps a little reading or a letter, though usually not, and the rest of the evening—2, 3, or 4 hours—out under the stars, sometimes walking far, sometimes standing on the bridge over the river, in what I hesitate to call prayer and hesitate to call meditation, both being so easily misunderstood. More of an opening up, a breathing in, or as Gibran says, "the expansion of oneself into the living ether." I have been happier, I think, than I have been since my first week out of prison—especially in those moments when the sense of my own insignificance in this mighty Mystery would become real and powerful. It is in those moments that things fit easily and clearly into their proper places, and life becomes a joy rather than a series of problems.

I have dwelt at some length on the beauty and happiness of my life on parole, to put in perspective what follows. Later in July my letter gave the first hint that the pendulum was about to swing back toward noncooperation: "I feel stronger and stronger the personal necessity to keep absolutely clear of Selective Service. It is probably foolish to act so strongly on that one point when I am so weak on others—but that's the way it is. And it is better to work toward a strengthening of other points than toward a weakening of this one." And then on August 11: "Things are happening inside me—maybe I'll see you soon."

Finally, on August 20, my last letter:

> Congratulate me, Larry—I am a free man! I sent, a few days ago, a letter to the parole board saying that I no longer consider myself on parole, that the obligations and implications of parole are no longer tolerable. This is no sudden decision—nor can I point to a moment in which the decision was made. I never decided—I have known within myself that this thing was inevitable for many weeks—and suddenly it was natural and right to go ahead with it, which I have.
>
> Though I am eager to leave the hospital for other things, I plan to stay here for a while, because there is a terrific shortage right now and it would be unfair to up and leave my responsibilities here without any notice. For at least two or three week I shall stay—bureau of prisons permitting.
>
> There is no need of my giving you "reasons" for my taking this step—you have felt this thing more honestly and deeply than I have. What I have found out during these seven months is that a real life requires the ingredient of a basic honesty—in the same way that human

life requires food. And now I feel freer than I have ever been—and that sense of being open and unchained and ready to move forward toward God—that sense must be nourished, be it out of prison or in, whatever it involves, wherever the singing road may lead. O when you walk along the street and look into a face—into eyes that have nothing to see—ears that do not hear a sound—into a spirit that dreams of God but has despaired of the search—when you look upon life that has forgotten its own wonder and grown tired of its own mystery, then you know that nothing matters, nothing matters at all, except a new life, not a temporary adjustment of the old, but a sailing out into the ocean of God and a colonizing of a new world.

My letter to the parole board said in part:

> In the last months it has grown upon me that I can no longer accept the implications and obligations of parole. In my weakness I have resisted this growth, but it has continued in spite of me, until now it is joyfully stronger than my weakness. And so I want to tell you that I no longer consider myself under the authority of the parole board. There is no special injustice in my parole situation that brings me to this step. I have been well treated—better than I deserve. Rather it is the fact of being on parole that has become intolerable. With all my heart I hope that the parole board will realize that I can be of far greater service leading the life to which I feel dedicated within society rather than in prison.

Shortly after this letter, I was rearrested by the FBI in the middle of an operation and, after a night in the Suffolk County Jail, was taken to the federal penitentiary in Lewisburg, Pennsylvania. There I immediately began a program of noncooperation that resulted in my being placed in segregation for the next twelve months, at first in a solitary cell and later in a large room with about twelve other noncooperating war resisters. During that time I refused to accept the policy of censorship, resulting in my not writing or receiving any letters. Then once again the pendulum swung, and in August of 1945 I ended my noncooperation, joining the prison population. As part of that decision I began to write letters again. In my second letter to my mother I wrote:

I work in the kitchen, preparing the vegetables. There isn't much physical exercise in this job—and naturally after a year in a canary cage I am eager to stretch my wings somewhat more vigorously, but it may be best to work in gradually. I kept in fairly good physical condition in segregation by doing about an hour's worth of calisthenics each day—not a very enjoyable procedure, but good discipline and certainly worth the effort.

When I came from segregation to population I wanted to avoid asking for anything particular in the way of job or living quarters, trying to make it as clear as possible that there was no element of bargaining or dealing in my decision. I did emphasize that I was unwilling to do "white-collar" work or anything that had institutional responsibility connected with it—since I wish to remain as unattached as I can in such a system as this. Just manual labor of some sort—something near the bottom of the prison hierarchy.

As for living quarters, I am now in a dormitory. You can imagine how good it has been to be able to sit down on a man's bed and talk with him—to live with him, rather than to watch him from a distance through a window. But one thing prisons teach—and dormitory life in particular—is that the human organism requires, if it is to be healthy and grow, the chance for privacy. . . . The final answer—the answer all men could have if we lived the Good Life—is to be in the heart of Nature, alone with the quiet life of the green, with the depth of the horizon, with the music of the life-sounds, where God sings.

Later in September I wrote:

Any "social reform," "non-violent direct action" or anything else is lasting in its effect only to the extent that it touches and changes man's spirit. Often such action may be necessary to reach man's heart—but at all times we must strive to focus our life upon the roots of the matter. Nor can we be effective in reaching the roots unless one's own spirit is worthy of speaking to another's. "And if it is a despot you would dethrone, see first that his throne erected within you is destroyed." Is this an "escapist" philosophy? No amount of words, but only one's life, can answer that.

The wonderful thing about the basic reality of the realm of the spirit is that the best in man cannot be smothered or checked any more than can the worst. Murder—and love—will out! These words of Gandhi's are more important toward understanding him and his greatness, than anything else I've read of his: "When that firmness and rarity of spirit which I long for have become perfectly natural to me; when I have become incapable of any evil; when nothing harsh or haughty occupies, be it momentarily, my thought-world—then, and not till then, will my non-violence move all the hearts of all the world." O we must learn to live fundamentally—that is to say, in the Kingdom of Heaven. Our great hope and joy lies in our knowledge that we have it in us to do it! Do you remember those words of Tagore's about each new baby being ample proof that God has not yet despaired of man? . . . .

Golly, all this seems horribly like a sermon, but I'm just trying to show some of the things I myself am slowly learning.

In October:

The real tragedy [of the war] is not just the life after life lost, and the home after home ruined—but it is the growth in callousness toward life and death and beauty, and the perversion of man's creative energy from the realm of love to the science of hate—which is the necessary foundation for all of this. And clearly no amount of outlawing of the atomic bomb and no amount of international "cooperation" (with the scientists of each State feverishly working on improving these weapons "just in case. . . .") will do one iota of good by itself. It is this callousness and perversion of life—something so much deeper than bombs or Big 5 Meetings—that has to be reached and overcome. O there is such tremendous potential for good and longing for God in each human being, but it is so smothered that men have actually lost faith in their own potential and are ashamed of their own longing.

And so I believe that a Dark Age is upon us—at least upon Western, civilized man, and the darkness seems to be spreading through much of the East. A darkness that can't be relieved by any number of electric lights or by the energy released from a pound of uranium. It can only be relieved by man's renewal of faith in his greater self, of longing for God, and of love for the green, clean, living things of God's creation. In the Middle Ages the monasteries kept the spark

of life alive. It is our greatest task now to find and nourish the modern
equivalent of the monasteries.

A look at the penitentiary population:

Men here are just plain people—with all their innate virtues and
superimposed faults. A wonderful cross-section of the American people—caught in the web of this competitive system and culture.
On our vegetable detail we go from a wealthy Californian real-estator
to a gas-station man from New Haven—from a soldier fresh from
France to a Tennessee home-spun farmer—from a Russian immigrant
to a youth with an education in the ivory-towers of Hotchkiss and
Yale . . . . and so they go—all criminals before Caesar, and all sons before God. And who is there who can lay claim to a nobler title?

I wish all those who want to reform the wicked criminal could have
been here in this dormitory one evening this week when someone
spotted a mouse scurrying across the cement—(not a frequent occurrence) and yelled "Catch him! Kill him!" Some—thankful for any
break from the monotony—jumped to the chase. But at the same time
several yelled "Lay off! Leave the little thing alone!" In fact such a
majority defended the mouse's life that the creature finally scampered
away very much alive. Later, one explained that he'd never kill a mouse
because once a mouse had kept him from losing his mind: once he had
spent 90 days in solitary in another prison and a mouse had been his
only companion, the only thing to keep him sane. Another, an English
limey, told me that a mouse had a right to live, the same as he—and
he wouldn't kill a mosquito or fly, unless he was sure it was its life or
his. Enemies of the State—punished by Caesar, loved by God. I don't
mean to imply that such an incident is typical—but people must learn
that prisons are not filled with kidnappers and murderers—but above
all with those who have been unlucky enough to be the losers and
scapegoats (—as are the slum-dwellers—) in this society of competition and mammon-worship. They are not guiltless, because no one is.

In November:

It is the value and necessity of suffering that makes the way of love
seem unrealistic and weak and doomed to failure. We avoid facing the

real nature of evil—and we shun the realization that the overcoming of evil must involve suffering on the part of him who overcomes—whether the evil be in others or in himself (and what we call evils in "society" reside actually in ourselves and the other individuals)—suffering and great joy!

What a wonderful, infinite path lies ahead of us—and the best of it all is that, in spite of atomic bombs, we will reach our fulfillment, though it be not until an Eternity has passed!

On December 20, 1945, with just six months to go, I was unexpectedly transferred from Lewisburg to the less severe federal prison in Danbury, Connecticut. The day after arriving in Danbury, I wrote:

Surprised? So am I. I thought my tour of the federal prisons was ended for a while—but one never knows, it seems, where one will lie down to sleep the very next night. Night before last I lay down in Pennsylvania—then a tap on the shoulder in the wee hours of the morning to tell me to get dressed—a 16-hour bus-ride—and then last night I arrived here at Danbury. As I was traveling it was good to think of drawing nearer and nearer to you—and also to Vermont. It was a truly enjoyable ride, provided one could sufficiently submerge the cattle-herding element and the handcuffs. You can guess how I feasted on the countryside—the heavy fall of snow had stopped a half-day earlier, and the sun had risen into a clear blue sky, making the whiteness sparkle. All day, as I watched the sun shining down on the snow I kept finding myself repeating the words of Sidney Lanier: "I am strong in the strength of my lord the sun; How dark, how dark soever the course that must needs be run, I am lit with the sun."

And then when the short daylight had gone and most people in the bus drowsed, it was good meditating on the ever-present love of God and the words of Brother Lawrence: "I can not do this unless Thou enablest me." The full moon came up beautifully clear, escorted by three bright stars, and Orion could be seen very well. We passed through the old stamping grounds of Newark and New York, and I felt more strongly than I had before what terrible prisons and life-denials they are.

As always happens, I didn't realize, until separated from them, how many valuable friendships I had acquired during those short three months in population at Lewisburg. For that reason I am sorry not to be able to stay there for these next five months. There was the Frenchman who had been in France through the German occupation and the beginning of the American occupation and who hates war with a vividness that comes from direct experience—and the man who was spending the time in prison in writing a book and was eager for suggestions and encouragement—the guy my age who had spent almost his entire life in orphanages, boys' reformatories, and prisons, and by some miracle had retained a powerful humankindness. Then, too, I miss being with the men who really have to drink prison to the dregs—the lifers and long-timers, who are not sent to these "Correctional Institutions." When one has to be in prison, one finds it good to be with them. If for no other reason, to keep one from self-pity! Though it goes deeper than that.

In January of 1946:

I have left Quarantine for "population"—so here I am, all set for these five or six months. I'm working on the farm—for which I am thankful. You can imagine what it was like to work out in the pure, clean air for the first time in over a year!—and the good, earthy, tobacco-free smells—and above all the sight of the surrounding hills, the snow and the trees, and the sky.

There was less external pressure of confinement and regimentation at Danbury than at Lewisburg. Most of my working hours were spent on the farm or in the greenhouse planting and transplanting. Internally, there was always that pendulum threatening to swing back to noncooperation. But I think that by then the three years of prison-to-parole-to-prison, and of population-to-segregation-to-population, had matured me enough to realize that the swinging of the pendulum was not the swing between right and wrong, but between the two sides of the same road. Sometimes it seemed better to travel on one side, sometimes on the other, sometimes in the middle. The important thing was to stay focused and sensitive and ready to shift. So there was always tension, but not the sapping stress of self-doubt or of constant wavering. And underneath it all was a growing sureness of purpose and a deepening vision. Thus in February I wrote: "I wish I could tell you how happy I've been for the last three days—it's as if I had just reached the crest of a hill, in the life-long pilgrimage to the Holy Mountain, and saw a fresh, wonderful view spread out before me." And in March:

> Life and all this natural creation are good, beautiful and holy—indeed it is a flowering, an expression of the Universe of Love. And that, I feel, is the emphasis of the truest, highest mysticism—not to discard life, but to regenerate it, to live it in its pure, essential form. Not to seek Heaven by rejecting Earth, but to know that we are in Heaven even now, if we are but pure enough and loving enough to see it—for Heaven is love.

Finally, a week before my release in June and nearly four years since my initial incarceration, I wrote to my father in China:

> On the 11th I shall walk out of here in work-clothes, as I requested, and after spending a day or two "hardening my wings" among the green hills of Connecticut I shall hitch hike eagerly to Auburndale, there to spend a couple of weeks with Mother and others of the family. Then my plan is to go up to Vermont. . . . I can't but see how everything is working together for good, and in this suffering, groaning world I wonder if there is anyone so blessed as I.

It is difficult to describe the emotion of walking out the gate of a prison with no strings attached! Happily, I don't need to try, since I can make use of the letter I wrote to Larry Gara after I arrived at my mother's home:

> The hour I left Danbury the rain clouds broke up and the sun shone down from a glorious sky, with just enough rolling cumuli to add majesty to the scene. All this made the beauty of the day really brim over! I roamed the Connecticut hills all that day—feeling, thinking, seeing, hearing, smelling—exploring the trees and wild flowers and the birds, knowing tragically few by name—but that was all right, because they didn't seem in the least offended—in fact they

didn't know my name, so we were all in the same boat and got along fine. That evening I climbed a hill from which I'd be able to see the sunset, the stars and the dawn—but the thunderclouds loomed up suddenly, and what a deluge! The thickest foliage didn't keep me from being utterly drenched; so finally I swam back to the road and found a barn where a farmer was tucking his cows in bed for the night. He gladly let me clamber up to the hay loft, where I wrung out my clothes, wrapped up in a horse blanket, and laughed with glee to think of how different all this was from the way most would want to spend their first night out of the clink! The next day, with that incredible after-rain scent, I set out while the birds sang their hymn to dawn. I enjoyed the hitching greatly. It was good to sit at the side of the road and play the shepherd's pipe I brought with me. I had sewn together a crazy-looking sheath for it, to be carried over my shoulder. The reaction of people to such lunacy and good spirits was really interesting. Once seven or eight tiny kids gathered around and kept me busy for half an hour playing all the Christmas carols and nursery rhymes I could think of. Anyway, I finally arrived, and it is really good to be with Mother for these few days—and my brother John arrived the day before me, just released from the army!

I hope that this inadequate narrative points to the fact that beneath the frustrations and boredom, beneath the struggles external and internal, prison was for those war resisters who chose that path a maturing and deepening experience as well as a call to humanity to turn from its violent self-destructive path. I personally cannot measure the privilege of sharing friendship and hardship with some of the finest persons of our generation in a cause that transcended and still transcends our individual lives. Now, a half-century later, my basic convictions remain the same, although I hope that they are clothed in a greater humility and a deeper appreciation of those who have been equally dedicated but who have chosen a different path. Certainly I would now use different terms and different symbols to express these convictions, whose roots have grown deeper and wider over the decades.

Was our protest and our witness of any benefit to society? Perhaps the answer lies in the findings of the new science of chaos and complexity, which has discovered that something as apparently insignificant as the fluttering of a butterfly's wings can trigger a cascade of events that in due time drastically affect the weather halfway around the globe. We flapped our butterfly wings in prison. Who can know their effect in our interconnected world?

How the War Changed My Life

*The struggle of man against power is the struggle of
memory against forgetting.*

—*Milan Kundera*

THE STORY OF MY experience of World War II is on the order of a
picaresque narrative with ups and downs—a bit funny in places,
sometimes embarrassing, sometimes painful, impossible to explain
in wholly rational terms, but not without meaning and interest. The
ultimate effect of the war on me, on the other hand, is much more
depressing to think about. The war certainly changed my life and set
me on a very different course, yet I do not regret having had the
experience of it.

When World War II began in the fall of 1939 I was a senior in
high school at Woodstock, perched on the frontal range of the Hi-
malayas at seven thousand feet, with a rather lofty attitude toward
the world I was about to go down into. As an American missionary
kid, having grown up in India, I had the vague notion of studying
agriculture at Cornell and going back to India as an agricultural missionary. If I had managed to carry out that plan I might have been
back in India in time to be a part of the famous green revolution
of the 1950s and 1960s. However, by 1942 I had just finished my
sophomore year at Bethel College in Kansas when I decided I was
a conscientious objector to war and that I would draw the line at
resisting conscription. I refused to register for the draft and wound
up spending three years in prison. After that I became a printer for
eight years, and then a college English professor. So much for agriculture.

LAWRENCE H. TEMPLIN (b. 1922)
After prison, Lawrence Templin worked for several years as a printer. He then
attended graduate school at Indiana University, where he earned a Ph.D. From
1961 until his retirement in 1988, he was professor of English at Bluffton College.
He has been a war tax refuser and active in Peacemakers and several local peace
projects. He and his wife, Orletta, live in Bluffton, Ohio.

The war forced me to think a great deal about who I am and eventually why I had come out where I had, and it precipitated my feeling of being a stranger in the American culture. I realize now I am a hybrid person: I grew up and have lived in two radically different cultures, I traveled a good bit in my formative years, and I do not feel rooted anywhere in particular. For the kind of exiles or hybrids represented by writers like Salman Rushdie or V. S. Naipaul, there is no home. The whole world seems strange, often in surprisingly wonderful and even magical ways, but mostly in terrible ways. That has been pretty close to my feeling. As a result I probably see World War II, and the world in general for that matter, quite differently from the way most Americans do.

For one thing, I have never been able to think patriotically, and could not see either the German or the Japanese *people* as enemies. Nor was I able to see Pearl Harbor as an unexpected and treacherous surprise attack on an innocent nation at peace in the world. It is difficult for me to think in black and white terms, for or against any people in the world. While I am not blind to the evil natures of world leaders like Hitler, Stalin, or Saddam Hussein, and the damage they can do in the world, neither am I blind to the seemingly benign schemes of most of the leaders in the so-called free world. If I am more critical of "my own people"—that is, of Americans in particular—it is because I live here in America and I feel and understand more strongly the wrong that my own countrymen do to people in other parts of the world. I have always seen "us" as the prime aggressor nation in the world in the twentieth century. Yes, I have a real love-hate problem with my own people.

Finally, in retirement, I have been able to return in memory to my past and to the implications of my nurture on the Indian subcontinent. Reflecting on my story, I realize with a certain regret, is not at all the same thing as going back to India to be a missionary and doing agricultural work. I would like to have been useful. Instead I aspire, a bit late in life, to be a storyteller. I would like a reader—just one reader would do—to assure me that story telling is also a kind of usefulness.

As I said, the war began for me late in 1939 when I was about to graduate from high school at Woodstock in India. War was declared in India on the same day Britain declared itself at war with Germany after the invasion of Poland. The Viceroy, Lord Linlithgow, was solely responsible for getting India into the war. The Indian people had no say at all in the matter, and consequently their loyalty throughout the war was problematic. Our German teacher, Fraulein Hahn, was soon interned as an enemy alien. She had put up a German flag with the swastika on it in her classroom and was quite openly supporting the Nazis, not quite realizing where she was and what was happening, I suppose.

More relevant to my personal situation, all of us in the senior class at Woodstock were asked to declare whether we would be willing to fight against the Nazis if America came into the war alongside our British cousins. With great hesitation and soul searching I said that as a pacifist I would not fight in any war, no matter how just. I remember being very near to tears, feeling singled out with a few other pacifists, probably Mennonites (I later became a Mennonite and married one!), as being rather naive. It was the first time I can remember speaking from conscience under pressure. I should explain two aspects of the situation at that time: most American missionaries in India were inclined to be very supportive of the British government in India, almost superpatriotic, and being in India made us more than a little aware of the threat of Hitler's Germany in Europe and of Japan in the Far East. For several years we had been asked to keep news clippings about the Spanish Civil War, Japan's advance in China, Italy's war in Ethiopia, and German aggression in Europe. We were not allowed to ignore what was happening in the world. When I came to America early in 1940 it was surprising to me how little people my age knew about the world situation.

I had never before my senior year at Woodstock thought of myself as a pacifist. Looking back I can see the symbolic significance of a kind of rude awakening on the personal level that had happened to me a few years earlier at an American public school. We were home on furlough and staying for a year in Ann Arbor while my mother got her master's degree at the University of Michigan. I had never been in a public school, since I had been taught at home in India. For the first few days I was seeing a lot of fighting going on among the boys on the playground. It puzzled and worried me. Why was there so much violence? My turn came to be knocked to the ground without warning by a kid about my size. I squirmed out from under him. He kept trying to pin me down, getting angrier as he failed to keep me pinned and as I kept squirming out from under him. Pretty soon I was hearing cheers for "the India rubber man" and I felt proud to be called that. In a strange sort of way I had managed to win my challenge without actually fighting, which I imagine settled my ranking on the playground satisfactorily for the rest of the year. It was the beginning of my career as a playground athlete. Yet obviously fighting was not part of my family culture, and I thought of it as morally wrong.

I had another fight, this one in my senior year at Woodstock. One of my good friends and classmates was British, who as I found out later was from an old Anglo-Indian family. One of his ancestors had fought in the Indian Rebellion of 1857. His family was of course loyally pro-British, whereas my dad had gotten into the national newspapers as an anti-imperialist. If I remember correctly, my friend took it into his head to uphold his family honor against a pacifist and anti-imperialist American. I can't remember any other possible motive. This time it was a real fight. I instinctively gave up my pacifism for violent self-defense. I think we both surged into a rush of acute, unforgiving rage. There was no vindication or pardon on either side. Since it was near the end of the school year we simply went our separate ways, and I knew well from then on what rage and violence I was capable of.

Since as a pacifist I had nothing to back me up like the Mennonite or Quaker peace heritage, I have to credit my father with somehow managing to instill his nonviolence and a bit of his strength of conscience into me. During World War I he had volunteered for the Army Air Corps, though he would have been exempt as a student pastor. He felt he had to be part of "the war to end all wars." But after a seminary education, world travel, a good deal of reading of history, and the experience of being a missionary in India, he came eventually to the pacifist position and declared himself a pacifist in World War II for exactly the same reasons, he said, that he had declared himself a soldier in the first war: to end war and to save the world for democracy.

As I left India early in 1940, Indian leaders were in a quandary about their position with regard to the declaration of war imposed on them. If they were to support Britain in the war, they felt Britain should declare its position with regard to independence for India after the war. It seemed logical that if the war were truly being fought for the admirable democratic and anti-imperialistic ends declared by the British and their allies, then the time had surely come to end empire and give India her right to be a free nation. Part of this equation in India was that many Indian people could sense the Japanese advance through Asia might well spell the end of European imperialism in Asia. And that was not seen as such a bad thing, even if the Japanese did overrun India. In fact, many Indian soldiers in the British army went over to the Japanese side in Singapore and Burma later in the war.

I left India feeling rather confused, not because I didn't know what was happening in the world, but because I knew too much, too many contradictory impulses and voices. I believed in nonviolence; Gandhi was one of my earliest heroes, and I believed that India should be free. I disliked the British being in India. I knew that Hitler was a dangerous man who had somehow managed to hoodwink the German people into almost worshipping him and the Nazi party. I found it hard to dislike the Japanese people, particularly since I had spent two weeks in Japan with my parents on the way back to India in 1934. Another of our family heroes was Toyohiko Kagawa who visited in our home in India in about 1938. Yet I also knew something about the cruelties of the Japanese army in their advance through China. It seemed logical to me to always distinguish sharply between the militarist groups in every nation and the people they were not so much benignly protecting as misleading into war. That is a fundamental distinction that has stayed with me all through my adult life.

On an Italian ship between Bombay and Manila, I was booked with Kenneth Forman, a high school classmate, into a cabin with two Jewish refugees from Germany. We did not know how to communicate with each other except by sign language, yet they succeeded in making it quite clear to us what kind of horror they had managed to escape from in Germany. But they had no place to escape to in the

world outside. Where would they end up? The United States was refusing to accept them as refugees. Their uncertain fate haunted me
for many years. I felt both ashamed to be American and yet glad for
myself to have a safe home and a family in Kansas to return to.

In Manila, while waiting for an American boat to take us the rest
of the way to the United States, we met a few American sailors and
we played basketball in the YMCA gymnasium. They told us they
expected war with Japan at any moment. There had already been
skirmishes and close calls in the Pacific. We were told the same thing
on the American boat by our cabin steward. It seemed to be common
knowledge in the Pacific. Each side seemed to be constantly threatening the other. It was like my Ann Arbor playground experience,
but a much more deadly game of international chicken.

In Hong Kong we went up the inclined railway to the top of
the hill. It was a nostalgic hike for me: to find the spot where we had
been able to look down over the city and across the bay on our trip
back to India in 1934. Suddenly we found ourselves surrounded by
British soldiers. We had somehow managed to penetrate their de-
fenses. After a few phone calls to headquarters and a rather stern
grilling they let us go—two innocent missionary kids! It may have
been more frightening to them than to us, to think how easily their
security had been breached. Another reminder that we were actually
in a world at war.

In Shanghai there was no security lapse. My friend and I tried to
cross a bridge to another part of the city. We were immediately
stopped by Japanese soldiers. Their bayonets were very menacing—
a much more frightening reminder that the world was at war. A
couple of hours visit in Kobe the next day was very different. Japan
itself seemed quiet and lovely, much as I had remembered it. No sign
of war. The people seemed friendly as usual, and very busy on the
dock trying to sell us their beautiful and delicate things. The war
was out there in the Pacific and in China—a soldier's war, so far—
except to the Chinese.

America seemed very unreal to me, beginning with Honolulu. It
was hard to get used to the consumerism and the popular culture.
It was so different from India—exciting at first, but too garish for my
taste. Things I found difficult to get used to: indifference to the rest
of the world, no serious conversations, horror movies with Chinese

villains in them, consumption of hamburgers, cigarettes, beer, cars everywhere all driving on the wrong side of the road, loud talking, crude language, racism, the way girls talked and dressed and flirted, football games, cheating in classes, gum chewing, and the born-again Christianity I suddenly found myself grouped with in my first year in college (my family background was very modernist, liberal, social gospel, whatever those terms meant). "Modernist" was a bad word among these Christians. But I was expected to feel at home among them because I was a missionary kid. Something was out of focus. I had come to America out of a world at war. Suddenly there was no war in sight. Everybody was having fun, or being very Christian, or both. It was unreal. I almost forgot about the war—for two years!

In 1941 I changed from the Methodist college I was attending to a Mennonite college. I was among pacifists with a social conscience— some of them anyway. I felt more at home and found congenial groups to associate with. Pearl Harbor came along finally in the middle of my sophomore year. Suddenly the war was real here in America too. I had known and then forgotten about it in the effort to get acquainted with America. It didn't seem surprising to me that the Japanese would initiate an attack against their prime enemy in the Pacific. They had been at war since 1936, and they were serious about their war. What kind of game were the militarists in America playing? Almost everyone had been joking about Roosevelt saying in his posh accent, "I don't want war. Eleanor doesn't want war," almost believing him. Now the truth was out. It was a case of carefully engineered consent for the war. We had, in fact, been up to our ears in the war with lend-lease, and Roosevelt had been conspiring with Churchill to get the American people into the war (and, unsuccessfully, to get him to promise independence for India). Suddenly everything was ready: all the wartime laws needed to run the country as an efficient military machine were in place. We could no longer be in denial about being at war.

The Student Christian Association at Bethel College asked me to write a regular column for the *Collegian* called "On the Serious Side." Since we had been discussing the military draft on campus after it became a serious threat to each of us, I wrote a column about two Quakers who had refused to register for the draft and had spent a year in jail as a result, just one possible option in relation to the draft.

I was not advocating nonregistration. At the time I had thought I would declare myself a conscientious objector and accept service in a Civilian Public Service camp like most Mennonites. But I suddenly discovered I was not a Mennonite. I was almost lynched for that column. The townspeople in Newton had been waiting for an excuse to blast the college. They wanted me expelled at once. But it was the Mennonites they were after, not me. I had inadvertently released the pent up feelings of townspeople who were by now superpatriotic and out to prove the treachery of those German-speaking, pacifist slackers and cowards. It is a complicated story. Not really about me at all, though I had inadvertently opened the bag of hostility. This was another part of America I found difficult to understand: pent up hostility, sudden violent patriotism, persecution of groups like Mennonites (a victim people historically, hounded from country to country since the sixteenth century), and the internment of the Japanese on the West Coast. These were all good people. Didn't anyone understand the difference between people and militarists? There was something similar in this to the football game mentality: root for your team, or else! That "or else" can be very ominous and threatening.

Late in 1940 my parents had returned to America, hounded out of India by their mission hierarchy (not by the British) for their pacifist and anti-imperialist attempts to speak truth to power. They were now managing the School of Living in New York, along with Paul and Betty Keene who had both been my teachers at Woodstock. I spent the early summer of 1942 with them. The date for my registration for the draft was coming due soon. In daily contact with my father, who was corresponding with older pacifists about their refusing to register for the draft as a united and well-publicized group, I was thinking about what witness I should make as a pacifist.

I think what bothered me the most at the time was the fact that I knew the war was a "just war" for most people. I wanted to be somehow part of it, yet also a conscientious objector to the military part of it. There had been an attempt to establish a Quaker-run ambulance unit in Europe that could help out in war-torn areas without being involved directly with the military. But this was to be a "total war," meaning that everyone had to be involved in the official war effort and suffer the consequences of it, and no such free-wheeling groups could be allowed to muddy things up. The British, I knew, had a more liberal policy of exemption from the draft, with relatively free choice of service options for conscientious objectors. The United States with its draft law seemed to have determined that there should be no such broad exemption, but that COs should be drafted, pressured into the army if possible, and then tucked into out-of-the-way places where they could not be seen or heard by the general population, and where they were to be restricted at first to forestry service. That seemed to be pretty far away from helping out in the world wide struggle against fascism and violence and imperialism.

I decided finally to refuse to register for the draft as my personal protest against this homegrown streak of fascism. It took the court system only a month to indict and sentence me to three years. I found myself with about six thousand other conscientious objectors and about as many so-called draft dodgers spread out through the federal prison system.

There is space here for only a few high and low points in my checkered prison experience as I recorded them in letters and notebooks at the time.

July 14, 1942: I plead guilty—I am guilty—and proud of it, in the tradition of Thoreau and Gandhi. July 30: I am sentenced to three years in prison. The Judge and the courtroom listen politely as I read a four-page statement. The teachings of Jesus are my laws of life; I cannot disobey those laws even in time of war. I am on the side of those "tiny, invisible, molecular moral forces that work from individual to individual" (the words of William James and the motto of The School of Living). I am for the abolition of war. I do not believe that war is a necessary or inevitable characteristic of human society. It propagates itself. It does not settle problems, it creates problems. Conscription forces me to take part in the total war system. I can have no part in it. I have a faith to live up to.

I am led out of the courtroom by a United States Marshall, leaving my parents and some friends and well-wishers behind. I do not see their tears or their farewells. I forget to look back toward them. I begin a three year sentence in a holding cell with drug addicts and draft dodgers. So much for principle. Now another kind of reality begins. A lot of switches in me seem to be turned off suddenly. I am wary,

watching, not really afraid, but numbed at the thought of three years
in prison. What are you in for, kid? Draft violation. That's all they
want to know; its just an opening gambit to get my attention so they
can tell me all about their bum raps. We're all in the slammer together.
I learn to play down being a conscientious objector immediately, on
instinct—also my idealism, or any sense of worth I may have, anything that might be interpreted as a suggestion of being superior
in any way. I am no better than anyone else. This is the bottom rung
of democracy—perhaps the only real democracy in this country,
because we are voting with our lives, for whatever personal purpose, although we are encapsulated by walls and the rigid discipline
of prison authoritarianism. It costs a lot of money to discard us from
society by encapsulating us like this; it proves that individuals do
matter.

From a purely sociological point of view, I had a most interesting three years in prison—all three of them, with no time off for
good behavior. They were divided into six parts—six different kinds
of imprisonment—that gave me the opportunity to experience almost the whole range of federal prisons, plus parole, and a couple of
nights in county jails. During the first eighteen months I felt that far
too much of the frustration, anger, and rebellion of those around me
was rubbing off on me.

Before being shipped out to various types of federal prisons appropriate to the crime, all prisoners sentenced in the New York area
were kept in the Federal Detention Headquarters on West Street in
lower Manhattan, along with those either awaiting sentence or serving a short sentence. Most of the transfers spent about two weeks
there. I got stuck at West Street for more than two months. That gave
me time to get acquainted with Louis Lepke, boss of Murder Inc.,
some German Bundists, a handful of COs and Jehovah's Witnesses,
and an assortment of people who had gotten hooked on drugs,
money, or whatever they couldn't get enough of legally.

The building on West Street had evidently been a garage of some
sort—parts of the ramps were still visible in the walls—and now we
were being parked there in barred cells. The structure immediately
gave me the impression of being impossible to escape from, though
I had no intention of escaping. As though the massive concrete were

not enough, there were metal cages dividing up the area where cars had been parked or worked on and a metal screen that kept us from getting near the barred windows. Much of the lower part of the structure was without windows at all. We were certainly cut off from the outside world. On the roof there was a large cage in which we could play handball or walk about, communing with the sky; and every few weeks the *Queen Mary* would come into view, returned for another boatload of troops. She was one of the very few feminine things in the outside world we could actually see, other than in pictures or in the small glass windows through which we stared at our mothers, wives, or girlfriends.

Since I was presumed trustworthy, I soon acquired a special job: a sort of clerical job in a large room known as the Receiving Room. All prisoners who came into and went out of the building had to be processed in the Receiving Room. They were stripped of all their clothing and possessions, examined carefully to make sure they weren't carrying something on or in their bodies, and given a set of clothing. Jim Peck wrote about this experience in his narrative *The Ship That Never Hit Port.* He said, "In the receiving room we were stripped and told: 'Spread your cheeks.' Later I heard of a young religious CO who had come straight to jail from a sheltered home. When ordered to spread his cheeks, he put two fingers in his mouth and stretched." I was that young religious CO.

My job was to help keep records. One of the advantages of being in the Receiving Room was that it was a kind of nerve center where one heard all the latest gossip, got to see people coming in and going out, and had more freedom than most of the other inmates. We might occasionally be called out in the middle of the night to process a bus load of drug addicts, but that at least offered a bit of excitement in an otherwise drab existence.

Eventually I was sent to the Federal Correctional Institution at Danbury. It was a magnificent location on a hilltop above Candlewood Lake, a clean prison, utterly soulless. By comparison, West Street at least had a kind of soul.

At Danbury there were classes, movies, musical programs, services, ball games, work hours, times for recreation and for clean-up, for showers, laundry, commissary—all of it routine and regulated like clockwork. There was a campus atmosphere and plenty of space. The Jehovah's Witnesses met regularly to study the Bible in their systematic manner; the conscientious objectors met in small groups, much less organized, to discuss philosophy, vegetarianism, civil disobedience, decentralization, nonviolence, education, politics, God, sex, intentional pacifist communities, Gandhi, economics, cooperatives, and building low-cost housing. Somehow it all became desolately routine and boring in Danbury.

One thing that did not become boring was people. There were those who became part of the scenery of desolation, like the guards who hid in their uniforms or behind the wire screens along the outside wall, or the Jehovah's Witnesses who became the medium of their message, or many of the COs who were tirelessly articulate about anything and everything and seemed to lose their individuality to their ideas. But the one shining exception to routine and boredom was individuals who had character and who wore their individuality like a badge. There was Rabbi Malino coming in from the outside world once a week, humming through the Shema Israel and the rest of the service as fast as he could recite it in order to have plenty of time for his provocative sermons. Once he read a poem to us, "Amos in Times Square," that put the prophecy of Amos into appropriate modern language.

There were the black muslims roasting potatoes over the barrel fire which they kept going all day to keep warm while working on the new piggery, and they shared their contraband with their friends and managed to provide butter as well. I felt honored to become one of their friends. There was Mr. Wells, the construction engineer, with his thin craggy face, in whose office I typed endless lists of nuts and bolts that might be needed somewhere in the institution. I think he liked me, patient as he had to be with my amateur typing. There were the famous (or infamous) COs, Stanley Murphy and Louis Taylor, who wouldn't cooperate in any way with the prison authorities, even refusing to keep down the food they had been force-fed while on hunger strike. There was the tall, lean prisoner who taught me how to use a jackhammer, and who said that he had tried marijuana once but it only gave him a headache. There was Robert Lowell, the poet, who would have nothing to do with other COs, who got into a hilarious rage and threw a bucket of paint on another inmate. These and many others kept reminding me by their individuality that there was a real world in which there were real people and where I would some day be returning.

I am sure the "problem of prison" is expressed in many ways. Perhaps everyone who has had some experience of prison sees it differently—what is the hardest thing about doing time, what is the root cause of prison neurosis, and so forth. In federal prisons, at least, the problem in 1942 was obviously not the daily threat of physical torture, terrible food, filth, disease—though one did hear about such things happening at other prisons in the federal system, such as at the psychiatric hospital at Springfield, Missouri. It was equally obvious that the problem *did* have something to do with feeling deprived and smothered as an individual. How did they manage it? Being locked up, counted, watched, moved in lines, scheduled, classified, ordered about, quarantined—yes, regimented is the right word for it—all that is bad enough. One can, of course, fight it prudently and silently, think one's own thoughts, disobey a rule occasionally, and survive on a thin margin of self-respect. But the worst part is that one *doesn't* fight it, or soon gives up trying to fight it; one *adjusts*, smiles at the guards, and even finds a few rewards for being tractable. One of the occupational hazards of being nice, however—and most people were nice, including both prisoners and guards—is that it is far too easy to adjust to being regimented. But, if you think about it, you never stop hating yourself for being "nice" in the sense of being tractable in the context of regimentation. In prison maybe genuine happy-faced tractability is a gift; maybe having the guts to fight against the system, come what may, is also a gift. I found myself somewhere in the frustrating middle without a good grasp of what to do about it.

It occurred to me near the end of my first eighteen months in prison that by the same logic which had brought me there—refusal to be regimented by conscription—I should refuse to cooperate with the prison system itself. Here was a model, if somewhat benign, of a fascist state that I was living in. I had not the slightest idea what to do about it. Was I to accept what I had refused to accept outside of prison? Was I to accept the real, galling, and daily regimentation here in prison after having balked at accepting the less immediately physical aspect of regimentation involved in conscription? I was too sensible to want to do all my time in the Hole, but I was also getting increasingly depressed and bored with being in prison. I was losing my drive toward self-improvement, which I had expressed mainly through reading, writing letters to the outside, or in discussions with others.

At that moment a group of us decided to go on work strike over the issue of racial segregation in the dining hall. So, I was to be in the Hole after all, though in good company.

The incident has been described by Jim Peck in *The Ship That Never Hit Port* and in Lowell Naeve's book *A Field of Broken Stones*. There were eighteen of us; we must have each experienced the strike quite differently. Naeve seems to have been depressed by the other strikers: their hesitations about taking more extreme action such as going on a hunger strike, the friction among us over strike policy, frustrations with those who said, "take it easy, let's stick to the strike issue." He said in his book, "We were bitter, resentful, felt stifled. . . . I would call to George: 'I wish I'd never joined this strike.' A moan, a growl: 'Yea, the same for me.' Two weeks, three weeks, the eighteen of us in cells. . . . Sixty days passed. We heard nothing from the local officials. . . . We were accomplishing nothing. . . . How could we win?" I felt much the same way. The odd thing is that Naeve epitomized for me the cause of my own frustrations. How far could this anarchistic drive to resist authority go? The logic of it seemed eventually to self-destruct—at least in my mind it did. I was frightened by it, by the possible escalation of protest violence, by the inconsistencies of changing tactics, or going on and off protest as one felt up to it.

Jim Peck, from a background in the labor movement, and not afraid to take action on any injustice, was more experienced than most of us about strike discipline and sticking to the issue. This was his domain—bucking against the bosses. In fact, he saw the whole prison experience on the model of the class struggle. In prison "human consideration is not allowed at any point. And this whole prison machinery [which he describes in his book much as most inmates would experience it] is at the service of the upper dogs to suppress the underdogs and mark as criminal those who try to get rich without using a respectable front." I found no quarrel with Jim Peck; in fact, he was a fascinating person to nearly everyone in Danbury—totally sincere and always willing to lay his life on the line, as he did after the war in the civil rights struggle. But we came out of totally different worlds and hardly knew how to talk to each other.

If Lowell Naeve represented for me the self-destructing tendency of anarchism that I saw in myself, Jim Peck represented the tough, worldly, radical vision and discipline that was quite beyond my experience, but seemed inherently right to me. I felt pulled and pushed by such forces inside and outside of me.

About this time I was reading Erich Fromm's book *Escape from Freedom*. There were passages in it that spoke directly to my condition and depressed me to the limit. I was supposed to be an exemplary and radical individual, in the style of Henry David Thoreau, saying a resounding *no* to conscription, doing it deliberately, and on principle. Freedom was my banner. It seemed there should be a certain joy in protest. And yet the feelings of powerlessness, inferiority, and individual insignificance were growing in intensity. Could it be that my attempts to strike out against regimentation were simply masochistic tendencies? Was I masochistic by nature, or because the prison society was relentlessly forming me into an ideal victim of their sadism? There seemed to be very little glorious, healthy sense of freedom for any of us involved in the strike at that moment.

Fromm had quoted from Dostoevsky concerning the individual who finds himself free and alienated in a hostile world. He has "no more pressing need than the one to find somebody to whom he can surrender, as quickly as possible, that gift of freedom which he, the unfortunate creature, was born with." I had in a sense freed myself from my society at war, from most of my family (except my parents, who were always supportive), and was in the process of freeing myself from some of the excess baggage of religious faith. I was certainly in a hostile world. I was feeling more and more alienation, even from my fellow COs—I was profoundly *tired* of their talk! To whom would I surrender my precious gift of freedom? There wasn't even a decent person around to surrender it to! I have never experienced an odder mixture of irony, depression, confusion, and bitterness. I *had* to get out of prison somehow. My friend, Vic Schwartzman, had gone out on parole finally; why shouldn't I? I had to experience real, tangible freedom before I lost my desire for it permanently. Fighting for freedom from regimentation seemed to be leading me into a quicksand of confusion about why I was in prison.

The opportunity came almost like a miracle. Parole had been granted to me, except for the hitch that I was in segregation striking against the prison authorities. If I would drop out of the strike the warden could guarantee that the parole date would be set for release within a month; I decided to trust him. After all, he had come out of the Church of the Brethren, one of the three peace churches. He was surely not so far away from decency and honesty as to go back on his promise. I dropped out of the strike; but now I felt terribly guilty. Was it then the cause, whatever it might be, to which I had feared surrendering my freedom and now felt guilty about abandoning it? Had Jim Peck surrendered his to labor and civil rights causes? Lowell Naeve to his philosophical anarchism? I decided it was time to devote myself to mere survival for a while until I could find out for sure what I was really devoted to.

When my promised parole did come through, it was not to a farm as I had been led to expect, but to Mount Sinai Hospital in New York City. It was not difficult to sacrifice principle at that point: I had already broken from the strike for the sake of parole, now I could surely give up the notion of free choice of parole conditions for the sake of getting out of prison. Vic Schwartzman was at Mount Sinai, and I would be getting *out!*—that was the main thing. I remember the train ride to New York City I shared with A. J. Muste. He wanted only to talk about the COs in Danbury and what they were thinking. I wanted only to smell and taste my suddenly acquired, luscious freedom.

As it turned out, nothing really important changed. I still felt imprisoned. It was impossible to lead a decent kind of personal life apart from the long hours of working in a kitchen or as an orderly in the operating rooms. I was still emotionally depressed. And perhaps I felt guilty about leaving the strike at Danbury for the sake of parole. But I endured the Mount Sinai experience for five months when a sort of summer madness came over me: I broke parole, moved to The School of Living (my first choice of farm parole), and dared the parole authorities to come and get me. They did. They shuttled me back and forth between West Street and Danbury and finally decided to send me to Mill Point, a prison camp in West Virginia. I still don't really know why I broke parole, except that in an odd sort of way I had finally accepted "the cause" I was part of—being a conscientious objector to conscription. The second half of my three-year term was a much happier experience as it turned out.

I did the rest of my sentence in three places: at Mill Point in West Virginia, at a camp for juvenile delinquents in Virginia (where I was supposed to be in charge of recreation), and finally in the penitentiary at Lewisburg. I acquired a fantastic suntan and became gloriously healthy at Mill Point, working all summer on a new road; after a short stay at Natural Bridge I joined the general work strike of COs that was spreading through the prisons; and at Lewisburg I endured fifteen months of segregation, proving to myself finally that I had the guts to survive even the Hole. There was much of interest in this experience, and I felt much more at peace with myself and with my involvement with other pacifists. Some of this part of my story connects with what others have to say elsewhere in this collection of stories.

Finally the war came to an end, and my prison experience came to an end soon after. It was all over, and yet it was not over. We now seemed to be living in an even more dangerous world in some ways: threatened by nuclear holocaust, the spread of communism as well as the canker of anti-Communist hysteria in the United States, and an increasingly toxic environment due in large part to the huge military system we seemed to have acquired permanently. I became a reluctant activist. During the war years I was caught up in the pacifist movement simply by being a CO, and then in other radical actions in the United States during the Cold War period. I marched on Washington several times. I came to realize eventually that I was temperamentally not an activist, though I believed in the causes as I understood them: against involvement in Vietnam, disarmament, an end to conscription, a nuclear-free world, justice in places like El Salvador and Nicaragua, and civil rights. It was my conscientious objection during World War II that brought me into such very American activities out of the very different world I had grown up in.

Meanwhile I needed to get on with my life, my education, my family, and hopefully my community, somewhere, somehow. Often we talked about migrating to another part of the world; but there was nowhere to go, we said, away from what had been let loose into the world. In some ways I felt trapped both by what was happening and what I believed.

I believe in nonviolence as a weapon against evil and injustice in the world, a weapon which has barely been tried so far. As a pacifist I believe that war is tragically wrong—tragically because it is so often conceived to be a just war by the participants on both sides, but which results in unintended injustice and suffering on both sides. As a realist, however, I know that I have virtually no good, short-term, convincing answers to the kind of events in the modern world that have traumatized so many people into acceptance of war as an answer: Hitler's holocaust, Stalin's purges, Japanese cruelty during the war, ethnic cleansing, terrorism on all sides, and all acts of senseless violence committed against innocent victims, especially women and children.

I confess to a dilemma of conscience: the conscience of a pacifist sometimes in inner conflict with the social conscience of one who believes in acting for justice, not just hoping and praying for it. There is some real self-delusion in thinking that pacifism by itself is a form of social activism. In limited ways, yes. And then after the war it was the frustration of so many fronts—how could one be everywhere at once, protesting? There was no one crucial pacifist front, just one damned thing after another to protest against. What about doing something positive? Something useful?

My life had changed suddenly and permanently not so much because of what the war did to me, but because of what I did to myself as a result of thinking about the war and conscription and committing myself wholly to what I believed. I am proud of what I did, but I blame myself for not being very focused on long-range goals. And yet, it is not often that a twenty-year-old is focused on any goals at all. The nature of this great total war focused the lives of the young for them. It did not permit opposition, or even many options within the system. Being both for the war in a sense (its idealistic objectives and its opposition to fascism) and yet opposed to it as a pacifist, I spent most of my brain power for a good many years figuring out how to survive, how to face the moment without succumbing to that very sharp and simple focus imposed on all of us.

World War II seemed like one long, neverending struggle to decide what to do with my life. That struggle extended after the end of the war into the protracted Cold War and the nuclear era and finally into the messy and violent world we live in today, in which we seem to be reaping the harvest over and over again that we Europeans and Americans sowed during five hundred years of exploration, conquest, empire, genocide, balance of power struggles, great wars, militant capitalism, and rampant modernization. I have spent much of my time dealing with all the guilt (if that is the right word for it) about being a Westerner, an American, and a white man. And I don't regret the intellectual struggle to remain independent of imposed and makeshift ideologies, either radical or conservative, with respect to those aspects of my identity.

Circumstances forced me to change my occupational goals twice—to printing from the idea of agricultural work, and from printing to college teaching—and to concentrate on different kinds of thinking and values each time. Changes of occupation are not at all uncommon in this culture now, and I think that one of the factors involved is a kind of universal restlessness that was intensified by the experience of the war and the aftermath of cold war in the nuclear age. Stability seems increasingly like an old-fashioned virtue. Community is more a dream than a reality for most people. I think my feelings are much like what others feel in this respect, no matter what their background or their ideas.

I think I would add to my list of ways in which the war changed me that I am a rather protean kind of person. In one part of me is a kind of anger, protest, watching the world struggle through waves of violence, being an exile, a cultural hybrid, a bit gloomy and pessimistic; in the other part is the acceptance of family, local community, church, contentment, a degree of comfort, and satisfaction with the few good things that derive from the life of the mind. I work hard at the contentment side, but the other side is never very far away from my thoughts. Much of the time it is good to be such a mix; it gives an edge to what you do, since conscience speaks from both sides. When it seems uncomfortable, I sometimes wonder what it would have been like to be an agricultural missionary in India.

And that is my story, and how the war changed my life.

GEORGE YAMADA
_____

My Story of World War II

In saner periods we realize that war subverts whatever
pretensions to freedom a nation may espouse.

WHEN I VISITED Japan for the first time in 1992 I learned from my
elder brother, Ryozo, who was then eighty-nine years old, that my
father had come to America ninety years earlier because of his refusal to be conscripted into the armed forces of Japan, which was
then preparing to fight a war with Russia.

My parents were born on Kyushu, the southernmost and third-
largest island in Japan. The city of Kumamoto was home to countless generations of my ancestors and to my then-surviving brother,
his sons, and grandchildren. In 1945 the U.S. military had been
scheduled to invade Kyushu. However, the massive fire bombings of
major Japanese cities, followed by the atomic bombing of Hiroshima
and Nagasaki, brought the war to an end and spared Kyushu. I felt
dazed to visualize this gentle place as a battleground, but relieved
that, through an ironic twist, the bombs that razed Hiroshima and
Nagasaki had left this pacific countryside unscathed.

My visit to Japan was made possible because of redress paid by
the United States government for removing me from the West Coast
in 1942. At that time I was a conscientious objector conscript, having
been assigned on December 5, 1941, to Civilian Public Service Camp
No. 21 in Cascade Locks, Oregon.

I was born in 1918 in a farm shack outside the small town of Mina-
tare in western Nebraska. The area is flat sugar beet country, made
productive by irrigation canals cooperatively constructed by farmers
and landowners in the early decades of the twentieth century.

GEORGE YAMADA (b. 1918)
Since the war, George Yamada has lived in Mexico and Canada as well as various parts of the United States. A printer and publisher, he co-founded a cross-cultural magazine in Toronto in 1974. He has also written on subjects relating to issues of war and social justice. He is retired and, with his wife, Kathleen, lives in London, Ontario.

In 1992 I visited the family burial plot in the village of Kawashiri, an hour outside the city of Kumamoto in Kyushu. My nephew, Yasuo, accompanied me to the huge Buddhist temple surrounded by grave markers. That visit confirmed for me that my ancestors came from a Buddhist tradition. Upon arrival in America, my parents became firm Protestant converts. Family attendance at the Methodist church in Gering, a town of twenty-five hundred, was ritual, particularly Sunday school. But at twelve I ceased attending, much to my mother's dismay. I was not impressed by the social application in daily life of Christian teachings. From that age my interpretation of the Gospel of Christ was uncompromisingly pacifist, and I was determined to carry out the pacifist premises of the Christian gospel as I perceived them.

At the age of nineteen, I left the shelter of my rural Nebraska community for San Francisco, in part because of my father's reluctance to give me more authority in the management of the 160 acre farm. My father was a close friend and supporter of Maj. Masasuke Kobayashi, the dynamic founder of the Salvation Army's Nikkei (any person of Japanese ethnicity) branch in San Francisco. His letter of referral to Major Kobayashi put me under the Salvation Army's care during the first months of urban readjustment.

In San Francisco, I attended the Nisei (persons of Japanese ancestry born in the United States) congregation of the Evangelical Reformed Church in the center of the Nikkei enclave whose minister, Reverend Felkley, was not sympathetic to pacifism. However, his replacement, Reverend Nugent, was a stout pacifist, in addition to having been recently posted in Japan as a missionary, and his daughter was active in the pacifist Fellowship of Reconciliation.

On October 16, 1940, I was attending San Francisco State College when the first nationwide peacetime draft law induced me to declare myself a conscientious objector to all war. School brought me in touch with Alfred Fiske, a prominent campus professor in the philosophy department, at whose home I met A. J. Muste of FOR. I remember that Muste led us in singing "God Bless America," which made me wonder if God was not beseeched by every nation as well as America. My first contact with organized pacifism was heartwarming and I was grateful to Fiske.

My draft board on Mission Street in San Francisco was chaired by an ex-army officer. Because of his World War I experience with non-combatant conscripts he upheld my right to be a conscientious objector. His familiarity with the pacifist position was providential for me. Notification of my 4-E classification arrived soon after classes began in the fall of 1941, followed shortly by orders from Selective Service to report to Cascade Locks, Oregon Civilian Public Service Camp No. 21 on December 5, 1941. The state board ignored my request to postpone my induction for a few weeks to allow me to complete the college term. I was one of about two hundred war objectors assigned by Selective Service to a former Civilian Conservation Corps camp located along the Oregon bank of the Columbia River, some forty-five miles upstream from Portland. The Church of the Brethren and the Mennonite Central Committee sponsored the camp, whose work was supervised by the U.S. Forestry Service.

One of the men who crossed my path at Cascade Locks was Lew Ayres, the Hollywood actor. Risking his film career, he had refused to perform military service and was sent to CPS camp. Later he was allowed to serve in the Army Medical Corps, the assignment he had originally requested. He had the common touch, a man unaffected by fame. At that time I was twenty-three and he was thirty-four. He had an extraordinary and lifelong interest in other religions, including Buddhism. At his suggestion we read together the references to Buddhism in the Encyclopedia Britannica we found in the camp library. Ayres was an uncompromising vegetarian.

On December 7, 1941, few people in America were not shocked by the Pearl Harbor disaster. War always arouses patriotic fervor. Emotions were running amok everywhere. Even among pacifists? I overheard one or two fellow campers discreetly express doubts that I had legitimate reasons to be among them in a pacifist camp. But I also recall conscript Jim Gallagher's skepticism of the president's insistence that he had had no warning of the Pearl Harbor attack.

In camp I was assigned to the kitchen crew. Awareness of the raw emotions loose in the community kept me discreetly close to camp. I was too timid to be a troublemaker. Daily headlines were shouting the latent hostility and simmering hysteria in the community. But on February 19, 1942, when President Roosevelt issued Executive Order

No. 9066, trouble came to me. That order mandated the internment of all Nikkei in the states of California, Oregon, Washington, and parts of Arizona.

In the summer of 1942, I was singled out to be transferred to an internment center for Nikkei, administered by the War Relocation Authority (WRA) to fulfill the mandate of Executive Order No. 9066. The order, in the form of a telegram, directed the camp director, Rev. Mark Schrock, to release me to WRA. I objected to the racial discrimination as well as violations of my civil rights. After listening to my reasons for refusing to comply willingly with the military directive, Schrock declined to obey the order.

The resulting furor among socially conscious objectors throughout the CPS system successfully forced Selective Service to rescind its directive to Schrock to dismiss me from CPS. However, I complied with Selective Service transfer orders to another camp. I went to CPS Camp No. 5, sponsored by the Mennonites near Colorado Springs, and remained there for more than three years before being shipped to Germfask, Michigan, to non-church-sponsored CPS Camp No. 135.

While in Colorado Springs, my participation in a Congress of Racial Equality project involved me in a civil rights case over denial of equal rights to African Americans for public accommodations in a theater. I was jailed eight days in El Paso County Jail, charged by a justice of the peace with barratry, the "persistent incitement of litigation." Had it not been for Denver attorney Arthur A. Brooks, who came to my defense, I might have languished in jail until those reactionaries were satisfied that their intimidation had succeeded. Although it had not, they arranged for Selective Service to transfer me to Michigan. I wish at this point to say how much I appreciated two local pacifist ministers, Rev. Frances Bayles and Reverend Kennedy, who stood behind me all the way in that confrontation. More radical than I, Bayles urged me to refuse the transfer to Michigan.

Although I had a hard time among Mennonites because of vastly differing social-cultural backgrounds, I remember real satisfaction in communicating heart-to-heart with many of the men in that situation, even with one or two visiting Mennonite bishops. In retrospect, should not a recent rural Nebraskan have stayed out of trouble over racist social practices in the community? However, because I felt so strongly about the injustice of racial discrimination, I ignored the consequences.

In Germfask, I was educated quickly to the discipline and tactics of a work slowdown. It was something I had never seen before my association with reputed "troublemakers" like Corbett Bishop, Frank Hatfield, Gerald Dingman, Alfred Partridge, Morris Horowitz, Horace Kehl, and Ralph Pulliam—all fiercely independent, so freedom-loving, so imaginative, so *intelligent!*

Within six months I left Germfask in a "walkout" that resulted in my incarceration for a total of nineteen months in local and federal prisons. Nine of us walked out of Germfask over a span of four months. We were arraigned together in the Sixth District Federal Court in Grand Rapids. Attorney Frances Heisler defended all of us, presenting a legal brief to the court on our behalf. Each of us was sentenced to a three-and-a-half-year term. After ten days in Kalamazoo Jail, we entrained for the Federal Correctional Institution at Ashland, Kentucky. There we joined earlier walkout Ralph Pulliam and met Bayard Rustin, whom I had previously encountered when he visited Cascade Locks CPS Camp as a speaker for FOR.

While in Ashland, I witnessed adjacent cellmate Ralph Pulliam test his will and wits against the force and totalitarian power of the prison system. I doubt that Ralph had reached the age of twenty-one, but he was healthy in every respect, mentally, morally, and physically. He would exercise by bouncing up and down on his mattress, barefooted. He made no effort to tidy his cell because he did not consider himself a felon. He was imprisoned for *refusing* to kill. He acted on the premise that it was not his duty or obligation to help keep the prison clean. He stacked his food trays in a corner of the cell rather than returning them to the cell door. When a prison official shouted, "Pulliam, why don't you clean up your cell?" he quietly replied, "This is your prison, not mine. You clean up your prison." He was sent to the Hole and severely penalized by restrictions in food and comfort. When Pulliam refused all food or water, it was the doctor's turn to worry. For three days his physical condition was closely monitored before he was released to his former habitat, the cell next to mine. Except for some drastic discomforts, Pulliam remained his imperturbable gadfly self. No wonder the prison system wanted as little as possible to do with objectors. They were a headache, and generally not a mild one.

When we arrived at Ashland, Bayard Rustin was organizing a strike to desegregate the dining hall, something objectors had already accomplished in the federal prison at Danbury, Connecticut. The mess hall strike at Ashland ended when the Bureau of Prisons in Washington transferred us to various other prisons. Rustin, Rodney Owen, and I were driven to the federal penitentiary near Lewisburg, Pennsylvania, a maximum-security prison where Rustin remained to finish his sentence. During my memorable one-night stay there, I met a lanky, red-haired objector who greeted me with a warm handshake. "Are you George Yamada?" he asked. "I'm Larry Gara." In Lewisburg we had our first meal after the long road trip from Kentucky. The next day Owen and I continued on to the Federal Correctional Institution in Danbury, Connecticut.

The tough but mellowed associate warden at Danbury confided to me in his office about "the boys in Upper Hartford" (other resisters) like Lowell Naeve, Dave Dellinger, George Houser, and Jim Peck, for whose integrity he had acquired considerable respect. Whereas prison officials could demand obedience from conventional prisoners by granting or withholding "privileges," the principled conscientious objector, they learned, was just that—principled. Uncompromising.

In Danbury, Rodney Owen and I joined a distinguished company that included Bob Brooks, George Clemence, Wally Nelson, Worth Randle, Roger Axford, Lowell Naeve, John Stokes, Ernie Smith, Louis Lindenbaum, Joe Guinn, Cliff Bennett, Jim Otsuka, Len Mehr, Dave Wieck, Bob Hegler, Don Hurford, Ralph Abruzzizi, and Dave Zernoske. Among such a diverse group of personalities and social-political perspectives, discussions were always provocative.

Soon after my release from Danbury, I met David Dellinger at Glen Acres, his New Jersey printing shop and communal farmstead, where he published *Liberation* magazine. I was impressed by Dave's writing, speaking, and organizing skills. I consider Dave the neglected but deserving candidate for the Nobel Peace Prize by reason of his exceptional courage, intellect, and awareness.

When he entered my awareness in the early forties, while I was conscripted in Cascade Locks, Arthur E. Morgan's conceptual focus on small community profoundly reverberated in my thinking. Consequently I kept in touch with his eldest son Ernest—now in his nineties—who has continued the Morgan legacy at Celo Community in North Carolina as well as Community Service Inc., founded by his father in Yellow Springs, Ohio. In the midforties, I attended a memorable Quaker International Peace Conference in Yellow Springs, highlighted by the presence of Norman Thomas, Eleanor Roosevelt, William Henry Chamberlain, Murray Lincoln, and Arthur Morgan himself.

In assessing my wartime experiences, I believe that five years of internment in camps and prisons constituted a more valid education than five years in a liberal arts college. My exposure to the variegated strands of the American pacifist movement through the War Resisters League, FOR, Catholic Workers, Mennonites, Quakers, and nondogmatic socialists has enriched my life immensely. Throughout my three years in CPS I was privileged to meet and hear such speakers as Kirby Page, Morris Mitchell, John Swomley, Nevin Sayre, Douglas Steere, Caleb Foote, Frank Olmstead, Frederick Libby, and Maynard Kreuger, who were all part of the pacifist legacy I absorbed.

Because of my CPS experience I met the noble Mildred Jenson Loomis, who was a loyal ally during my subsequent four-year association with the School of Living as editor of the periodical *Green Revolution*. Ralph Borsodi, founder of the School of Living, wrote *Flight from the City* and *This Ugly Civilization*, books which were forerunners of a later back-to-the-land movement. Those volumes nourished me then and remain valid critiques today of our industrial culture.

In looking back over those years, I think of so many individuals whose courageous lives were an inspiration. One who stands out is George Clemence, who was escorted to the door of his Michigan home by prison officials despite his refusal to accept a change of prison clothes or to allow himself to be shaven before exiting. A personal friend of Merle Alexander, warden of the federal prison camp at Mill Point, West Virginia, Clemence had used his knowledge and skill to build the entire refrigeration system at the camp, expecting to be compensated for his work by "good time" release on parole. Instead, Washington reneged on its pledge. After that George simply refused to trust them and went into a noncooperative mode. "Keep me here for the full sentence," he advised officials. Eventually the prison system deferred to his tested and recognized integrity and he went out in style, his body and personal dignity inviolate. Although he was not a conventionally religious pacifist, I believe that his integrity was unalloyed.

My internment in Germfask coincided, serendipitously, with Corbett Bishop's presence there. I treasure the many chats I had with him, an inimitable, admirable "shit disturber." Once he had been incarcerated by the Bureau of Prisons, he refused to eat or do anything to assist in that incarceration. He epitomized, in spades, all the headaches handed to officials by war resisters.

One of my most admired heroes was Jim Peck, thinker, loner, powerful personality, with the unforgettable courage of a lion. Jim was the opposite of an aesthete. In the midfifties I met Jim and Paula Peck and Larry and Lenna Mae Gara in Mexico City and later was invited to the Pecks' Riverside Drive apartment to meet their sons and to savor Paula's gourmet cooking. Jim chided me for my preoccupation with perceived harrassment which persistently pursued me into my Canadian period. (Fascism is very much alive today.) I admired Jim's superb chutzpah and agitational skills.

How can anyone ignore the "One Man Revolution," Ammon Hennacy? During my Denver period, I ran into Ammon working as a day laborer in a dairy, wearing a Nehru or Gandhi cap, far ahead of me at the time. Later I met him again during the early fifties, working in the broiling Arizona sun when the Hopi had become the focus of his attention as well as mine, soon after I had spent a spring with Thomas and Fermina Banyacya on the First Mesa of Oraibi and the Second Mesa of Shungopavi, east of Flagstaff. Learning to know him turned me into a respectful, admiring friend. His contagious optimism and joie de vivre and his shining intellect could not be ignored. Even across many miles, Ammon was a powerful presence. His acceptance of the Premise of Reincarnation was an added dimension to our relationship. His empathy for Hopi traditions and history was extraordinary and unique, for which he had a legion of

admirers everywhere, among them Steve Allen of radio and televi-
sion, who became a supporter of traditional Hopi culture.

It was Jim Peck and Ralph DiGia who helped me distribute
the first thousand copies of my book, *The Great Resistance: The Hopi
Speak.* After visits to Hopiland at intervals over several years, I wrote
the book from the perspective of the traditional Hopi and printed it
at Allen Farson's shop in Cuernavaca, Mexico, in 1955. When I was
ready to put out a second edition I was disappointed to discover that
the linotype text I had set had all been inadvertantly melted down at
the print shop.

Another person who had a preeminently formative influence on
my life was Henry Geiger, who began a forty-year career as publisher of a weekly journal, *Manas*, on January 1, 1948. Later I worked
for Henry as a relief linotypist at Cunningham Press in Alhambra,
California. From one of his articles in *Manas* I borrowed his title,
"The Great Resistance," as the title for my book. Geiger's close association with the United Lodge of Theosophists introduced my in-
quiring mind to the beautiful and logical Doctrine of Reincarnation,
based on law, which provided for me a cogent and compelling rationale for the contradictions, contrasts, and conflicts encountered in
one's journey through many lives, but with the same evolving soul,
the enduring real person.

The transcendant event which overwhelmed me and 120,000
other Nikkei on the West Coast was Executive Order No. 9066, leading to internment in bleak concentration camps for the duration of
the war. The effect of racism on my childhood development in Nebraska was almost shattering at times, something a child can handle
more sensibly than an adolescent. Speaking from my own experience I must say that overt, or worse, subtle, covert racism takes its
toll on personality and on one's sense of identity.

When the Smithsonian Institution planned to document the contribution of Japanese Americans to the culture and history of the
United States as part of the bicentennial of the U.S. Constitution,
I wrote officials that emphasizing only the heroic sacrifices of the
all-Nisei 442nd Combat Team during World War II would distort
historical perspectives. There was harsh irony, I wrote, "in the hero-
ism of the 442nd, which fought for the honor of a nation which was
interning parents, brothers, sisters, wives, children and sweethearts

of those same soldiers and depriving them of the basic civil liberties ostensibly protected by the Constitution, solely on the basis of racial ancestry."

In saner periods, we realize that war subverts whatever pretensions to freedom a nation may espouse. For me, however, the premises of Birth and Rebirth as a logical explanation for whatever circumstances one may confront have given a positive outlook that has enabled me to surmount and transcend painful experiences.

Selected Additional Readings

Anderson, Richard C. *Peace Was in Their Hearts: Conscientious Objectors in World War II* (Watsonville, CA: Correlan Publications, 1994).
Contains quotes from men who performed alternative service. The material is organized topically, but the narrators are not identified.

Benedict, Don. *Born Again Radical.* (New York: Pilgrim Press, 1982).
Personal account of the only Union Theological Seminary nonregistrant to later change his position. As a United Church of Christ minister, he devoted his life to furthering racial and economic justice.

Cantine, Holley, and Dachine Rainer, eds. *Prison Etiquette: The Convict's Compendium of Useful Information.* (Bearsville, NY: Retort Press, 1950).
Extremely valuable collection of writing about prison by resister convicts. Should be reprinted.

Clark, Bronson P. *Not by Might: A Viet Nam Memoir.* (Glastonbury, CT: Chapel Rock Publishers, 1997).
A personal account of a tumultuous time in American history.

Dellinger, David. *From Yale to Jail: The Life Story of a Moral Dissenter.* (Marion, SD: Rose Hill Books, 1996).
A personal account by a major figure in the peace movement.

Goossen, Rachel Waltner. *Women Against the Good War: Conscientious Objection and Gender on the American Home Front, 1941–1947.* (Chapel Hill: University of North Carolina Press, 1997).
An account of women whose pacifist convictions led them to oppose World War II and serve as volunteers in CPS units and in other types of work unrelated to the war effort.

Hassler, Alfred. *Diary of a Self-Made Convict.* (Chicago: Henry Regnery Co., 1954).
A detailed account of a resister's life in Lewisburg Federal Penitentiary during World War II.

Kohn, Stephen M. *Jailed for Peace: The History of American Draft Law Violators, 1658–1985.* (Westport, CT: Greenwood Press, 1986).
Includes an excellent chapter on World War II draft resistance.

Lindner, Robert M. *Stone Walls and Men.* (New York: Odyssey Press, 1946).
A prison psychiatrist's work, including his highly biased analysis of several World War II resisters.

Marshall, S. L. A. *Men Against Fire: The Problem of Battle Command in Future War.* (Gloucester, MA: Peter Smith, 1978).
A military historian's study revealing that a large majority of American soldiers in combat during World War II failed to fire their weapons.

Naeve, Lowell, with David Wieck. *A Field of Broken Stones.* (Glen Gardner, NJ: Libertarian Press, 1950).
Valuable prison journal smuggled out of Danbury prison by a resister prisoner. Naeve, an artist, included his own illustrations. This one should be reprinted.

Peck, James. *We Who Would Not Kill.* (New York: Lyle Stuart, 1958).
———. *Underdogs vs. Upperdogs.* (New York: AMP&R, 1980).
Personal accounts of a life that involved countless acts of civil disobedience for peace and social justice.

Selective Service System. *Conscientious Objection.* (Washington, DC: Government Printing Office, 1950).
The official history with numerous documents of all types of objectors during World War II.

Sibley, Mulford Q., and Philip E. Jacob. *Conscription of Conscience: The American State and the Conscientious Objector, 1940–1947.* (Ithaca: Cornell University Press, 1952).
Still the most comprehensive, scholarly account of pacifism during World War II.

Tracy, James. *Direct Action: Radical Pacifism from the Union Eight to the Chicago Seven.* (Chicago: University of Chicago Press, 1996).
The first attempt at a scholarly overview of the contributions of activist World War II resisters in the postwar world.

Wetzel, Donald. *Pacifist: or, My War and Louis Lepke.* (Sag Harbor, NY: The Permanent Press, 1986).
A beautifully written account of the prison experience of a World War II resister.

Wilson, Adrian. *Two Against the Tide: A Conscientious Objector in World War II, Selected Letters, 1941–1948.* Ed. Joyce Lancaster Wilson. (Austin, TX: W. Thomas Taylor, 1990).
Candid letters by a conscientious objector who served in alternative service projects and later became a major figure in theater on the West Coast.

Wittner, Lawrence S. *Rebels Against War: The American Peace Movement, 1941–1960.* (New York: Columbia University Press, 1969).

Includes an excellent discussion of CPS and imprisoned World War II resisters.

Zahn, Franklin. *Deserter from Violence: Experiments with Gandhi's Truth.* (New York: Philosophical Library, 1984).
Memoir of World War II resister who continued his work for peace and justice after the war.

A Few Small Candles

was designed by Diana Dickson; composed in 10.5/13.3 Palatino with Optima display on a Macintosh Power PC system using QuarkXPress by The Book Page; printed by sheet-fed offset lithography on 50-pound Glatfelter Supple Opaque natural stock (an acid-free, recycled paper), Smyth sewn and bound over binder's boards in Arrestox B cloth, and wrapped with dust jackets printed on 100-pound enamel stock coated with polypropylene matte film lamination by Thomson-Shore, Inc.; and published by

The Kent State University Press

KENT, OHIO 44242